60 0413420 0

UNIVER... ...NGHAM

WITHDRAWN

FROM THE LIBRARY

Students and External Readers	Staff & Research Students
DATE DUE FOR RETURN	**DATE OF ISSUE**
29 6 72	

**Any book which you borrow remains your responsibility
until the loan slip is cancelled**

D1337199

WITHDRAWN
FROM THE LIBRARY

THE GOLDEN RAM

THE
GOLDEN RAM

A

Narrative

History

of the

Clothworkers'

Company

*

1528-1958

HD 9901. 1 G4

BY THOMAS GIRTIN

UNIVERSITY LIBRARY
26 APR 1960
NOTTINGHAM

©

THE WORSHIPFUL COMPANY OF CLOTHWORKERS

FIRST EDITION APRIL 1958

SECOND EDITION NOVEMBER 1958

PRINTED IN GREAT BRITAIN

*D*edicated

BY THE MASTER ⁄ WARDENS ⁄ AND

COURT OF ASSISTANTS

OF THE

WORSHIPFUL COMPANY OF CLOTHWORKERS

IN THE WORDS OF HIS MAJESTY

KING JAMES I

TO

All good Clothworkers and all
good Clothwearers

*

*In the ancient manner of the members of the
Clothworkers' Company
this work is offered by the author
to their Patroness, the
Blessed Virgin Mary of the Assumption,
of the Mistery of Clothworkers*

*

CONTENTS

* *
*

CONTENTS

LIST OF PLATES

* *

*

ix

Though Jason's Fleece was fam'd of old,
The British wool is growing gold:
No mines can more of wealth supply.

DRYDEN: KING ARTHUR

PROLOGUE

*   *
*

ON the afternoon of St Catherine's Day, 25 November 1531, three senior members of the Company took boat from Clothworkers' Stairs by the Steel Yard, just above London Bridge, and were rowed towards Westminster.

They were the Master, Oliver Claymond, and two of his Wardens, Christopher Cherborne and John Perle, and this was the culminating point of weeks and months of activity, of coming and going by river between Clothworkers' Stairs and the Temple, between the Temple and Westminster. Now, at last, the new book of the Statutes of the Clothworkers' Company was ready for signature by Sir Thomas More, the Lord Chancellor.

There had been another such occasion – an abortive mission – earlier in the year, after a Chancery Lawyer named Johnson had prepared the first draft of the Statutes. The Clothworkers had been involved in much expense – even the porter at the door of the Star Chamber had required 1s before he would admit them to the Lord Chancellor's presence – and then all they had got for their pains was an order to go away and see the Lord Chief Justice.

The Lord Chief Justice of the King's Bench, Sir John Fitz-James, was approachable only through two clerks, each of whom had had to receive a reward 'to help the Clothworkers to show His Lordship their book'. Fitz-James himself had been graciously pleased to accept the gift of a brace of capons, a brace of geese, and three brace of quails for his dinner, in exchange for advice no more concrete than to go away and take counsel's opinion. After this aggravating setback, the Clothworkers had employed *the Recorder in their affairs, and, not before a considerable amount of time and money had been spent, a new set of Statutes, twenty-seven pages written on parchment and neatly bound in vellum, had been prepared. It was this book that they were taking up the river to Westminster.*

Nothing had been left undone to ensure that, this time, their mission should be a success. A certain Mr Roper,* for example, had been given 6s 8d for himself to clear the way to the Lord Chancellor, and he had been given, in addition, £2 to buy the Lord Chancellor a hogshead of wine.

At Westminster, where they were joined by the Recorder, there was a slight delay. His Lordship was at dinner. The Clothworkers adjourned to The Clock House and themselves dined simply. After dinner they returned to the Star Chamber. Again the porter received a tip before admitting them, and again they stood before Sir Thomas More. This time their preparations had not been wasted; their book of Statutes was signed both by Lord Chancellor More and by the Lord Treasurer, the Duke of Norfolk. And, on the Sunday following St Catherine's Day, after Mass at St Paul's, Sir John Fitz-James and Sir Robert Norwich, Chief Justice of the Court of Common Pleas, added their signature in approval of the Company's Statutes.

Now, nearly four years after Incorporation, the Clothworkers' Company possessed a legally constituted authority.†

* Presumably Sir Thomas More's son-in-law, Mr Anthony Roper.

† This authority was placed before the Court of Aldermen on the following 17 January, for recognition.[1] The Statutes were generally accepted although in September a few of them were considered 'objectionable'.

INTRODUCTION TO THE COMPANY

* *
*

ORIGIN

AT this moment it may be convenient to consider the nature
and origin of the infant Company.

The trade guilds of London were societies existing to foster
primarily good trade and to give security to the workman by
preventing him from being undersold in the labour market; they
controlled the number of apprentices that might be kept, they
searched London for ill workmanship, they laid down conditions
of employment, they acted as domestic tribunals, benefit and
funeral societies and, generally, as social institutions. They were,
in short, not trading but trade societies which, incidentally, pro-
tected consumer as well as producer from fraud.[1]*

Originally, and perhaps to avoid the dangers of being charged
with illegal association, they had formed themselves around a
religious core, attaching themselves to some church or monastery
and adopting a heavenly patron. Those in the cloth trade had
chosen as their patroness the Blessed Virgin Mary, Mother of the
Holy Lamb, whose fleece was symbolical of their calling.[2] By the
very first Ordinance of the Clothworkers' Company thirteen
tapers of wax were to be kept burning before an image of Our Lady
in Christ Church monastery. The election of the Master and
Wardens was to take place on the Sunday following the Feast of the
Assumption and, in general, the feeling of religious dedication was
strong. It was from this religious background, too, that the livery –

---

* Throughout this book superior figures refer to the Source Notes contained
in Appendix G.

I

the distinctive costume of the guild – had been evolved. Its pattern had been taken from the gown worn by the various orders of monks; it was parti-coloured and, generally speaking, in bright hues, and members wore their hooded livery, 'the roundlets upon their heads, the skirts to hang behind on their necks, the tippet to lie on their shoulder or to wind about their necks'.[3]

These trade guilds had arisen from simple associations formed to help the members bear the misfortunes of life. There had to be enough members of the trade in the association to secure, by their entrance fees and subscriptions, sufficient money to pay the fee that the Crown demanded for the right of association. Guild meetings at which new rules could be made, and breaches of existing rules punished, had to be held. Halls had to be built for the better housing of the meetings. Those connected with the wool trade seem to have been the first to become organized in this way,[4] and, as their wealth and power increased, so their organization began to be aimed towards the creation of monopolies. Their governing bodies began to draw up ordinances and rules of conduct that gave them complete mastery in their own house and a control not only over standards of workmanship and rates of wages, but over domestic disputes as well. And, as their power grew, so did it become the more desirable to wield these powers from the security of a properly constituted authority. The trade guilds began to petition the Crown for the grant of charters to define their legal rights and responsibilities. The Weavers, who were the first of the cloth trade to do so, secured their charter as early as 1130 – a charter that authorized them to regulate the trade of 'cloth-workers, drapers, tailors and all various crafts and mysteries that belong to cloths'.

But there were still many associations that had, deliberately or not, entirely overlooked even such details as the necessity of obtaining a licence to associate, and, in the reign of Stephen, eighteen 'adulterine' guilds in London were fined for this offence; amongst them was the guild of Clothworkers★ who were fined one Mark.[5]

★ Possibly Cloth Finishers; the Gild Parariorum.

The early history of the trade guilds, as their influence ebbed and flowed in the changing economic scene, in alliance and counter-alliance, is obscure, but of matters concerning the cloth trade, this much, at any rate, is clear. In 1479 the Shearmen, a guild who had been in existence* certainly since 1360, sought a charter of incorporation. They sought, too, an extension of their rights of search to those who did not belong to their guild. In the face of this threat to their sovereignty the Drapers and the Tailors, who throughout the fourteenth and fifteenth centuries had been rivals for power, sank their differences and joined together to oppose the Shearmen. But, even as they did so, their cause was weakened by the defection of the Fullers, a guild flourishing since 1376,† who now withdrew and also sought a charter of incorporation.

Of the two guilds seeking charters it was the Fullers who were successful. Not only did the Shearmen fail to receive a charter but Edward IV went so far as to promise the Drapers that the Shearmen should not be so incorporated. He also severely restricted the Shearmen's rights of search.[6]

But when these jockeyings for position were over, a peace, in a country boiling with civil war, seems to have come to the rival Companies. Both victor and vanquished alike sat down in friendship, with the Drapers and Tailors in supremacy and the Fullers and Shearmen in subordinate roles; certainly, for many years to come, Fullers and Shearmen were still joining the Drapers' Guild. But twenty-five years later, the claims of the Shearmen for incorporation were too strong to be denied. On 24 January 1508, after repeated demands, the Shearmen at last received their charter.[7]

The struggle for the balance of power in control of an industry which, as will be seen, had become of the greatest importance in the Kingdom, continued. In 1515 a dispute over precedence‡ arose between the Shearmen and the Dyers which was settled by the

* They stood forty-second in the list of guilds in 1376.

† The Fullers were fifteenth in the same list.

‡ Precedence depended neither on age, numbers, nor wealth. The Weavers and the Saddlers, the two oldest Companies, were placed in the grand allocation of precedence in 1515, forty-second and twenty-fifth respectively. The Merchant Taylors and Skinners ranked sixth and seventh in alternate years.[8]

Lord Mayor, Sir William Boteler, decreeing that the Dyers'
Company should 'lovingly and cheerfully follow the Shearmen
without any further strife or debate'.

Inter-guild rivalry, however, continued, and eventually, to
strengthen their hand in the contest against the Drapers and Tailors,
the Shearmen and Fullers agreed to unite in one Company. The
amalgamation was not achieved without opposition; the Mayor
and Court of Aldermen were against it. As late as 29 July 1526,
'touching the Bill put to this Court by Shearmen and Fullers that
they might be united into one fellowship . . . this Court will in no
wise assent to it'.[8] But assent to it, in due course, they had to. On
18 January 1528, in the nineteenth year of the reign of Henry VIII,
the charter of incorporation was granted to them, they to be known
as 'the Guild or Fraternity of the Assumption of the Blessed Virgin
Mary of Clothworkers in the City of London'.

Although junior in foundation the Shearmen came first in the
charter of the new Company. The Clothworkers succeeded to the
precedence of the Shearmen and took the last place among the
twelve so-called 'Great' Companies. The Dyers continued as the
first of the so-called 'Minor' Companies. Such then was, in brief,
the lineage and the ancestry of the Guild or Fraternity of Clothworkers.

BACKGROUND

The new Company found themselves heirs to a situation, both
national and international, that was filled with complications and
dangers. The whole of the first reign – that of Henry VIII – in which
they had their being, fell within 'the Age of the Italian Wars',
which continuously involved the greater part of Europe in the
struggle.

Spain and France were constantly embroiled. In the twenty years
immediately preceding the emergence of the infant Clothworkers'
Company, Henry VIII had managed to fight three wars, two with
France and Scotland and one with Spain. The first of these wars had
absorbed the whole of Henry VIII's considerable treasure and large

sums of money granted by Parliament as well. The second war, by paralysing the trade and commerce of the country, resulted in heavier taxation, and the third war crippled at the source those riches on which taxation might have been levied.[1] As Maitland says:

a war, happening between England and the Emperor, it put an entire stop to the trade with Spain; whereby the Clothiers became such sufferers that, not being able to dispose of their Goods they were obliged to dismiss their servants which had liked to have occasioned insurrections in divers Parts of the Kingdom; wherefore the Cardinal Minister ordered several of the principal Merchants of this City to attend him, when he simply threatened, that if they did not take off cloths &c. from the Clothiers, as usual (notwithstanding the Merchants being as great sufferers by the war as the Clothiers, by their not being able to export one piece to the Imperial Dominions where formerly their principal Commerce lay) the Cloth Market should be removed from Blackwell Hall in the City to Westminster: However, it was neither in the power of the King nor in that of his Minister to execute the aforesaid injunction. Wherefore Commerce continued on the same foot as before till the conclusion of a Peace.[2]

Peasant insurrections in the south-east and east of England had, in fact, led eventually to the withdrawal of the new taxation and had put an end to the King's campaigns. It was a time of desperate economic difficulties although, given a peaceful Europe and a contented Kingdom, the opportunities for gain were immense. For the England into which the new Company emerged had undergone, at the end of the fifteenth century, a process of development that has been described as 'an industrial revolution hardly less momentous than the later and more familiar one'.[3]

Largely self-supporting, England was, at the same time, one of Europe's primary producers – even though its chief product had changed. The wool exports, which had once been the most important economic factor of England, had fallen to a tenth of their mid-fourteenth-century peak. The wool that had once helped the merchants of the Staple to maintain Calais, England's bridgehead on the Continent, the wool that had gone to the looms of Flanders, now went to the looms of England to feed the country's own cloth industry. In 1490 legislation had given priority in the purchasing of wool to the home market, and in the hundred years from the middle of the fifteenth century England had become a large-scale producer and exporter of woollen cloth: at the beginning of the sixteenth century England was exporting 80,000 cloths a year. It has been estimated that perhaps ten times that number were produced for the home market. It is impossible to over-emphasize the importance of the cloth trade in the national economy.

Originally, trade with the Continent had emanated from every leading seaport in England to widely separated ports along the Continental coast. But, gradually (and partly as a result of the hostility of the German Hanseatic league), the export trade had, by 1460, become forced into a single central channel, the passage to the Netherlands. It was natural, therefore, that the harbours of south-east England, the harbours most nearly concerned with that passage, should become of more importance than those more remote and that the influence of those merchants using and supplying those ports should increase. London in particular, ever the greatest port and with the richest merchants, set out to exploit the new conditions. It was the London merchants who had originally opened up the Antwerp trade; they regarded it, therefore, with a proprietary air and they opposed strongly any attempt by provincial rivals to break into the market.

A rudimentary London organization of 'Adventurers', as merchants specializing in the export trade were called, had already come into being.

In 1486, the Fellowship of Merchant Adventurers was formally created in the City. The fellowship aimed at establishing an entire monopoly over the Antwerp trade, a monopoly sustained by the device of making the fees for admission to the Company, by redemption, so high that the provincial merchants, to whom admission by apprenticeship or patrimony was in practice impossible, were discouraged from joining.

Not unnaturally there were strong protests from the provincial merchants, who found themselves crushed by the monopoly. Their complaints reached the King and as a result, in 1497, by an Act of Parliament, the fee was reduced. But this very Act of Parliament, in reducing the fee, established by implication the rights of the Merchant Adventurers to control the export trade. The way was open for the State monopoly. The Merchant Adventurers were on the royal road to becoming the new Staple.[4] Nor were all the other repercussions of the export drive fortunate. The ever-increasing demands for wool for the cloth trade led inevitably to a reduction in the acreage available for food production. Henceforth there was to be a constantly recurring shortage of wheat, and, as the sprawling bulk of London began to encroach upon the countryside, demanding, as yearly it engulfed ever more agricultural land, victuals from a continually widening area of the country, a problem was created that still existed in the twentieth century.[5] From a population of 75,000 in the year 1500, London grew in only one hundred years to a city of 200,000 inhabitants;* as it grew, the financial interests of city and country began increasingly to clash.

It was the rural manufacturers that benefited most greatly from the export drive because the foreign demand was mainly for an unfinished cloth that could be dyed and dressed after it had reached the Continental market. The rural districts were able and ready to supply such undressed cloths, whereas the manufacturers of London and the provincial cloth-towns, thinking naturally of the interests of their own finishing trades, wished to market their cloth already dressed and dyed.

The export trade was at that time spasmodic; shipping of cloth, previously collected from the makers to the Netherlands took place only twice yearly, in time for the fairs at Antwerp and Bergen-op-Zoom. This shipping of the cloths was the business of the Merchant Adventurers at Blackwell Hall. The actual buying of the cloth for the merchants and the collection of it from the manufacturers led to the creating of a new middleman, the cloth dealer,

---

* Of 172 youths apprenticed to Clothworkers in 1624 less than twenty were from London or its immediate suburbs. The remainder were drawn to the magnet of the city from as far afield as Cumberland.

who scoured the countryside to satisfy the demand of the shippers for undressed cloths.

In 1487 the townsmen had already secured legislation to prevent the export of undressed cloth, and the struggle to obtain a secured export market for dressed cloths continued unabated for another two hundred years. It coloured the whole history of the Cloth-workers' Company. It divided the members of the Company one against the other, as the interests of the mercantile members of the Company clashed with those of the manufacturers, and it led to class-warfare in what had originally been a comparatively class-free society. The struggles of the Clothworkers against the Merchant Adventurers, in their efforts to prevent the shipping of un-dressed cloths, continued almost as long as the two Companies still had any active control over the cloth trade. In the fluctuations of the struggle the history both of the Company and the nation was written. To recall this background will be an aid to the under-standing of the pages that follow.

STRUCTURE

It is to be regretted that, of the first eight years of the Company's existence, only fragmentary evidence remains. The Great Fire of London which destroyed those early records, left unburned of the Company's papers previous to 1536 only a few pages of accounts.

The general form of the Company is, of course, known. They were governed by a Court of twelve (in addition to the Master and four Wardens), 'of such as have been Masters of the said Mystery of the Clothworkers and of the said late Mystery of Shearmen and Fullers and of either of them'. They were to meet at the Common Hall and 'there they, among themselves and none other, to nomin-ate such person as shall be Master for the year following'.[1]

This restriction of voting power to the Company's past Masters was a development not called for in the charter, but it was a restriction in keeping with the trend of development of the Livery Companies, for a characteristic of the new types of association was that the legal status of incorporation gave them the right to hold property in land,[2] 'to purchase receive demise and alienate in fee and perpetuity lands and tenements rent and other possessions whatsoever',[3] and it was the most successful merchants and land-owners – the sort of men who became Masters of the Company – who were obviously the most suited to conduct such new business.

The posts of Master and Wardens, too, generally devolved on those who were the wealthiest, for the majority of members of the Company found it quite impossible to bear the expenses connected with the office.[4] A new gentry of England was arising from the moneyed ranks of the City Companies.

The Clothworkers were now divided into two classes: the craftsmen who devoted themselves to the finishing of cloth and the merchants who bought the unfinished cloth from a clothier and employed the craftsmen of the Company to finish it – a business in which their chief rivals were the Merchant Taylors. Doubtless, they sold some part of the cloth produced direct to the consumer, but for the most part they dealt with the Merchant Adventurers and the Drapers.[5] The resulting oligarchy was to lead to con-stitutional crisis. Laws were demanded – and obtained – by the craftsmen for the better securing of their livelihood, laws which were often – particularly in the case of those regulating the export of undressed cloths to the Continent – contrary to the interests of the governing body of merchants. It was a system that was to lead to endless trouble.

*   *

*

In the earlier days, even after the Shearmen and Fullers had attained incorporation (an indication that there was a well-to-do trading element present among the workmen), they were both of them still socially overshadowed by the Drapers.

The majority of the larger cloth merchants belonged to the Drapers, and, like calling to like, this tended to draw away to the ranks of the more influential company the richer members of the Shearmen and the Fullers. An example of this had occurred in 1515 when Alderman Bayley, free of the Shearmen, was translated to the Drapers' Company soon after his election. His brother-Shear-men, in their disgust, called him a perjuror, for they said 'he had solemnly declared that he would live and die a true Shearman'. For publicly insulting him, Shearmen had been fined and imprisoned.

But from the amalgamation of Shearmen and Fullers a new Merchant Company had arisen. Soon the Clothworkers were to boast an Alderman of their own. The days of envious inferiority were ended, but so, too, was ended the carefree solidarity of the Company. The class barrier had been raised with disastrous speed[6]. The body of the Company now consisted of men amongst whom discontent, though hidden for long periods (for who would raise his voice in complaint against his master when work was short and the cost of living was high?) was always liable to break out in active shape.

The members of the Company soon became divided into four degrees. First, and most junior, came the *Apprentices*. Their con-ditions of employment were controlled and inspécted. The number that each householder was allowed to employ was restricted, not only to control the numbers entering the trade, but also because, being forbidden to take wages, they might have provided a plenti-ful supply of cheap labour to the detriment of the second group, the *Freemen* of the Company. These freemen, sometimes called the *Yeomanry*, some times the *Company of Bachelors*,★ were journey-men or servingmen who undertook not to work for any foreigner – that is to say, for anyone who was not a freeman of the craft. This usually meant working for the third group, or *Householders*, the men who had been given licence to set up house on their own, to employ journeymen and, generally, to be small master-cloth-workers. They had to show, not only that they were of sufficient means, but that they were able and ready to instruct the apprentices in the art of being Clothworkers. (By definition, a Clothworker was one 'able to wet out or damp the cloth in the stocks, then put it over the perch and rough it sufficiently with card or teasle, then

---

★ They were organized on parallel lines to the Livery with their own Warden and officers. Thus the Clothworkers consisted really of two companies within one organization.

set it and afterwards shear it by hand or frame with the broad shear and to finish the cloth by planing or pressing it'.)[7]

Householders of sufficient rank might be elected, if they could afford it, to the fourth degree, the *Livery* or *Clothing* of the Company – those who were entitled to wear the gown and hood – and it was from the wealthy members of the Livery that the Master Wardens and Court of Assistants were elected.

In theory, it was possible to rise from Journeyman to Master: in practice, though instances of such promotion were not unknown, it was of overwhelming difficulty, and, as time went by and the classes and orders of society became more and more rigidly marked by boundaries of wealth and breeding, it became virtually impossible.

Such then was the ancestry, background, and structure of the Guild or Fraternity of the Assumption of the Blessed Virgin Mary of Clothworkers in the City of London when, on St Catherine's Day in the year 1531, Oliver Claymond, Christopher Cherborne, and John Perle stepped out of obscurity and set in train the history of the Company.

CHAPTER ONE

THE FORMATIVE YEARS

* *

*

THE journey to Westminster to Sir Thomas More has been chosen as the Prologue of this story for the reason that it is the earliest clear and connected account of an incident in the corporate life of the Company that remains on record. It stands out – in addition to its importance to the Company's being – as the first detailed incident to have survived the destruction of the Company's earliest records in 1666. For the rest of those early years there remains nothing but little scattered allusions to things once known.

From these minutiae it can be gathered that, three years after the amalgamation of the two parent companies, both the old Halls were still in use: for there is a reference, in 1531, to 'conveying the 1531 great fire pan from the other Hall by four porters'. The Hall in Mincing Lane had been bought by the Shearmen in 1456.* By inference, therefore, the other Hall which stood in Billiter Lane (now Billiter Street), close to one of the ancient estates of the Fishmongers' Company and to Ironmongers' Hall, was that of the Fullers. From the scanty records it can be gathered, too, that the new Company had established itself in the Hall in Mincing Lane, and that in the garden, where rubbish was burned in a trench, a vine grew upon a frame and there was eglantine; that, at the election of the Wardens in the Hall, a gallon of Bastard was drunk, and that, on our Mass Day in 1534, the whole company – some 264 members, including ten brethren and three widows – drank five kilderkins

---

* The earliest title deed relating to the Mincing Lane site is dated 1391 when it was apparently privately owned. On 15 July 1456 it was conveyed to certain individual Citizens and Shearmen in fee simple.[1]

13

of good ale, an average of nearly three pints per head; that the Company, whose gross income for the financial year 1529–30 was £69 16s 8d, used the seal of the Shearmen (which represented Our Lady) and adapted it, probably in 1551, with a roughly-inscribed 'Clothworkers'; and that, after Court Meetings, the Company would adjourn to the Cardinal's Hat in Lombard Street or the Boar's Head in Eastcheap.

From the sombre background of the events that were shaking the nation such trivia are almost all that have survived. The stories of social disorder, the immense increase in the number of public executions, the growing poverty and dishonesty, the outrages committed by soldiers returning from the wars, the very Reformation itself, find no echoes in the Company's records. Of the effects of that vast unemployment that led the Duke of Norfolk to write to Wolsey on 4 May 1528[2] that 'divers substantial Clothiers' had been with him

that day complaining that they had had no sale for their cloths at London, and that unless remedy were found they would be unable to keep their work folk in work more than a fortnight or three weeks – the scarcity of oil alone, they said, would compel them to give up making cloth unless some came to them from Spain

of all this no word remains. To all the sensational events of those first years, but one reference remains, an account, for the 15th day of May 1536, for 6s 8d, 'spent at the Pope's Head in Crooked Lane on certain of the Company that waited on my Lord Mayor to the Tower when the Queen* was judged'.

The same year the garden was new-set with Rosemary and Spyke, and on the reverse of one of the Warden's Accounts is written in wry criticism of the accountant: 'Thys ys ove a rude and sympull hande'.

* *

*

But in any case, as will be seen, great national events were seldom referred to directly in the Company's early records. There are inferences and allusions, but for the most part the story is one of the

* Anne Boleyn.

Here followithe the last charge
for the seid boke

Item to j recordeys clark to wryte o boke new in ...
... levys off pap and acts lyke as yt now stondithe ... xxxs
... boke of ...

Item geven to my lord norwiche for a reward — ... xls
Item in lyke wyse to my lord cheyffe justyce of
the kyngys benche — ... xls

Item to mayst Johnson for wrytyng owte of this — ... xls
boke in length in perchement

Item for glewyng the ij vollams to gy ther — ... iiijd
Item ffor o dend at westmynst for vs ... — ... vjs
Item spent at the iij drawys at ... other tyme — ... viijd
Item for bote hyr vp and downe that day — ... vjd

Item delyverd to j clopper to helpe vs to loke to my — ... vj s viijd
lord chauncelor for vynyng of o boke —
Item spent at the cloke howse that day for o dend — ... xxd
to tary tylt my lord had dyned —

Item rewarded to ... a ster cloper to ... — ... iijs
my lord a goffs hed of wyne —

Item spent on saynt katheryn evy d vpe downe — ... xxjd
ij dyned tyme to the tempull & other charges —
Item for j recordeys bote hyre to westmynst on o — ... iiijd
saynt katheryn day at after none —

Item geven to the porter that kept the ster chambre dore ... iijd
Item the sonday after saynt katheryn day for j — ... vj s viijd
recordeys labour for to ... vs ij chaborne ... perll ...
& one penny to my lord cheyffe justyce whow the
... o boke —

Item for j recordeys bote hyre ij pollis & my sylffe — ... iiijd
Item Edwayrd his servante that wayted on j recorder — ... iijd

Sū — ... pt ...

narrower scene. The early minutes particularly are concerned with recording the accounts of domestic disputes. If one member accused another of calling him a 'false churl and knave' in the middle of Lombard Street, the Court made them be friends again. If two members were at variance over a debt, the Court settled the amount to be paid and the manner of payment. If an apprentice accused his master of some breach of the terms of his apprenticeship, the Court put the matter right. If there was any disagreement over the sale of goods, or about rent to be paid, the Court judged the matter and the disputing parties accepted the judgement as they would have accepted that of a Court of Law. Orders in restraint of trade were imposed, money was lent out at 9 per cent, and fines were levied for the illegal setting-up of house or for the ill workmanship of cloth which had been confiscated during the official search. But this idyllic picture of a Company obedient to its rulers and, after being at variance, dutifully doing as they were bidden, 'to take each other by the hand and, in time coming, to be lovers and friends and no more to have no such Rebukings the one to the other', is but one side of the medal.

The country, as a whole, was in a state of social disorder and the Company, in particular, proved no exception.

Social Unrest

On 20 September 1538 the Master and Wardens assembled at the Hall to give a solemn warning:

1538

Forasmuch as there is divers and many obstinate and misruled and riotous Journeymen and Servants, and also apprentices, the which maketh many vagabonds within our Craft, the which Journeymen at their own wills and pleasures at divers times will not work without they may be hired for a certain time but will rather sit in Ale houses and haunt ill company, and also play at unlawful games, the which is great hurt and hindrance and an undoing to all young men and an ill example for many servants – and also a great slander unto our Company. For the which it is ordained and agreed that no man within our Craft shall not keep nor set no foreigners at work without he can get no friend or else to ask licence of the master and wardens.

Also if that any master hath any need of a Journeyman and knows where that he is, and if the said Journeyman will not work without he may be hired for a certain time take him and set him at work as long as your work will last and it be for one day or two. And if that there be any such Journeyman that will not work after this Rate but had rather play and go up and down like a Vagabond let all such be sent into prison and there to tarry the pleasure of the Master and Wardens a day or twain for the first fault. And for the second like fault to be in prison five days. And at the third to be tied at a cart's Arse and beaten naked through the City like a vagabond. And to be banished the City for seven years and a day by my Lord Mayor's commandment, and this to be used without favour. And to the contrary to be fined at my Lord Mayor's commandment and the Master and the Aldermen.

Furthermore there be divers and many house holders the which receiveth and taketh apprentices to be bound unto them and, within short space after, they do let the said Apprentices have so much of their will that they run abroad and in conclusion their masters cannot rule and order them. Wherefore all such masters that hath any 'prentices, or here-after shall have any, the said masters shall charge and give in command-ment unto their 'prentices that on holidays they shall truly wait upon their master or masters to the church and there to serve God.

And after, to wait upon their master and masters at dinner and supper – And in no wise to go from their master's house or door without the licence of their master. And that their master shall give no licence to no 'prentice to go forth to no place without he know whither he goeth, and in what company he goeth in, that he neither haunt tavern nor alehouse nor bowling-alley nor none other suspicious place.

And, if the said 'prentice do, the charge to be laid to the said master and [he] to be punished for the said 'prentice. Also and if any master hath any apprentices that keepeth any ill rule [such] as haunting of whores or any other unlawful games and cannot Rule the said 'prentice nor by punishment neither by fair words that then the said master shall com-plain unto the Master and Wardens and bring him to the Hall before the Master and Wardens, and there shall punish him according unto his offences openly in the Hall. . . .

This is the first of the very many occasions on which it becomes increasingly apparent that Merry England did not consist entirely of happy, carefree men and women only too ready to do a full day's work for a full day's pay, with some maypole dancing thrown in for good measure on high days and holidays. In fact, the

conflict between the two interests of the Company – the mercantile and operative – was now beginning to take shape.

Economic conditions were making it difficult for the smaller
masters without capital – and many were in a very small way
indeed* – to maintain their status and many of them were forced
into becoming journeymen to pay their debts.[3] For these same
economic reasons – which included the expenses of entrance fees,
of dinners, of 'a drinking', and so on – it became more and more
difficult for a journeyman ever to become a master.

This state of affairs, true to many of the Livery Companies, was
particularly marked in the cloth trade, where, therefore, the class
feeling was most accentuated. It had led to the organization of
Yeomanry or Bachelors existing below the Livery, and, in practice,
agitation by the Yeomanry craftsmen would lead to legislation
which the merchants of the Livery would then ignore. Parliament,
to whom the craftsmen appealed, fluctuated between a desire to
check the too rapid rise of the new mercantile gentry and to
regulate trade as it stood: its policy was, therefore, constantly
changing.

The first evidence of this state of affairs of the house divided
against itself comes in 1540 when two craftsmen, John Pillsworth 1540
and John Draper, brought in a supplication to be put before the
King. It was read to the Court for their approval and 'They liked
it well save in two or three points'.

In spite of this qualified approval John Draper began to find that
his connexion with the supplication was doing him harm in his
relations with his employers; they resented the animadversions he
had made against the behaviour of those who did not uphold the
laws that had been made for the benefit of the craftsmen. Two
months went by and John Draper appeared in a very ill humour
before the Court.

This H all [he said] is a place of Secret and what person, whosoever he
were, should open or declare abroad any words out of this house it were
almost his head were worthy to be set on London Bridge.

* In some cases, the admission fee of 10s could only be collected in quarterly
payments of one shilling.

He then addressed himself to the Master:

Whereas you say that I said that there be many heads on the Bridge and [that] if there were three or four more it made no matter: so I said, for it were better that three or four more should perish than twenty or forty hundred should.

For the King's grace – God save him! – for the common wealth of his Grace's subjects (being of the poor handicraft of Clothworkers within this realm), with all the Honourable Council, hath made an Act and proclaimed that no person should send nor convey nor cause to be sent nor conveyed into the parts beyond the sea any white Woollen cloths above the price of £4 nor coloured cloths above the price of £3 and upward, unrowed, unbarbed and unshorn upon pain of forfeiting the value of the said cloth or cloths so carried and conveyed into the parts beyond the sea. And if there were six or eight that do steal and convey away the living of the King's poor subjects [it was right that their heads] be chopped off and set upon the Bridge in tokening of all others that follow that trade and which they do contrary to the King's Acts. . . .

Secondly, you say that I said [that] the head of the assistants of the Company was under your girdle. And so I say again because of your being Alderman and taking yourself as head and ruler of the Company and bretheren of this house of Clothworkers. And so do all the Assistants, and the whole body of the craft, take you as their head and ruler over them in keeping and setting forth good order and in increasing and maintaining of a common wealth for them.

Thirdly, you said that I said there be many murmurings against you and grudges; Aye! Forsooth! And even so I may well say so if it be, as I understand, by against you, hearing it recorded that you, being in this secret house of council, revealed what I and my fellow did shew you touching the Associates of this house. In which matter, the two of us were not seeking our own advantage but the King's. Therefore if you did reveal it you were not worthy of being told anything that is to the King's advantage.

No more is reported of this affair,* but it is one of the greatest significance.

The following year legislation was introduced to restrict the

* Though, later, it was ruled that proceedings at Court meetings should not be divulged – a victory for the complainants.

export of undressed cloth – and again it was tacitly ignored by the merchants.

The class warfare that this behaviour gave rise to makes the Livery's policy towards their Yeomanry more readily understandable.

In March 1543 an attempt was made to remodel the Yeomanry.

It is agreed that the Wardens of the Yeomanry now being shall bring in their box with their money, their cloth and their torches and the Master and Wardens to choose four honest men, being Journeymen, and they to be as Wardens of the Journeymen only and they to have the cloth and torches in their custody and that there be four Journeymen yearly chosen to the said room by the Master and Wardens for the time being.

Several inferences can be drawn from this action. Obviously the Yeomanry no longer consisted entirely of journeymen. By choosing their officers for them and by excluding from the election the small masters who were members of the Yeomanry, the position of the latter in the affairs of the Company would be considerably weakened.

This intention failed, however, for the existing organization was too firmly entrenched to be remodelled. By 1546 it had been reluctantly agreed that the Yeomanry should choose their own wardens as they had done before. But they still remained financially dependent upon the goodwill of the Court, and in 1553 new ordinances for their 'governance and good ordering' were promulgated. They were to have four wardens of their own who were to collect 6d quarterage from householders other than Liverymen. (Of this quarterage £16 per annum was to be paid to the Master and Wardens of the Company.)

The wardens of the Yeomanry were given limited disciplinary powers but in the use of these they were strictly overseen by the Master.

Their finances, too, were controlled for there was provided

a chest with three locks and three keys, two of the said keys to be in the custody of two several wardens of the said Bachelors and the third key to be in the custody of the Master of the said Company for the time being to the intent that when any money shall be either put into the said chest or taken out of the said chest, the said Master may be made privy thereof.*

*   *
*

These fluctuations in the attitude towards the Yeomanry came about as the Company gradually tended more and more to pass into the hands of the merchant class. But even though the control was changing, it was not at first possible for the Clothworkers to become an utterly mercantile Company like that of the Drapers or the Merchant Taylors. The whole reason for the Company's corporate existence lay in the claim to represent the craftsmen against the merchants: the small master craftsmen in the Company could, and did, insist that the authority of the Company should 1587 protect them. By 1587, the structure of the Company had again changed as the result of compromise. The merchants still governed and the industrial element was still subordinate to them. But the Yeomanry had emerged from the struggle a different organization. Whereas it had at one time been thought possible for it to be an organization for journeymen only, it was now composed for the most part of small masters. These small masters administered such funds as that for supplying teasles at cost price to poor house-holders, they controlled the admission of householders to the Company, and to them fell the examination of apprentices.

By 1587, in a short sixty years, the strata of society had settled into fixed and rigid bounds. The new ordinances provided that journeymen, who previously had been forbidden to marry or set up house – living in their masters' houses like servants and sharing bed and board – might set up house on their own if they could prove that they were worth £10.

But, in their wording, the ordinances showed that the journey-men had sunk still lower in the Company's scale, for they spoke of electing yearly four Yeomanry 'for the better regiment, rule and government of the said Yeomanry and Journeymen'.

* More than 400 years later the chest still survived in good and usable condition.

The journeymen now played a subordinate role to that of the Yeomanry. Certainly they had ceased even to express their grievances through their appointed officers, so they can have had no sense of solidarity with them.

This rapid evolution, by which a company formed to represent the interests of the manufacturer had fallen into the power of the merchants, led to other problems. As a mercantile corporation, its interests clashed even more violently with those of the Merchant Taylors – a company containing many merchant employers. The latter challenged most strongly the claim of the Clothworkers to regulate the industry, and, as will be seen, the two companies remained rivals during the whole period of their industrial importance.

* *
*

While the classes of society were gradually, almost imperceptibly, being sifted, the everyday business of the Company was continuing and developing in scope as the corporation grew in complexity. From 1540 to 1550 there is great preoccupation with legislative detail. Trading laws were gradually formulated – some on moral grounds, others as a practical policy for the protection of the handicraft interests.

Domestic Legislation

For example, in 1541, restrictions on Sunday working enacted that no man should

1541

from henceforth sell or suffer to stand upon his tenter any cloth or cloths or carsey upon a Sunday between Candlemass and Halloweentide [2 February to 1 November] nor hang any cloth to dry upon any pale, hedge or rail without the City upon pain to forfeit and pay 2/– for every cloth.

All householders having apprentices and journeymen were instructed – at the Lord Mayor's order – to see that their servants were well-behaved; they were warned that they should only keep servants who were of honest behaviour and they were to 'see them indoors before ten at night and not out before four o'clock in the morning as they would answer at their uttermost perils'.

1547   Possibly from the moral code, too, arose restrictions placed in 1547 on the public employment of women: nobody was

from henceforth to suffer either his wife or any of his maidservants to work openly either in his shop or at his tenters or else to suffer any of them to carry either Kersey or Broadcloth through the streets or shears to the grinding.

From the additional order: 'Any maid or womankind is forbidden to work in any shop, tenter or other open place', it would seem that 'openly' was the operative word.

For the protection of the Company's property, it was decreed that no man 'having a key of the Common Stair should★ lend his key to any stranger, being none of the Company, to wash bucks nor for no other intent upon pain to forfeit 6/8d'. (A member who attempted to evade this order by having his own servants bring other men's 'bucks' to the Thames-side was discovered and fined.)

1543   In 1543, attempts to secure, for the future, the controlling interest in the trade began to be made and a Bill or Petition was presented to the Lord Mayor and Aldermen

that all who occupy the handy-craft being free of other Companies may be translated over to our Company, or else that all the apprentices may henceforth be bound to one of our Company and so set over to them that they shall be [trained] withall. So always at their years' end they may be made free of this Company.

Two years later no satisfactory reply to this petition had been made and the suit was renewed. The Company were, in fact, finding their feet and beginning to employ their own stratagems in the subtly waged warfare of inter-guild politics. Amidst all this welter of legislature, of the hearing of disputes and of punishing offenders, and of the ever-tightening grip upon the controls of trade, the social side of the Company still continued, and from the records of those social activities there does come, for a moment, the faint savour of the perpetual roistering that is apt to be associated with Tudor England.

★ For details of Clothworkers' Stairs, see Appendix E.

There come such items as the election of wardens when hippo-
crass was drunk and minstrels played; of the accounts of how Mass
at St Dunstan's-in-the-East on the Sunday after Lady Day was
followed by bread spiced with pepper, saffron, and Mays, white
buns and butter, and a barrel of Ale; of how, when the Clothworkers went to Westminster, they travelled in a chartered barge
glorious with silken banners and streamers, the bargemaster in a
hat bedecked with ribbons.

These were pleasant, homely occasions and, although, particularly after searches had taken place, the members of the Company
resorted to taverns, most of their activities, of course, were
centred round their Hall: dinners were held there (although, since
the cost of dinners had risen by twenty-five per cent, they sometimes had 'a drinking over-night' instead); and it was there that
pageants were performed at midsummer when twenty-four men
in straw hats held the cressets that flared outside the Hall all the
midsummer night long. Indeed, one of the domestic factors that
must have contributed largely to the Company's growing confidence in themselves and in their actions was the building and
occupying of a new Hall of their own. The use of the Shearmen's
Hall had at best been a makeshift, the occupation of another's
house – a house designed for a smaller Company and now, by
Tudor standards, outmoded.

On 8 April 1548 it was agreed that a parcel of the Company's
land should be sold to raise funds for the building of a Hall. The
old building was to be pulled down immediately and a contract
sought for the erection of the frame for a new one on the same site
in Mincing Lane.

Three months later a bricklayer bargained – presumably after the
frame had been constructed by a carpenter – 'to bring up and make
the sides of the walls with brick and all other workmanship of
brick and he to have for his labour £20 and he to find scaffolding-
stuff and all other charges of workmanship and make it 18 feet
high'. By some miscalulation, as it chanced, the builder made the
walls two feet higher than he had bargained and was out of pocket
by doing so. But the Court were in generous mood and paid him

23

the extra forty shillings he was asking. The carpenter, too, had made a mistake and found himself ten pounds out in his costing. 1549 This, too, the Court made good and in 1549 the Hall was ready for occupation. A new Parlour had been built in 1538 – there was a clear distinction made between the Parlour and the Hall: the Parlour was used for business while the Hall was devoted entirely to the public and social meetings of the Company.*

The Hall garden, enriched with twenty loads of dung, was new made with hyssop, spike, sage, daisies, and other herbs; and, since no expenditure was then too small to be itemized, it was recorded that 4d was spent upon 'lyttle basket and a waterying potte'.

* *

*

The Reformation Meanwhile, in the harsh outside world, a world typified by those thin-lipped, unsmiling portraits by Holbein, stirring events were going on that the writers of the Clothworkers' minutes, perhaps with the silence of fear, found it wiser to ignore. At their meetings reference must surely have been made to some aspect of the Reformation, yet in the minutes there is none. The little whispered prayers: 'Jhus', 'Jhus Amor', 'Jhus Maria', 'Jhus have mercy on all Xpen souls', with which the clerks dedicated their pages, are quietly discontinued. For one year only, from 15 May 1546, the new style, 'by the Grace of God King of England, France and Ireland, Defender of the Faith and in the Earth Supreme Head of the Church of England and Ireland' is used in the heading of Court minutes. But then that, too, drops silently away.

Obits and candles and masses disappear for a while and some layman is given the tenancy of what had been a priest's house. But of the revolt of some counties against the religious laws enforced by Protector Somerset in 1549 nothing is heard, though, perhaps, there is an inkling of it in the precepts of the Lord Mayor that the Companies should provide themselves with handguns and artillery

* 'The diffensive body, viz. the Yeomanry or Journeymen, paid for their sports, recreations, and assemblies in this Hall; nay, they were permitted sometimes the use of the Hall upon their good abaring to the Master, Wardens and Fellowship.'4

and that every man should make provision of victuals for his house for one month.

Of the fall of Thomas Cromwell all that appears is the record that the Company in 1543 bought some of his attainted lands beside Austin Friars and paid £666 13s 4d for them. From the reign of terror instituted by the 'upstart Nobles on the Council of Regency'[5] no word comes except the injunction to the whole Company 'that they should have no unfitting words of my Lord of Warwick nor of any other of the Council upon the pain and peril that will fall thereof. And that they see their servants keep in due order as they will answer'.

Of the Army necessary to subdue the rebels and to support a projected alliance with the Emperor, when his struggle with France was renewed in 1543, there remain orders for soldiers to be supplied and equipped. 'Five Billmen and a Bowman equipped for the King's wars, with swords, daggers, white kersey caps etc.' was one detachment. Another call was for twenty-eight soldiers and, indeed, there are many of these evidences of conscription.

Of the confiscation of the monastic houses there is no mention, yet this was a factor that contributed enormously to the ten years of unparalleled prosperity that the Company enjoyed. The dissolution of the monasteries provided those in the wool trade with an additional source of the land they needed for pasturing the number of sheep that were now necessary to supply the increased demand of the clothiers. The monastic buildings, too, were bought by business men and adapted for the uses of industry.* William Stumpe took over the Abbeys at Osney and Malmesbury where, wrote Leland, 'Every corner of the vast houses of office that belonged to the Abbey be full of looms. . . ' The spacious halls, outbuildings and mills enabled the industrialist to concentrate in one establishment workmen and processes previously dispersed.[6]

Industrial Results of the Reformation

They were the first factories, as we understand them to-day. With the enormous increases of production it was inevitable that there should be a diminution in the quality of the goods produced.

* Some monasteries had already established 'factories', such as that at Cirencester with its fulling mills, which were taken over as going concerns.

As the village manufacturers were called upon for more and more output, so it became necessary to employ more part-time and untrained workers. There were endless complaints about the quality of English cloth.

There was a certain Red cloth brought in by Gilbert and Smith, partners free of the mystery and Company of Drapers, to be viewed and overseen whether that the faults in the same cloth were by means of the Shearmen or else by means of rowing. Which cloth was viewed and seen by Mr. Small and Mr. Rogers, Wardens, Mr. Davy, Mr. Pettinger, Mr. Wagstaff and John Benloss, who found that the cloth was marred and hurt for lack of rowing and ill-shearing in the country before it was dyed and no fault in the shearing here within this City.

1549   By 1549, workmanship had so greatly deteriorated that the city authorities found it necessary to issue a 'Proclamation concerning True Dying and Dressing of Cloth'.[7] Among many other remedies, were such regulations as:

Every Clothier to seal his Cloth declaring the just length thereof to be tried by Water.
No Tenter keeper or cloth stretcher to stretch a cloth above a yard in length and half a quarter of a yard in width;
No one to sell a cloth which when wet will shrink more than the above measurements.
No iron cards to be used in Rowing.

The Aldermen of the Steel Yard in London for the time being were to search all packhouses of the Steel Yard 'and shall prove in the water as many cloths and kerseys as they shall suspect whether they be drawn or strained' contrary to the Proclamation.

The Wardens of the Clothworkers to search all Clothworkers at least once a quarter.

No doubt these and similar measures did something to lessen the evils arising from the increased production, an increased production from which there emerged a new figure, the Master Clothier, the industrial tycoon of whom John Winchcombe – 'Jack of Newbury' – remains as an example that has become almost legendary.

Another fillip to the cloth industry was given by a debasement Prosperity of the coinage at home and an exchange depreciation abroad. The Continent was able to buy more English goods in general and English cloth in particular.

During the reign of Henry VIII the export of short-cloths from London had more than doubled: a great part of this increase occurring in the last ten years of his life. The climax was reached during the late 1540s when a truly amazing expansion had been achieved. By 1550 the foreign sales of the London trade had reached 132,000 short-cloths a year.

Pleasant though this situation might be for those in the cloth business and invigorating though the atmosphere of prosperity must have been to the Company – particularly when in 1549 a further debasement of the coinage led to a further leap in the exports of cloth – the financial gains were somewhat offset by the concomitants that followed a too sudden prosperity: the growth of materialism, a decay in business ethics and in public morals, a neglect of the Christian virtues, and an outbreak of vice and crime. But, if the weakening of the moral fibres of the country could be generally ignored, except by a few gloomy prelates such as Latimer, the economic situation itself contained unhealthy aspects which carried within them the germs of great danger – and that was something that could not be overlooked.

London was gradually destroying England. London was hand-ling four-fifths of the whole of the national commerce. London allied itself with the rural cloth-industry against the provincial cloth-towns. London imported such foreign goods as the felt hats demanded by the fashionable and, in doing so, drove native crafts-men out of business.

The whole national economy, concentrated into the cloth-business, was becoming, in the view of many – including such a scholar as John Hales – lopsided. All the country's eggs were in the one basket of the Netherlands trade, a basket that could be upset and the contents smashed by forces quite outside English control. For this reason the Subsidy Act of 1548 (equivalent, roughly, to the twentieth century's Finance Act), which voted revenue raised from taxation to the Crown, made an attempt, common enough to-day but then a novelty, to control economic planning by taxation. At Hales's suggestion, a tax of 1d per sheep, a halfpenny a pound on wool used for cloth-making, and 3s 4d on every exported broadcloth was imposed. The sum that, it was anticipated, would be raised by such a tax amounted to £112,000 a year: a sum nearly equal to the entire revenue of the Crown.

But in 1549 the Subsidy Act was repealed, 'as the result of vigorous lobbying by clothiers and sheepmasters', and the very next year that blow to the country's economic position which had been feared came crashing down on the heads of those who had been merely living for the day and ignoring the reckoning to follow.

Slump   A further debasement of the coinage led, this time, to a slump in foreign exchange. The cost of living at home had, in two short years, been doubled. Attempts at price-control led to black-marketeering and all that that involved. The high price of the cloths produced, coupled with a saturation of the Antwerp market, led to a sudden check in the export market. It is a pattern that is sadly familiar. Merchants began to complain of over-production. The boom was ended: the slump had begun. Yet, by a natural dispensation, some good resulted from this gloomy scene. England, and Englishmen, were stimulated by the economic collapse to a revival of maritime enterprise and seamanship, which was, on more than one occasion, to save the very existence of the Kingdom.

1551   In 1551 a further blow fell upon the export trade. Devaluation took place by the drastic method of marking down the coinage to fifty per cent of its face value. The foreign sales of short-cloth fell immediately from 132,000 to 112,000. The next year they had fallen to 85,000. The warehouses were full: customers were few. Prices and standards of manufacture were cut in an attempt to halt the glissade. The clothiers sold their wares at a loss and still no increase in sales resulted. Unemployment followed rapidly, and, in an attempt to remedy the situation, restrictive legislation was enacted to control the standards of workmanship and the time – seven years – to be served by an apprentice before he was allowed to weave broadcloth.

In the collapse of all the prosperity that had been built up and enjoyed during the ten years of boom conditions the Clothworkers' Company were grieviously involved. Furthermore, the confiscation of lands devoted to so-called superstitious uses dealt a terrible blow at the Company's finances, for the capital outlay needed to purchase the lands back from the King was considerable. In 1549 the Clothworkers had to pay £405 3s 4d to the Crown for the purchase of quit rents amounting to some £20 a year.

By 1552 the Company were financially in difficulties and

it was agreed that no general dinner be kept till such time as Mr. Hind shall be Mayor except it shall be for some special cause. And that every Master yearly between this and the said time shall pay towards the charges of the house £6.13.4. and every Warden to like use £5.

Mentioned that this order was taken in consideration that the house was at the present day in debt to the sum of 13 score pounds and above.

Not for very many years were the Company to be free from the dead weight of debt.

*   *

*

For a Company in a parlous financial condition, continual and expensive litigation – principally against their great rivals, the Merchant Taylors – was an added and crippling burden.

The Struggle Against the Merchant Taylors

This rivalry which, as has been shewn, had been occasioned by, and grown in force with, the evolution of the Clothworkers into a Mercantile Company, was first directly referred to in 1545; the same quarrel, scarcely abated, still continued 160 years later.

The first shots in the battle had been fired on 12 March 1545, when a Bill of Petition had been made to the Lord Mayor and Aldermen for the translation of all apprentices engaged in working cloth to the Clothworkers' Company.

To control apprentices entering the trade was eventually to control the trade itself, and of all the Companies it was the Merchant Taylors who reacted most strongly in opposition to the Petition.[8]

29

As a result of their manoeuvring the matter was repeatedly adjourned and it was not until early in 1548 that a committee of twelve persons selected as arbitrators from different Companies met to pronounce upon the dispute. Three years had already elapsed and another three years were to be wasted in the innumerable fatiguing delays of the law. In the time of waiting tempers ran high and there were one or two riots between supporters of the two Companies. Once the Clothworkers had to be called together and given 'commandment that they should be quiet among themselves and keep their servants in due obedience without any contention or words of reproach by any of them to be spoken'.

It was not until 21 April 1551 that the final report of the Committee of Arbitration was published. The Arbitrators pronounced unfavourably upon the Clothworker claims and, in spite of several stormy meetings at which the Company roundly declared they would never submit, their resistance suddenly collapsed.

It was meekly agreed that the Common Seal of the Company should be given to abide the Lord Mayor's decision, and a month later it was decided that all variance between the Clothworkers and the Taylors should be decided by the Lord Mayor. First blood was clearly, as might have been expected, to the older and more experienced Company. The terms of the settlement, though not mentioned in the Clothworkers' records, are to be found in the City Repertories.

But the Clothworkers were not entirely defeated. One of their grievances left outstanding had been that the Taylors were flooding the market with apprentices when, by limiting the number to two per master, the Clothworkers had hoped to maintain a monopoly. They appealed to the Court of Common Council, and in 1552 the Lord Mayor did, in fact, order that no more than two apprentices should be kept by any householder in the trade, and that no male servant above twelve years of age should be kept without being apprenticed. Otherwise, victory was to the Merchant Taylors.

Once or twice the Clothworkers kicked officially against the pricks. In May 1552 they attempted to obtain legislation to prohibit those 'persons using to Row at the Perch or to Shear with the

Broad Shear from taking an apprentice not bound to a Cloth-worker'.[9] But their proposal was rejected as being contrary to the liberties and custom of the city. For the time being they made no further attempt to extend their jurisdiction.

There are a few reports of acts of individual disobedience by rebellious journeymen, but they were unofficial and they were punished. Generally speaking there reigned, for fourteen years, an uneasy peace.

CHAPTER TWO

THE DOMESTIC SCENE

*   *
*

THERE follows a brief period of domesticity when the story of
the Company looks inwards upon themselves rather than out-
wards to the political scene.

If the Clothworkers were prevented from extending their
jurisdiction to include the members of other Companies in the
City, they had, in fact, a sufficiently strict control over their own
members. Before a Clothworker could go to law, he had to seek
the permission of the Court. It was the Court who, in the days
before there was a police force in the country, gave permission for
one Clothworker to arrest another. It was the Court who could
arrest their own members and have them imprisoned. They did
so with Robert Barrett to whom a cloth had been put – by a
Merchant Taylor – for a first coursing –

which Barrett carried the said cloth to the dyers being never touched
with shear, wherefore, for as much as the said Barrett craftily to the
slander of the whole Company would have suffered the said cloth to
have passed unwrought

he was committed to the Ward.

It was now that the washing of 'bucks' – or laundry – at the
Common Stair became strictly forbidden. The habit had been the
chief contributing factor in the decay of the Stairs, the repair of
which was a continual drain on the Company's resources. Now,
too, the fustian sellers were warned to employ none other than
regular fustian shearers who were on the official list. Cottoners and
kerseymakers were forbidden to use iron cards.

New ordinances for the Yeomanry were drawn up to come into force at Christmas 1552 and their wardens were elected.*

All this was in addition to the settlement of disputes, the granting of leases and all the administrative details of an increasing organization. Who will, therefore, grudge the Court the 'pottle of Muskadell' they drank on Court days? But although the Court may have been looking to their own affairs, the outside world kept breaking in.

Against a background of 'irreligion, irreverence and immorality 1550 on a truly terrifying scale'[1] England was again involved in the first armed contest for the Crown in fifty years.

At a Court Meeting held the 13th day of July 'in the first year of the reign of our Sovereign Lady Queen Jane', the whole Company were assembled and warned to keep their servants from unlawful assemblies and not to talk about the affairs of the Privy Council who had proclaimed Lady Jane Dudley as Queen.

The Council, whose forces, under Northumberland, had marched against Mary at Framlingham, fell back in the face of 'the greatest mass-demonstration of loyalty ever accorded to a Tudor'.[2] Without a battle the Council reversed its decision and proclaimed Mary Queen of England. The fortnight's reign was ended.

At a cost of £4 6s a new stand was made for the Company to witness the entry of the Queen into the City. A present – assessed on the Company by the Lord Mayor at £34 – was given to Her Majesty, and, when she came by water from Westminster, the Clothworkers' barge was out on the river sailing with the rest of them.

Within a very short time religion was, so to speak, denationalized

* The election of the wardens of the Yeomanry by the Court was not an infallible way of ensuring their loyalty. When one of the Yeomanry in 1555 'had the garland set upon his head and was chosen warden according to the laudable custom used, he openly in the face of the whole company then present disobediently as well as by unseemly words as also by other misbehaviours refused to take and receive the garland'. He was sentenced to have the garland taken off his head in front of the whole company, to be dismissed and committed to Ward to purge his contempt. There is a strong note of relish in the report that 'the Master, Wardens and most of the Assistants repaired here to see the said order performed accordingly. Which order after dinner was fully in every point, performed'.

and members of the Company were being warned 'that they should strictly charge and oversee their servants that they misuse not themselves towards priests . . . upon pain of imprisoning and straight punishment'.

The return to Catholicism, was, in fact, accompanied in London by little disorder. It was quite another factor that was to lead to one of the most serious attacks aimed at the Tudor monarchy. A hatred of foreigners was the particular feature of the Tudor Englishman's character, a hatred that was only gradually watered down in the softer centuries that followed.

1554

The reaction, therefore, in 1554 to the proposed marriage of the Queen – with all its constitutional problems – to a foreigner, Philip of Spain, was instantaneous and alarming. Within a fortnight of the signature to the marriage contract, the rebellion of

Wyatt's Rebellion

Sir Thomas Wyatt had broken out. Of the series of risings he had planned, all, except the one in Kent, misfired. Against this threat to the capital, the City, in the last days of January, raised an armed force.

As far as the Clothworkers were concerned, the expedition verged upon the farcical. Considerable care had been spent in equipping and arming twenty-eight men for service against the rebels. But what happened on that valiant occasion can best be judged by the Minute, one month later:

Order was taken that all such persons which were sent out of this Hall into Kent which came Immediately home again, shall bring in their harness and weapons which they had, forasmuch as they went not whither they were sent, forasmuch as their Captains were gone away before they came, who were in number that came again, six which were known.

Some Londoners had gone over to Wyatt, but the personal courage of the Queen caused the majority to rally in defence of the City.

The Clothworkers raised and equipped fifty-six men 'warded within the City when Sir Thomas Wyatt lay in Southwark', and when, with the end of the rebellion, in due course, the Prince of

Spain came to the City, all the Clothworkers were there in strength upon their stand, with a couple of cloths hung on the rails in front of them, to greet him.

Once again they settled down to the daily domestic round. New rules about the keeping of apprentices were formulated and partnerships were forbidden. The use of 'cards' was constantly punished and a restriction placed on the purchase of teazles. Warning was given against such unlawful engines as the pin and ring.

Strong disciplinary action was taken against a householder named John Reynolds who had

lately taken into his house divers cloths of a merchant to work. And he craftily and deceitfully, to the great slander and defamation of the whole Company shore the said cloths at the one end and so pressed them and tacked them up colourably as though they had been thoroughly wrought. And took of the merchant for the workmanship of them.

For this offence he was forbidden to keep house any longer but permitted to go out to work as a Journeyman.*

Even marital disputes were brought to the Court: a husband and wife who had appealed for arbitration after living apart for two years were 'with many Godly lessons and persuasions exhorted . . . to live together as man and wife ought to do whereby they should not only win again the good report and fame of the world but also thereby obtain the favour of God. With other Godly persuasions.' But godly persuasions, perhaps at a discount in the dissolute London of the day, were in vain. The Court therefore not only ruled that the wife should have back some of the goods she had contributed to the marriage, but was actually involved in drawing up an inventory for the separated couple.

*   *
*

* At the next Court, however, considerable clemency was shown to him and, on condition that he never committed any such offence again, it was agreed that, after a couple of months, he should be readmitted as a householder.

Enough examples have now been quoted to give the picture of the everyday business of the Tudor Company. Greater issues were now forcing their way forward, but in dealing with them it has always to be remembered that there, in the background, are continuing the quarrelling and law-giving, the feasting and the drinking, the demands for money from the State and the gifts of money to the poor.

It is convenient here to state again the form that the Elizabethan Clothworkers' Company had taken. That it had fallen from its original object of representing the craftsmen to become the instrument of the merchants has been shown, and there were now, in all, three main classes represented in the Company. They have been well stated in Unwin's *Industrial Organization in the Sixteenth and Seventeenth Centuries:*

1. Craftsmen: the rank and file: journeymen and master craftsmen. Generally, they were set to work by other members but, in times of unemployment, those with a little capital would buy cloth and set their own servants to work and sell it to the drapers and merchants.

The conditions of employment for Journeymen were strictly laid down in Ordinances made by the Company in 1553:

Item: That every Journeyman of the same Mistery working by the month, by the quarter, by the half year or year be of good behaviour to his master and not depart out of his master's house neither holiday or working day without licence, except it be to divine service, and his said master to keep him from all unlawful games and assemblies as near as he can upon pain of 20/– and if any Journeyman do refuse and will not follow and keep this ordinance then he shall be fined and punished at the discretion of the Master, Wardens and Assistants.

Item: That every Journeyman come to his work at 4 of the clock in the morning both winter and summer and leave in summer at 7 of the clock at night and in winter at 8 of the clock.

Item: That every Journeyman shall be of good behaviour as well to the Master and Wardens as to his master and shall not use any unlawful game or unlawful assembly and if he do and thereof being warned by the Master or Wardens or by their officers will not leave it shall forfeit

and pay at every time so offending 13/4 and if he refuse to pay it the said fine then no man being warned to the contrary shall set him to work nor give him wages till he hath paid his fine upon pain of 20/-.
Item: That no Journeyman of the said Ministry rebuke his master upon pain to forfeit 6/8.
Item: That no Journeyman of the said Company rebuke or slander another in open audience otherwise upon pain to forfeit and pay 20/-.

In addition to these stringent rules there were penalties enforced for non-attendance at Company meetings and for non-payment of quarterage.

2. Merchant Employers: they bought unfinished cloth from country clothiers and employed fullers and shearmen in finishing it. After they had finished it, they would sell it to the merchants for export. This class performed the useful function of helping 'the clothier at a dead market, the handytrade to work at a bad time and the merchant upon his present occasion'.

3. Exporters: 'Those which mantle, fold, put in buckram, and pack all such cloths as are dyed and dressed in London as also those that came out of the country ready dyed and dressed – of which sort are all Suffolk cloths, Stroud waters, Coventry and some others.
'In these people very great trust is committed both by the clothier and the merchant. For the clothier sendeth up his clothes to the Hall where he pays his duties and himself cannot stay until the market serveth him best but leaveth his cloths to the care and order of those clothworkers who have in their charge, sometimes six months or twelve months for a market, five hundred or a thousand cloths. ... And the merchant giveth order to him likewise to cause the clothier to make such and such colours. ...
'Also if the clothier at any time want money the Clothworker is the instrument to furnish him and if the merchant be unknown to the clothier and would have credit the Clothworker doth advise him of his sufficiency. ...'

Such were the three main classes and such the structure of the Clothworkers' Company when Mary died and Elizabeth I came to the throne. But since no company possessed a complete monopoly over all those employed in the trade it represented, there were also in the Clothworkers' Company those who followed other trades. There were also a few retailers, such as the twenty-four householders, engaged in the buying and selling of fustians and silk, who were called together before the Lord Mayor and told to serve better pennyworths.

*   *

*

The interests of all these classes had to be reconciled in formulating the policies of the Company. And, of these classes, it was those agents who supplied the export trade whose interests were very nearly identical with the interests of the Merchant Adventurers. They received as much profit on a country cloth as they did on a London one. But whereas the country was ready to supply them with the undressed cloths for which there was more demand on the Continent, London, with its interests in the cloth finishing business, was not. It was only natural that they should turn their attention towards the country when the export market was hanging fire.* There is, therefore, reason to believe that there was some truth in the complaints that were made that the merchants in the Company evaded the law without consideration for the rank and file.†

Restraints of Trade

Nonetheless, the interests of the craftsmen could not be wholly neglected, and reports of the restraints of trade and opposition to the introduction of machinery, made on their behalf, would not have been out of place at a twentieth-century trade union meeting.

1560

In 1560,

a Venetian came to this house and brought and shewed a certain gin devised for the rowing of broad cloths and offered to this Company

---

* In 1566 complaint was made to the Lord Mayor that cloths were being bought and shipped in Suffolk – and were being dyed and dressed there – to the detriment of the Company.

† The evolution of this rank and file of the Clothworkers had somewhat followed the pattern of the Company as a whole. Whereas in 1543 it had been intended that the Yeomanry should be confined to journeymen, by 1559 it had become necessary to appoint assistants to advise the Yeomanry wardens who, being merchants, knew little or nothing about the manufacturing side of the trade.

upon condition that they would provide him his necessaries he would
teach this Company his feat of workmanship. Whereupon the Master
and Wardens called certain of the Company, being the most expert
men, and shewed them the said device and gave time to advise them,
who, after deliberate advice taken, thought it would be a great decay
unto the Company. Whereupon the Master and Wardens gave the
stranger great thanks – also twenty shillings towards his charge – and
so parted.

The Court were in fact ready to consider, sometimes sym-
pathetically, the petitions of the craftsmen and to deal with such
points in them as were not of too revolutionary a character. There
was the example of the Supplication of the Yeomanry on 4 August
1562. This claimed that searches had not been carried out whereby
'true workmanship is sore decayed. And by that means good
workmen be little esteemed which is one special cause of the decay
of the said Company'. They asked, for redress, that two of the
youngest Wardens should go on a monthly search with the
wardens of the Yeomanry,

and that such as be found offenders may pay their fines without any
favour in that behalf to be shewed.

They also complained that the Ordinance that a Journeyman
could not set up house unless he could show that he was worth
£10, that he knew his job, and was capable of teaching his servants
theirs, was not being enforced and that

divers and sundry unapt and very unskilful persons have lately set up
house. And because of their unskilfulness and extreme necessity have
been driven to work much better cheap than they have been able to
maintain their charges. And so have not only undone themselves but
also others who by their means have lost their workmasters. . . .

Thirdly, they complained that the Ordinance that

none of the handycraft being lately set up shall jointly occupy together
as partners nor . . . take for the first two years more apprentices than one

was not being observed.

Fourthly, the rules for the conduct of Journeymen (noted above) were not being observed.

the said Journeymen now for the most part [are] grown so far out of rule and all civil order that without your Worships do extend your authority upon them your poor Orators shall not be able to keep them for now they be at that point that they will come to work and leave off at their pleasures, yea, and moreover control their masters if they be not served and have such fare as their poor masters be not able with their ease to provide for them.

Fifthly,

of late days a great disorder hath grown by reason that the most part of the householders of the handycraftsmen of this Worshipful Company have used and daily do use to stand and wait at their masters' doors and in their shops more like drudges and labourers than men of occupation and science, greatly to their own shame and also disworship of the whole Company,

'Which Bill was divers and sundry times read' and the Court 'lovingly granted and agreed Articles 1–4 and the fifth article to stand as void till further consideration be thereupon had'.

Exports of Undressed Cloths

The interests of the handicraft were also, in theory, forwarded – when an unruly stirring amongst the rank and file made such a tiresome step necessary – by the sponsoring of legislation in Parliament to ensure that the many laws concerning the export of undressed cloths should be enforced. Always a source of dissension,

1565 the matter came to one of its periodical heads in July 1565 when some journeymen agitating on this very point, 'unlawfully consulted and assembled themselves together, and . . . absented themselves together from their master's service'.

The ringleaders who had already been warned not to 'meddle' were sent to the Ward for four days but clearly something constructive had to be done. At a meeting in November 'all the workmen being here present had commandment to do their work justly and truly for the honour of the Queen's Majesty and the Realm and for the worship of this Company', for, so they were assured, the Company were now 'earnest Suitors' to the Council for a redress of the wrongful export of unwrought cloths.

Piteous complaints of the unemployment caused by the export by the Merchant Adventurers of undressed cloths had indeed been put before the Council which, in Tudor England, was regarded as the Court of Appeal for any Englishman who felt himself aggrieved. At a meeting at which both parties were present, the Merchant Adventurers, in defence of the shipment overseas of unwrought cloths (which they could hardly deny), alleged that English workmanship was not as good as that of Flanders.

There may have been an element of truth in this allegation, for, as has been already stated, standards of workmanship had fallen with the great expansion of trade. The Council decided that a trial of 500 cloths, rated between £4 and £6 a piece, should be made during the following three months – and completed before 1 March 1566 – 'at such reasonable prices here as they have the like wrought in Flanders having consideration to the charges of victuals and other necessaries and the difference in the manner of living here and there'.

The Trial of Cloths

It was promised that if the English craftsmen could 'shew an equality in the dressing of the said 500 cloths in any wise comparable to the workmanship of Flanders', they should have an increasing number of cloths to dress for as long as they continued able to compete with the foreigner. It is perhaps significant to note that no suggestion was made that the laws of the Realm, already made and re-stated on a number of occasions, should be enforced. Arrangements were made for judging the cloths and the Clothworkers asked that the material should be delivered to them 'as soon as may be for that the great frosts, chancing commonly in the dead of winter, may be to them a great hindrance in their working'.

A meeting was fixed with the Merchant Adventurers for the following Thursday, both to arrange delivery of the cloths and to settle the price to be charged for working them, and in preparation for this a small committee of Clothworkers met 'to consult together what price and answers this Company shall make to the said Merchants'.

Another committee of thirteen was appointed to have the oversight of these cloths 'which workmanship is to be circumspectly looked on for that the wealth of the whole Company dependeth thereon'.

In spite of this rigorous inspection, not all the 500 cloths were well wrought. Fifty of them were left with the workmen for as long as nine weeks, and even then some of them were badly worked. In such case, the offending workmen were punished but, generally speaking, the test proved a successful one: the English workman, as has always happened in time of crisis, proved that he was quite capable of competing with the foreigner. The Committee reported on 5 July 1566 that they had viewed 300 cloths and found them to be 'very well and substantially finished in all things concerning workmanship. And . . . we which have used the trade of drapery a long time have not seen cloths of that price and value better wrought and coloured in any place'.

It was perhaps a little disappointing that after this successful trial the Merchants should have continued to export undressed cloths exactly as they had always done before.*

* *
*

There now occurred an incident of a quite fantastic nature – an incident which might well have resulted in the Company becoming something quite other than the great corporation that was still to develop. The incident happened in the course of the daily struggle against the Merchant Taylors: it developed suddenly and without warning and it assumed proportions entirely unforeseen and of disastrous implication.

In the normal course of jockeying for position with their rivals, the Clothworkers promoted a parliamentary measure which was designed to give them, *inter alia*, complete authority over all those in the London cloth trade without having regard for any other Company of which the workmen might be members. The Bill, its promoters maintained, was for the securing of good workmanship and 'the avoiding of sleight' – for which reason they desired

---

* The Merchants of the Steel Yard, for example, exported 5,000 unwrought cloths by royal warrant in 1566.

'to have the Search of all such persons as occupy the handycraft of clothworking'.[3]

The Company of Merchant Taylors understanding of this Bill and not contented withall procured the matter to be brought before certain Committees, being some of the said Committee of the Queen's Majesty's Honourable Council and other worshipful, being of the Parliament House to the number of 12.

The Committee met at the house of the Chancellor of the Duchy, Sir Ambrose Cave, on 8 November 1566 and, on the point of search, 'though good that as well the said company of Clothworkers as the said Company of Merchant Taylors shall severally search all persons occupying the said handicraft of Clothworking'.

This suggestion so outraged the sense of authority of the Clothworkers that, in the heat of the moment, they actually offered the startling observation that, rather than accept any search by Taylors, over their members, they would prefer 'to surrender and deliver up all the poor handycraftsmen of the Clothworkers to the Company of the Merchant Taylors'. At a distance of time such an observation sounds no more than a bad-tempered expression of disappointment at the unacceptable nature of the Committee's proposal – and perhaps even at the moment of utterance it had not really been meant – but it was taken entirely seriously. The Council asked the Lord Mayor to call the Clothworkers together and find out if they really meant to stand by this remark.

Perhaps something that had been said at the moment of anger had now become a matter of pride: they affirmed that they were entirely serious. Armed with this affirmation, the Lord Mayor called the handicraft together to hear their views on the subject. Some 140 of them turned up at the meeting on 13 November 1566 and the proposal was put to them: whether or not they would like to be translated to the Merchant Taylors, 'at which motion some of them seemed to be scant well pleased'. However, they agreed to do whatever their Master and Wardens arranged.

Three days later the triumphant Merchant Taylors came before the Lord Mayor and said they were ready to take over the handicraft of the Clothworkers provided that they might have with

them 'a competent store of goods and lands to relieve them withall'. They insisted, too, that 'no person within the City of London
or within three miles compass [should] from henceforth work any
cloth but only they', and they made the further proviso that the
great Translation of men must not mean that they were to be
'taxed or sessed at higher and greater impositions than they, in
time past, have been'.

A Committee was set up by the Lord Mayor to draw up articles
between the two Companies, but when they produced their draft,
the Clothworkers thought they were too 'straight' and made a
draft of counter-proposals 'very indifferent and reasonable'.

Eventually, on 4 December 1566, the Clothworkers withdrew
their almost incredible offer to give up the members of the handicraft and reconciled themselves instead to a mutual search extending to retailers as well as craftsmen, 'as well for ill-workmanship as
for falsehoods of making and dying and stretching of cloths'.

But the matter continued to be disputed for another hundred
years.

Why had they done it? Were they really serious in their offer to
surrender control of the handicraft? Was it because, at a time of
unemployment, of high living-costs and of debt, the Company
thought to rid themselves of the considerable cost of relief to poor
artisans? Was it because the merchants wished to be done with
obligations to the handicraft and enjoy the comparative freedom
enjoyed by their opposite numbers in the Merchant Taylors? The
only thing that emerges clearly from the whole extraordinary
incident is the complete dependence on the will of the merchants
of the handicraft element, some of whom complained bitterly –
and not without reason – of the attempt to be rid of them.

By a curious twist of human nature the Company emerged
from this fantastic incident much more unified than ever they had
been before. The ruling body now showed itself ready to take its
obligations to the industry much more seriously. The *status quo*
remained but the rule was not an entirely oppressive one. They
might, if it suited them, close their eyes to breaches of the laws, but
they were always ready to help in the fight to obtain those laws in

Parliament, and in Court discussions the interests of the craftsmen were always taken into some consideration even though there were few, if any, craftsmen on the Court. This basic unity was to save the Clothworkers' Company during the following century when other corporations were breaking down and losing their powers.*

* An indication of this unity occurs when in November 1567 the Court arranged to appoint 6, 8, or 10 searchers to view cloth worked by the members and to seal, with a leaden seal, cloths that were well-worked and up to standard. Searchers were to collect one penny off the workmen for every cloth they sealed and no cloths were to be folded, tucked, or delivered until they had been sealed. It was a measure that might have been expected to arouse fierce opposition but the handicraft accepted it without dispute.

CHAPTER THREE

THE DAYS OF ADVERSITY

*   *
*

U NITY was a quality greatly to be desired during a period
when it was becoming increasingly common for the State
to interfere both with business corporations and with the private
individual.

First, Henry VIII had seen, in the City Companies, a source of
wealth for financing his expensive military schemes. In 1544, the
twelve Great Companies had raised, according to Herbert, more
than £20,000 on land mortgaged by them to assist the war against
Scotland. An Alderman who had objected was conscripted, sent as
a foot soldier, endured great hardship, was captured, and had to pay
ransom – an object lesson that did not go unnoticed in City circles.
Moreover, the confiscation of lands held on trust to provide
income for such supposedly superstitious uses as praying for the
souls of the dead and the subsequent resale of those lands to their
original owners, had provided an example which puts to shame any
twentieth-century confiscations by the State.*

Then Mary had demanded, in 1557, a loan of £20,000, secured on
certain Crown lands, and a year later a further £200,000 for the
French wars. Henceforth, the Companies were pillaged in every
conceivable way. Precepts were issued through the Lord Mayor
for money for projects ranging from setting the poor to work and
erecting the Royal Exchange, to an adventure to Virginia (aimed
at getting rid of some of the surplus population). Money was

---

* Even the mechanism of bureaucracy is familiar: there were forms to be filled
up and 'commissioners', as they were called, to go around the country and investigate.

WILLIAM LAMBE

demanded for ships, for arms, for gunpowder, for corn, for coal.*

In addition to their money, their persons were likely to be seized either by Lord Mayor's precept or by the press gang. The Company involuntarily provided forced-labour gangs for the camp at St Quentin; they maintained fifty-six soldiers in constant readiness; they sent twenty-eight soldiers to Calais and another fourteen men to Berwick; more peaceably they provided men for a muster before Queen Elizabeth at Greenwich where they paraded with arms and armour hired from the Tower. Thirty-three of the Company were pressed on 27 July 1562 and set towards Newhaven on 19 September. The Company gave each man 5s to carry in his purse and a 'reward' of 20s was given to the 'Sergeant of the band that served under Captain Leyton – because he should shew favour to our men'. Favour he may have shown to the men but soon the Company were paying pensions to their widows. *Conscription*

But, apart from these direct attacks on person and pocket, the State now shewed the will to control more closely the actions of the individual. Sumptuary laws there had always been to control any excess in the clothes the citizen wore. Now fresh attempts were made to have them enforced: the statutes were constantly read at meetings of the Company. On one occasion, when austerity was being preached, the Queen gave further command 'that they should be circumspect in excess of fare as namely at Christenings, Banquets made at the Lying-in of their wives and at their wives' Churchings'. *Austerity*

Just over a year later, a Precept was received (21 May 1566) to appoint 'three sad and discreet personages' to join three Fish-mongers at Ludgate and there, from 7 a.m. to 11 a.m. and from 1 p.m. to 6 p.m., to stand and have 'a diligent eye' for anyone 'using or wearing any great or monstrous hosen, silk, velvet or *1566*

---

* The provision of coals and corn was an admirable project. In order to provide a constant supply of coal for the use of the poor in times of scarcity the Companies were ordered to lay up, during the summer months, stocks of coal which, in times when it became both scarce and dear, were sold at the Lord Mayor's controlled price – but not at a loss – to the poor. Since the Companies' store-depots were scattered about the City, the idea was practical as well as charitable.

weapons restrained and prohibited' by various Acts of Parliament. Offenders were to be arrested in all their forbidden finery and dragged away to Guildhall. Daily watch was to be kept until further notice.

Behind these laws there may have been, at any rate partially, an economic reason. In exchange for cloth sold in the export market, the country was receiving not gold and silver but foreign luxuries that went to bedeck the wealthy citizen. Moreover, there was a school of thought that maintained that the vast sums spent on clothing – generally far superior to the station of the wearer – by proud persons merely meant that they extorted more from their tenants or ran up bills that impoverished their creditors.[1]

Economic Planning

Certainly there was now a very determined attempt at economic planning. Sir Thomas Gresham was a prime mover in the attempt to bring the Netherlands' trade – in which the Clothworkers were particularly interested – under the control of the Crown. It seemed to him, after the experiences of boom and slump following on devaluation of the coinage, that prosperity was bound up in the rates of exchange. He himself was a Merchant Adventurer and, as such, was chiefly familiar with the exchange rates between London and Antwerp, exchange rates that were governed by the flow of cloth to Antwerp set against the flow of foreign goods from Antwerp to London.[2]

He planned therefore, firstly, that the Merchant Adventurers should be given a monopoly which was achieved in 1552 when the trade with the Hanseatic League became blocked. Secondly, he urged that customs duties on cloth should be increased; they were increased in 1557.* Lastly, he thought it desirable that the trade should be in as few hands as possible to make it the more easily controllable: in 1564 a reorganization of the Merchant Adventurers resulted in an oligarchic control of that Company.

These reforms provided one measure of economic control in the planned economy. There were others. A system of price controls was instituted. Householders of the Clothworkers engaged in the

* It will be remembered that Hales, with his plans for a levy on sheep, had failed in 1549.

retail trade in silks and fustians were told that the Queen had found great fault in the high price of silks and had said, threateningly, that the fault lay greatly with the Clothworkers' Company, being the one with the biggest membership. Acts were passed that discouraged or prohibited entirely the import of many articles of clothing, of ornaments, and of weapons.

The coinage was reformed to its original state of purity. There was some attempt at currency control by a weekly computation of statistics. These were forms to be completed every Saturday by wholesalers and retailers, of money paid to strangers – how much it was, what day they paid it, and in what kind of money their payment was made.

But of all the planned economy of Elizabethan legislation, the most important and effective was the Act known as the Statute of Artificers. This Act has been compared, not unjustly, with the National Service Act of the 1940's, and indeed in general tone it is strongly reminiscent of that Act. The principle underlying the Statute of Artificers was that of the universal obligation to work. The Act aimed at mobilizing the entire labour force of the nation and in a programme of 'full employment' directing it into appropriate callings in a strict order of priority.

Agriculture, and its ancillary trades, came first, followed at a short distance by cloth making. At the bottom of the scale came the professions. In official favour the husbandman was the most, and the merchant or lawyer the least, socially useful citizen.

But the Elizabethan man-in-the-street with an obstinacy that after four hundred years showed no signs of decreasing felt a strong inclination to reverse this order of things. Not for him the arduous tilling of the soil for fifteen hours a day. He sought rather a 'black-coated' (and then better-paid) job in trade, industry, or the professions. This desire for employment in the less back-breaking jobs led to an increased pressure to enter them – a pressure that had to be relieved by creating residential or property qualifications. Regulations were made to stabilize employment and check mobility among the workers. Seven years' apprenticeship became universal; employment was no longer by the day, week, or

Statute of Artificers

month, but by the year, and anyone seeking employment had to produce a certificate, signed and countersigned, to say he was at liberty to take such employment. Only in the City of London was exemption made to some provisions of the Act: a person there who was 'free' of one trade was at liberty to follow another since the City needed scope for individual enterprise.

But the success of economic planning at home depends, tiresomely enough, on other factors and other nations beyond the control of the planner. The Antwerp trade, on which almost the whole of the English economy rested, was facing increasing difficulties which arose from upheavals in the Netherlands and the tyranny also of the Spanish Governor. Each time there was a disturbance in the Netherlands it meant, sooner or later, trouble in England in the cloth industry, where it was common knowledge that 'the people that depend upon making of cloth are of worse condition to be quietly governed than the husbandmen'.

It became increasingly obvious that an attempt must be made to open up other fields of trade. As Cecil said, 'it were better for this realm for many considerations that the commodities were issued out rather to sundry places than to one'. It were no bad thing he thought, too, if the type of trade were to be changed, if there were less emphasis on cloth. Any resulting unemployment could be dealt with by the colonization of Ireland.

Unemployment

Great unemployment there already was in the Company: unemployment and poverty arising firstly from two trade embargoes that had closed the market first between 1564 and 1566 and then again between 1568 and 1571, and secondly from the fact that the Merchant Adventurers were still resolutely refusing to carry out the Statute, again restated in 1567, that at least one in every ten cloths exported must be dressed.

In addition to wilful evasions of the law by the Merchants, there were exceptions made to the law by the Crown. Lord Cobham, for example, was given a licence to export 2,000 Kentish cloths a year contrary to the Statute, and, although the Company sent a letter to Sir William Cecil asking him to use his influence against it, no relief came from that quarter.

In addition, the Council asked – and the Company were in no position to refuse – dispensation for certain others: for the Queen's Merchant, Thomas Allen (who had to export quickly to the East some 400 Suffolk and Kentish cloths), for Merchants of Spain, Moscovia, and Danzig, who had bought cloths before the laws were enacted and now could not get them wrought in time for export.

By 1570, when Elizabethan England was in the middle of its greatest crisis, the Company were in debt to the extent of £450 and more. The following year the financial situation had further deteriorated and it was reported that many of the Company were in the greatest decay and want, and the Council were urged once again to see that the laws were enforced. The Company themselves owed £500 and were having to borrow from the Bishop of London.

One of the main difficulties in enforcing the export laws concerning undressed cloths lay in the fact that once the merchandise was packed there was no undoing the bales to see that the Merchants were observing the law, and it was to remedy this unsatisfactory state of affairs that, in 1575, certain of the poor handicraftmen petitioned the Queen for relief by word 'to be had according to the Statute'. This petition, which included the request that a packer might be appointed to oversee the actual baling of the cloths and ensure that the Statute was being observed, was made without the consent of the Court and contained what was considered a slanderous attack upon the rulers of the Company. It caused fearful offence and was described as being of great prejudice to the City. It was in due course rejected and the artisans were told to 'sue the Merchants by gentle means and ways for their relief', and when, later in the year they did so through the proper channels, the Court granted their assistance in the affair.

The Company were, in fact, enduring a period of considerable adversity. For, in addition to their difficulties with the Merchant Adventurers, they suddenly were compelled to face a shrewd blow aimed at their very existence by the Merchant Taylors who were attempting to procure legislation to ensure that at least a half of

1570

Financial Crisis

Adversity

51

all work done in woollen cloth should be put to the members of their own Company. They had got the support of the Lord Chief Justice and were making clandestine suit to the Lord Keeper when the scheme, in spite of the most careful precautions for secrecy, came to light just in time for the Clothworkers successfully to lobby the Lord Keeper against a scheme that 'would utterly undo the Company'.

Hardly was this threat circumvented than more disturbing news was received – this time to the effect that Sir Francis Walsingham had been granted a licence from the Queen to export 30,000 unwrought cloths. It was suggested suavely that, in view of Sir Francis's long friendship towards the Company in their suits, perhaps the Company might see their way to grant him a dispensation in spite of the Statute.

1579 This was asking too much: with a creditable firmness (and hoping that it would be taken in good part), the Court refused. On 14 April 1579 the Company had a meeting with Sir Francis, a meeting at which the great poverty among the members of the Company by lack of employment was pointed out. An agreement was reached that, although out of the 30,000 cloths to be exported by the Merchants the Company were legally entitled to the dressing of 3,000, they would content themselves with the dressing of only 1,400 of them, and there were to be no coloured cloths exported unwrought. The agreement was, moreover, not to be taken as a precedent. Against this very moderate score was to be reckoned the counter-agreement that the Merchant Adventurers were to be able to choose their workmen and get the work done as cheaply as they could: there was to be no invoking the laws about price control.

*　*
*

But, if the Company as a corporate body struggling against such adversity was sinking deeper and deeper into debt, there were still plenty of wealthy members of the Court upon whom the burdens could be placed. For, though the cloth trade might be suffering, the years 1575–85 were, for the country as a whole, boom years. There was, indeed, an amazing spirit in the air. The world was suddenly unfolding and its boundaries extending. Shaking herself free from a too-deep immersion in the waters of the Scheldt, England was breasting the oceans of the world. Trade routes with vast potentialities reached out to the Baltic, the Indies, the Levant, North Africa, and the Americas. Into the distant Pacific swept British flags, fluttering from ships of an almost incredible smallness. Drake and Hawkins, Frobisher and Raleigh – merely to read their names is to feel the imagination begin to stir – sailed out into the glittering new world and brought back with them gold and jewels, spices and costly furs. Above all, they brought back with them tales that gave a new spirit of ambition to a nation that was much in need of it. Additional zest was given to the voyages and the explorations by the fact that they involved conflict against the hated Spaniards, a conflict of power-politics and religion, a conflict in which even the most minor victory could fill the contemporary mind with exultation.

While the men of action were ransacking the treasure houses of South America, at home the 'back-room boys', the geographers and chroniclers, were planning new worlds to conquer and new adventures to promote, were celebrating and publicizing the glories already achieved. And here, too, the Clothworkers' Company played a small but significant part.

Richard Hakluyt

It was in 1551 that, a precept being issued to the Company 'for the finding of a skoller at the University', the sum of five pounds was yearly set aside for the purpose. Various scholars came and were supported at the University and went their way, until on 13 August 1577 there came the entry:

This day also was granted to Richard Hackluyt being a scholar in Christ Church in Oxford, who, as he saith, is already proceded Master Of Arts* and is entered into the study of divinity. Upon condition that he proceeded Master of Art as aforesaid and do study divinity and so continue the same study the next avoidance of the pension of £6.13.4.

* Born in 1552, Richard Hakluyt the younger had gone in 1570 to Christ Church, Oxford, with an exhibition of £2 13s 4d from the Skinners' Company, of which his father was a member. He had become Bachelor of Arts in February 1574 and Master of Arts in June of the same year.

granted to Mr. Wilson, Scholar, and which he now enjoyeth, when the same shall become void by death resignation or otherwise. He to enjoy the same during the Company's pleasure.

This caused great anxiety to Mr Wilson who pleaded great indigence and hoped the Company did not intend to remove his pension from him. On 21 January 1578 Mr Wilson's scholarship was, in fact, extended for another two years. Hakluyt, however, did not have to wait all this time, for the accounts for the year 1578-9 show that he received his pension for the whole of that year from midsummer to midsummer. It seems likely that he had influential friends on the Court of the Company who were pulling the strings for him. In the absence of any evidence, there is nothing to show whether these Clothworkers, of whom he speaks with gratitude or with whom he is subsequently found in acquaintance and friendship, were friends made before or after the granting of the scholarship.*

That the Company was investing in an exceptional scholar – a scholar able to read works in Greek, Latin, Portugese, Spanish, and French – soon became apparent.†

The next year in *A discourse of the commodity of the taking of the Straight of Magellans* he was arguing with all the weight of authority that, because Spain might cut off our cloth trade with Africa, and 'the tyranny of the Muscovite' might cut 'our vent of cloth in Russia and Persia', a North East passage should be developed. And in 1580 the great map-maker Mercator was writing to Hakluyt

* In his Epistle Dedicatory to the Favourable Reader of the *Principal Navigations* he acknowledges the help of Master Edward Dier and Master Richard Staper. There was an Edward Dyeher, Master of the Company in 1576. Alderman Richard Staper was Master in 1590 and a governor of the Levant Company. Perhaps the ground had been prepared that day when the Company shared a barge to Westminster with the Skinners.

Later, in 1605, Hakluyt is to be found in the company of Spero Pettingarre at a meeting of some of the Gunpowder Plot conspirators (there is no reason to suppose that either man was cognisant of it – they left the room before the meeting proper began). A Pettingarre or Petynger was Master of the Company in 1571 and was at the Court Meeting at which the grant was given. He, too, could be a connecting link.

† Trevelyan has written: 'The most influential writer in the age of Shakespeare, if it were not Foxe the Martyrologist, was Hakluyt.'

on the same subject. The study – and practice – of divinity upon which the Clothworkers had insisted was, however, not neglected: geography for him had still to be an unofficial study.

In 1580, the year that he procured the publication of Cartier's first two voyages, he was certainly tutoring in divinity at Oxford, for in the case of Gabriel Bowman – a poor scholar of Magdalen who was granted an exhibition to study divinity by the Company at the request of the Governor of Christ's Hospital – it was stated: 'Mr. Hackluyt to be his Tutor if it may be'.

On Lady Day 1581 he preached the Lambe sermon before the Company in Lambe's Chapel, receiving 6s 8d as his fee for the sermon and £1 6s 8d for 'his charges up and down from Oxford'. That the occasion was a success may be inferred from the fact that he was invited the same year to make a sermon for the Company on election day.*

Another mark of the Company's rather wary favour was shown by the order on 2 September 1581 that 'Mr. Hackluyt our scholar at Oxford shall have our books of St. Augustine's works, out of this house, for the furtherance of his study, putting in sufficient sureties for the safe delivery of the same again upon demand'.†

In 1582 still supported by the Clothworkers, he published *Divers Voyages touching the Discovery of America*, and the following year he received an appointment abroad that would have normally brought his pension to an end. But on 10 September 1583,

at the request of the Right Honourable the Lord Treasurer of England, signified by his letters, it is ordered and agreed that Mr. Hackluyt of Oxford, the Company's scholar, who is appointed to go with the Lord Ambassador into France shall have his pension of £6.13.4. yearly paid unto him during his abode there in the service of the said Lord Ambassador. And that Mr. Warden Brande shall pay him presently his

* As Dr J. A. Williamson has pointed out, this is the first evidence that Hakluyt was ever, as he described himself, a preacher.

† These works of St Augustine in twelve volumes travelled several times between London and the Universities. They were then relegated to a cupboard and, in a clearing-out of accumulated rubbish two hundred years later, eleven were presented to the Library of Sutton Vallence School, where they still remain: it was reported in 1653 that one volume had for a long time been missing.

quarter's pension due at Michaelmas next. And so from thenceforth quarterly or as it shall be demanded.

It was demanded until 25 March 1587 when 'by his own voluntary consent' he surrendered it.

This intervention by the Treasury on behalf of a minor official on the staff of the English Ambassador to France is mysterious indeed. It is possible that Burghley may have been engaged on some intrigue of his own or that Hakluyt was employed as a commercial spy whom the Lord Treasurer wished to be paid in a manner at once unobtrusive by reason of its continuity and unrecorded in the accounts of the Treasury. Certainly, in the listening post that was France, Hakluyt amassed a vast amount of information. Mercantile, geographical, statistical – the news was collected and sifted by Hakluyt. Frequently he returned as courier to England – returning perhaps at the same time as a trading spy to report to the Government the intelligence he had gathered. But his stay abroad had other importance in his own words: 'During my five years abroad . . . I both heard in speech and read in books other nations miraculously extolled for their discoveries and notable enterprises by sea but the English of all others for their sluggish security and continual neglect of the like attempts'. English publicity on the Continent was bad, and there was no other Englishman able or willing to disprove such foreign allegations. Hakluyt was the one man who could and did remedy the situation.

That the Clothworkers' Company should have helped to support, at a time when he was of 'poor estate',[3] a man whose genius has been spoken of in the same breath as that of Shakespeare and Cervantes, is a matter for self-congratulation: it was a splendid start to the Company's long history of enlightened educational policy.

*   *

*

Stirring times meant stirring deeds.* The voyages to South America and the West Indies had led inevitably to serious clashes

_____

* Sometimes too stirring. In 1575, Clothworkers Edward Osborne and Richard Staper, amongst others, complained of piracy committed upon their ship *James*.[4]

with Spain to whom a Papal decree had allotted the sovereignty over the New World. At the same time France was in the throes of a religious civil war and the Netherlands in a state of revolt against the dominion of Spain. From 1572 onwards there were always companies of English volunteers in the Netherlands, and after 1585, when the war against Spain may be said to have properly begun, there were never less than 6,000 British troops there. Military Conscription

Such military expeditions – which included the inevitable forays against the Scots – and the preparations for them naturally affected the Company. Money was perpetually being demanded for soldiers or for arms.

In November 1569 'the worshipful and wealthy of the Company were sessed towards the charges of 56 soldiers sent against the rebels of the North'.

One member who kicked against paying 40s was sent to the Ward until he came to his senses. In a spirit which was still extant in the twentieth century, the soldiers were allowed, after demobilization, to keep their uniforms, coats, and 'galley sloppes of broadcloth' for their own use. Each soldier was equipped, in addition, with a caliver with powder flasks and a touch box, a morion (or helmet), a sword, and a dagger, but these remained the property of the Company and were normally stored in the Company's armory.

In 1574 came a precept for twenty-two able, tall, and warlike men, well and thoroughly furnished with calivers and shot to be kept at one hour's readiness. At once thirty-two journeymen were pressed ('for the more better assurance and certainty of the said number of twenty-two'), given a shilling a-piece, told to be in a state of perfect readiness, and, after their names and addresses had been taken, sent back to their masters' houses, 'amongst which number of men one Roger Roberdine, Journey-man, upon his appearance before the Table after he was pressed gave to the Court such stout, stubborn, opprobrious and seditious words concerning his said pressing that for the same he was forthwith committed to Ward' – where, in less than a week, he had cooled down sufficiently to apologize. 1574

Eleven of the men were called up a week later into the Queen's Guards: a message sent by the Lord Mayor ordered that they should have coats of blue kersey with white and black laces, gascoin fashion. But when they turned up on Parade their turn-out was regrettably not as smart as was expected. 'Because many of their hose are very uncomely and not uniform like which will be disliked by their Captain' – possibly an understatement – the Company were ordered to make 'sliders to draw upon their own hose to be forthwith made of the same blue cloth of kersey that their coats be of'. Properly equipped at last, in due course they were posted away to deal with the rebels in Ireland.

1578 Four years later came the demand for one hundred able and sufficient persons, journeymen or apprentices and others who were freemen of the City, 'the same being of Agility and honest of behaviour between the ages of nineteen and forty', who were 'fit to be trained for Arquebus, shot, every one of them having a Morion, a sword, a dagger and a caliver with furniture for the same and a half a pound of powder, beside touch-powder'. Twenty-five of them were to be householders and a return was to be made of their names and addresses together with a list of any Captains suitable for training.

A training directive on the use of the arquebus arrived from the Lord Mayor with the general instruction that, in assessing the contributions towards this force, even if it meant that a larger burden fell upon the rich, the Company were to spare the poorer members. Rich or poor, there were, of course, always those in the Company who complained about having to pay their share towards these military preparations and the cost of training so many men: but fortunately the Company did not lack means for persuading them. Their indignation was understandable for there is no doubt that the burden fell very heavily upon them. A soldier's pay was, in regard to the comparative value of money at that time, amazingly high. The hundred men and their officers were being paid on the following scale:

One Captain at 13s 4d a day
One Lieutenant at 6s 8d a day

Two Sergeants at 3s 4d a day
One Clerk at 2s a day
Drum, Flute, Ancient at 3s 4d a day each
100 Soldiers at 8d a day.

For the eight days' training in the arquebus, for which this Company was responsible, the pay roll alone amounted to nearly £43, and the total cost of supporting the fifty-six soldiers sent against the rebels in the North had been £252 6s 10d for one month – a horrifying figure.

It is not to be wondered that the Company could not afford such a drain on their corporate resources and had to raise such amounts by a poll tax upon their members. For, to a Company already greatly in debt, the cost of living and in particular the cost of legislation were appalling. The Statute about the Dressing of Cloths which the Clothworkers had managed to get through Parliament in 1567 was a case in point.

High
Costs of
Legislation

Imprimis given to Mr. Onslow, Speaker of the Parliament, for his friendship for the preserving of our Bill to be read ... £10.

Item: given to Mr. Seymour, clerk of the Parliament House to prefer our Bill ... £3.

Item: to my Lord Keeper for his fee for that our Bill passed the Parliament House ... £13. 6. 8.

Item: given to Sergeant Hales, keeper of the Parliament House door in reward ... £1. 10. 0.

Item: for two sugar loaves given to Master Bell ... 8. 0.

Item: for a gallon of burnt Sack bestowed upon Master Seymour ... 2. 6.

Item: for a Swan for Mr. Speaker ... 10. 0.

In addition to these more obvious charges, there were all such expenses as dinners for the Company lawyers – to say nothing of their fees – at the King's Head in Fleet Street, and the cost of a fine satin doublet given to Mr Gray of the Custom House for his 'friendship'. And, after the Act was passed, there were the costs of the general rejoicings which included the price of a butt of Muscatel.

Yet, with all this money spent and the Company so deeply in debt that the ordinary dinners had to be done away with, all that there was to show for it was an Act which nobody observed and which led to further expense in opposing Lord Cobham's licence.

There were the bills to be met in 1579 for the Costs of getting the Queen's Letters Patent in confirmation of the Charter:

To the Attorney General for his office pains and friendship   £8
To Mr. Sonkye his man for to remember his Master of our busi-
ness being at the Court   £1
To Mr. Secretary Wilson for his friendship and furtherance to get
Her Majesty's hand to our Charter   £30
To Godfrey Wilson, Mr. Secretary's brother, for his friendship
to his brother in our business   £6

'Friendship' in Tudor England was no cheap commodity.

Even by Poll Tax these sums were, by reason of human un-reliability, hard to collect. 'All such of the Company as had promised any money towards the suit and charges of the Queen Majesty's Letters Patent were called hither for the same. Whereof some promised payment thereof with speed, some at Days and some others utterly denied their promise.' For those responsible for the Company's finances, the times must have been worrying indeed.

It was not that there was, in the mid-twentieth-century phrase, 'no money about'. (On the contrary, the Queen, having raised by enforced loans more than was needed for her immediate purposes, had made a forced loan of the surplus back to the City at 7 per cent.) But so bad did this reluctance, or inability, to pay become that a 'Book of Stops and Stays' was instituted. The name of any-one who refused to pay this contribution towards a precept was recorded in this Book and he became ineligible for any aid from the Company until he had paid in full. But, unable, even by economies and unwelcome austerity, to balance their books, the Clothworkers were now faced with another serious expense. The problem of Concealed Lands was upon them.

*   *
*

'Concealed Lands' were, so the Crown alleged, lands that the Com- Concealed Lands panies had overlooked, deliberately or otherwise, at the time of the 'Reformation' when a return had to be made of all lands left in trust to the City Companies for supposedly superstitious uses. These lands had been first seized by the Crown and then sold back to their rightful owners in a manner which, even to the mind attuned to national confiscation, seems somewhat extortionate.

After four hundred years it is perhaps impossible to determine whether the Companies were, in fact, guilty of making incomplete returns: guilty or not, they were to be a prey, for many years to come, of any man who could secure a patent from the Crown to indulge in a little legalized blackmail.

In 1582 it was rumoured that a Commission was afoot to enquire 1582 into the position. The Court had already in 1569 looked through the wills of benefactors to see what yearly payments went out of the Company's land 'for the finding of Chantrey's, Obits, Lamps, Lights and such other like charges'. Moreover, they asked their lawyer, Mr Blackwell, to procure a conveyance of all such lands and payments as were re-purchased from Edward VI after the great confiscation.

Now, alarmed by this fresh activity over something which they had long thought to be settled, the Clothworkers decided to take counsel's opinion. Hardly had they done so than the Patentees of Concealed Lands were appointed – men who, for a payment or as a mark of their Sovereign's favour, were granted the right to collect such sums as they could extort from landowners. The Company were asked if they would agree to a composition with the Patentees.

The Company's position, if all consciences were clear, was theoretically unassailable but practically speaking hopeless. The Court replied that, although the lands brought in question did not exceed £40 per annum, and that, although both in their own and in their counsel's opinion they did not think there was any doubt as to their title, 'yet to avoid Suits and to promote Goodwill and to get a certain Title to the property they [were] prepared to pay his Lordship something to be good to them'. They were afraid, they added, that they could not promise more than £200, but this sum would carry with it the prayers of the poor of the Company.

1584 Two years later, in November 1584, after being called upon to produce copies of the wills concerned – which they refused to do – they agreed to a composition of £160. At the same time they sought a five-year purchase and, presumably in payment of this, agreed to an additional impost of 100 marks (£66 13s 4d).

Did the Company really hope, with the helpless trust of blackmailed to blackmailer, that this would be positively the last demand?

* *

*

War Against Spain

With the outbreak of war with Spain, the boom years of plenty for the country came suddenly to an end. Many outlets were closed to the exporter and for the trade in those markets that remained there was a desperate scramble. Moreover, for a country having to provide itself with the necessities of life, the war caused a great strain on the manpower available. The Company were continually called upon for men and money. Sometimes the demand for money came in the form of a State lottery with the note that, if the members did not voluntarily raise the money for a share in the lottery, they would be compulsorily assessed.

On one such occasion, the Clothworkers' offer to subscribe £20 to the lottery was refused and they received the sinister request for a list of the members from whom a greater sum would be levied. The wardens were thereupon instructed by the Court to appear before the Lord Mayor and tell him how greatly were the Company in debt, how poor were the members, 'and yet, rather than to certify the names, to yield to augment' the offer of £20. They paid, eventually, £30 and the wardens themselves had to make good such money as they could not collect.

In fact, during the whole of this time of the war with Spain, the Company were obsessed with their own financial troubles. The outside world where, with its shattering defeat of the Armada, the course of history was being changed, hardly intruded except in the form of a further demand for money: a levy of 2s in the pound 'towards the provision and setting forth of the ships that were sent to Sea at the charges of this City towards the resistance of the Spanish Navy', which amounted to £13 6s 4d. But no record appears in the Company's own archives of that occasion when, on 26 June, according to Stow:

arrived at London deputies for the States of the Netherlands [to present the Sovereignty of the Netherlands to the Queen at Greenwich three days later] and were lodged about the Tower Street and had their diet worshipfully appointed at the charge of her Majesty in the Cloth-workers' Hall.[5]

There is evidence that the Company were represented at the funeral of Sir Philip Sidney from the fact that 13s was spent on trimming and scouring the graven corslets and other things used at the burial.

But for most of the time the Company were looking inwards **1588** towards the desperate state in which they found themselves. In 1588 the Queen demanded from them a six-months' loan of £6,000 to be raised by a poll-tax. The members were called to-gether 'as well of the Livery as the Yeomanry ... and made acquainted with the sums of money set upon them. ... Whereof some yielded but the most part refused.'

Later came a letter saying that all who refused were to be com- **1590** mitted to the ward. An initial payment of £4,000 was made and in 1590, as the result of what in a war 350 years later would have been called Navy Week, the Company found themselves with an assessment of £419 towards the purchase by the City of six ships and two pinnaces.

There was discontent amongst the Yeomanry, not only at such **Growth of** levies but also at the growth of abuses and disorders; 'foreigners' **Discontent** were working as journeymen, apprentices were not being en-rolled, men were working without masters, illegal partnerships were being set up. It was suggested that either one of the wardens or one or two of the Court (whether they were trained craftsmen or not) should sit with the wardens of the Yeomanry at their meet-ings for the better government of the Company and for the reformation of the abuses complained of.

Throughout the last years of the century unrest and disaffection grew among the body of the Company. Alarmed perhaps by the strength of this discontent, the Court dealt more firmly with efforts by the Merchant Adventurers and the Merchant Taylors to get concessions that were not theirs by right. There appears to have been a moral ascendancy gained over both these other companies.

1589 First, to prevent the illegal shipment of undressed cloths, three searchers at the waterside were appointed and, two years later, four of the Yeomanry were appointed to supervise their work.

Next, some Merchant Adventurers came and asked that, in cases where they were compelled to have one cloth in ten dressed and wanted to get the order shipped more quickly than the cloths could be dressed, they might have permission to ship the undressed cloths first and the dressed ones as soon afterwards as possible. 'To them the Company answered they could not give any such leave'.

Moreover, as an additional check, four of the Yeomanry were 1591 appointed to seal all woollen cloths that the merchants sent to the Company to be dressed for export: all Clothworkers were instructed to send for the sealers when their cloths were ready. No charge was made for sealing as it was 'only meant for to have true workmanship done in the Company'.

A Merchant Adventurer who, being caught in breaking the export laws, was sued by the Clothworkers in the Court of Exchequer, 'submitted to the Company' and was fined £15. The Merchant Taylors, noting this new efficiency, were inspired by it to do likewise: they appointed two of their own searchers to share the work in the port. They demanded, too, a share in the searching and sealing for good workmanship – a request to which the Clothworkers retorted that, if the Merchant Taylors wished to search and seal for good workmanship, they were at liberty to 1592 do so but 'that this Company would not in any sort join with them. . . .' It seems likely that the pressure from below was becoming uncomfortable and that the Court were being forced to a stricter observance of the laws.

It was at this moment that the voice of the blackmailer was heard again.

* *
*

Notification was made in 1591 that Mr Tipper, the Patentee of Concealed Lands, had some of the Company's properties entered in his book. Once again the Company made no attempt to fight the claim – an acceptance of the impost which might argue a sense of guilt in any age other than that of the State Omnipotent, to the demands of which resistance was both useless and expensive. A meeting with Mr Tipper took place in 1592. He produced his 'Book of Concealments' and a long debate took place, at the end of which, 'in consideration of his friendship and charges in altering his former patent and passing the same again with such words as our Counsel thought good', the Clothworkers agreed that Mr Tipper should receive £70. *The friendship of Mr Tipper* – and for only seventy pounds!

Concealed
Lands

1592

* *
*

It is almost a matter for surprise to find that, with all these distractions and with all these expenses and debts, the Company were still able to spend money upon their own embellishment.

In 1587 the College of Heralds was approached concerning a crest and supporters to be added to the Company's arms and the same arms to be imposed in the new Book of Ordinances 'for beautifying of the same'. The Clarenceux King-of-Arms received £5 and the Company were granted two griffins pelletes as their supporters and a ram, a golden ram, as their Crest. The Hall, too, was beautified – in 1594 there could be no dinner. 'only a drinking for that the hall and parlour and all the house is in such order that there cannot be any dressing of meat there or provision for that purpose'. Now the parlour was to be wainscotted anew and 'to be ceiled plain white with roses according to the former proportion'.

The Hall itself, where the Earls of Shrewsbury and Cumberland had been made free of the Company, was, in the last year of the old century, redecorated – the upper part in perspective work – its

The Arms
of the
Company

1594

screens painted and gilded, and provision made of forty buckets decorated with the Clothworkers' arms. The Garden was paved 'for to walk around upon the pavement three in a rank, and also with a walk in the middle for two to walk in [with] a Grass plot at either end as big as may be'. Then it was new-stocked with jarmanders, with rosemary and double primroses, with daisies, mastick, and angelica. It provided an idyllic setting, as the great Elizabethan age drew gently to its close, for the new passionate upsurge of unrest amongst the Company.

CHAPTER FOUR

THE TYRANNY BEGINS

* *

*

THE Elizabethans had grown rich too quickly. As always, the aftermath of great extremes between newly-acquired wealth and grinding poverty led to unrest and class warfare. The social distinctions had come too fast and the discontent had been increased by the unsettled attitude of soldiers returning from the wars.

In the Clothworkers' Company at the end of the sixteenth century, there must have been many journeymen who had heard their fathers tell of the old days when the Company had been a company of craftsmen. Now the spirit of unrest, the new spirit of democracy, began to make itself felt.

This had led, amongst other things, to the revolutionary idea of having a secret ballot at the elections: in 1596 a balloting box was provided 'to decide all doubts and questions in variance without any disliking or cause of offence to be taken in the same'. And, in view of the famine and unemployment and poverty that ushered out the old century – great taxation, plague in 1592, 1602, and 1603, and the poor harvests of five out of the last seven years of the 1500s, all contributed their share – the Lord Mayor commanded the Clothworkers (no doubt with one eye on those disaffected) to 'leave off their great dinners now in this dear time. And the moiety of such money as should be spent on those dinners to be . . . distributed to the relief of the poor.'

In 1598 a great petition was made by the Yeomanry to the Court. They demanded that steps should at once be taken, firstly for a revision of wage scales according to the latest legislation and for the

1596

1598
Yeomanry
Petition

67

payment of wages quarterly, and secondly for all manner of cloths 'dressed to the proof' anywhere in the City for export to be viewed and sealed by the Company's sealers, four of whom they nominated.

To the second part of this petition the Court agreed, with the proviso that, should any dispute arise between searchers and workmen, arbitration should be made by a committee of six workmen appointed by the Court. On the wage issue they were not yet prepared to give way: they would take counsel's opinion as to whether the new legislation applied to the Company, and, if it did, they would hold a conference with the Flanders Merchants, the Merchant Taylors, and Drapers.

So far so good: there was clearly an air of reasonableness and concession to the new spirit of the age. But the discontent continued; it showed itself in a number of bad-tempered actions and slanderous statements recorded in the Minutes.

There was an allegation that the Beadleship in 1598 was got by bribery. Lewis Jenkins, an unsuccessful candidate for the post, maintained that the 'Beadleship cost Ellis Jones £40. And that one man of this Company had for his part 20 nobles'.

1600   In 1600, slanderous speeches against the Court and Wardens, separatim and seriatim, are recorded, and William Judson told Warden Jackson 'that this table had made a wise choice to make him Warden of this Company and they that sit at this table do keep all the Company of the handicraft in slavery but for my part I care not a louse for any of them'. He was fined £5.

Later came the Wardens of the Yeomanry complaining bitterly of lack of work and demanding that the Court sue for relief to the Privy Council. The Court answered that they had made such petitions frequently without result and suggestion that the Yeomanry should organize their own petition this time: with a gesture of liberality they voted the Yeomanry £10 towards their expenses.

But liberality did not entirely stifle the malcontents. More slanders, spoken publicly in a tavern this time to make it worse – and by one of the Livery – were to follow. The Court were accused of being 'Pelicans who did suck out the blood of their dams and

weed out the profits of the Company's lands which of right be-
longeth and was given to them by the handytrade of this
Company'. Another agreed 'they should be ashamed of their
doings and they would make them ashamed and if they were
rightly served they should be thrust out of the hall for place had
they none there'.

A member of the Court was fined for foul language and for
striking one of the Livery; and one of those on the mercantile side
of the Company was committed to ward for 'slanderous words to
the discredit of all the handicraftmen of this Company in their
workmanship viz: that there was no good workmanship in the
City but that foreigners might teach them, being all botchers'.

Yet, if there were bad feelings among the Company, it was not
until 1614 that they broke out, as will be seen, with an unexpected
and new violence that overshadowed all other business of the
Court. In the meantime, however, there was a new Monarch and
new considerations to keep them occupied.

On Saturday, 7 May 1603, twenty-nine Members of the Com-   1603
pany 'well mounted on horseback and apparelled in velvet coats
with chains of gold attended the Lord Mayor and the Aldermen to
Stamford Hill amongst other Companies of the City to receive the
King's Most Excellent Majesty being his first repair to this City'.

*   *
*

From the Union with Scotland there came to the Company no
immediate effect: the old economic order continued, changing but
little and almost imperceptibly during the first forty years of the
seventeenth century. But there were two great factors which were
to be reflected in the history of the Clothworkers' Company.

The first lay in the great financial difficulties which beset James I.
The second was the beginning of the permanent expansion of the
English race overseas.

Virginia, New England, the West Indies, India, Northern Ireland – colonies and trading stations were established in them all.
And towards the 'Adventuring' to such places the Company was to
contribute greatly.

69

Financial
Needs of
the Crown
The financial difficulties of James I were due, quite apart from his profligacy, the expensive immorality of his Court, and his lavish entertainments, to several inter-related causes. The expansion of mercantile enterprise, as we have seen, had made the English economy vulnerable to continental events quite outside English control. Peace that came with the first year of James I solved some problems, but the great rise in prices that had taken place meant a time of hardship for many. This price revolution had seriously aggravated the plight of the royal exchequer. The King was no longer solvent.[1] In the absence of Parliamentary legislation, he had to fall back on raising money by various devices – the exaction of penalties for the breach of obsolete laws or, more generally, by

Monopolies
grants of monopolies. These patents of monopoly were granted for cash or given to the royal favourites in lieu of wages or pensions. Many of them were, most injudiciously, entrusted by Parliament to the discretion of the patentees.[2] All too often the patentees, whose interests were frankly financial, compounded with law-breakers in the name of the King.

1606
Such monopolies were a consistent source of social unrest: the outcry against them gradually increased until in 1606 a Committee of Grievances was set up. The most serious grievance (and the one that perhaps best illustrates the defects of the system) was the 'Patent of Aulnagers'.[3]

Patent of
Aulnagers
Aulnagers were officials who, as early as the thirteenth century, had been appointed to see that regulations in the cloth trade were carried out: their functions were to test every cloth and see that it conformed to the prescribed standards. Satisfactory cloths were sealed, the rest were confiscated. In the seventeenth century the Duke of Lennox procured the surrender of the existing patent and was granted a new one which was gradually extended to cover eighty new and different kinds of cloth. The patent was granted by James I for sixty years. There were fines of 20s for the sale of un-sealed fustians – 10s of which went to the Duke – and the Duke and his men had power to enter and search, to seize materials, and hold them until forfeits were paid. For resisting the searchers, fines of ten shillings could be imposed. Power was delegated by Parliament

to the Lord Treasurer or the Chancellor of the Exchequer to make
new Ordinances to aid the Duke. According to a petition[4] by the
Fustian Makers, the Duke's men were acting unjustly, they were
exacting money for sealing or demanding 'annual rents' as protection money 'to be at peace'. 'And,' said the outraged Fustian
Makers, 'where they exact money they force the parties to give
them a general release'. Some of them were compelled to 'take
from them a stamp to seal their own Fustians withall and become
their tenants at a yearly Rent for they never care for the Sealing of
the Fustains so they may get money'.

To such lengths did the abuses go that, so it was said in Parliament
in 1624, seals were publicly sold by the bushel.[5] The original design
of the institution had been entirely lost sight of. The monopoly
had become a simple method of extortion by the individual and a
source of revenue for the Crown.

The Statute of Monopolies in 1624 did something to regulate
the gross abuses that had arisen, by making illegal all monopolies
'for the sole buying, selling, making, working or using of anything'
and by limiting the grant of any monopoly to a period of fourteen
years. But, as is usual with all legislation, particularly in the time
of the Stuarts, there were many loopholes to the Statute through
which patentees quickly wriggled, and monopolies continued,
their powers of annoyance only slightly curtailed.

* *
*

In addition to monopolies there were also, to bolster the King's   Forced
finances, a number of forced loans levied upon the City.   Loans

In 1604 a forced loan of £15,000 was raised from the City, and   1604
the Clothworkers were assessed at one thousand guineas, a sum
which, in their strained position, they were quite unable to raise.
Money had to be borrowed at 9 per cent, and members were
assessed not only for the raising of the interest but also – and it is
apparent that James's insolvency was common knowledge – for
what sums were to be raised from them 'if the King pay it not'.

These gloomy forebodings proved only too accurate. Early in   1606
1606, when the King was due to repay £900, the Court appointed

two members to go to collect the cash, but at the next Court the pair returned the King's seal as the debt had not been honoured. Those who had underwritten the loan were called upon to make good the loss.

Concealed Lands   With the Crown in such financial straits it was only a matter of time before the name of Concealed Lands again raised its head. But this time the City and the Companies did not meekly accept the blackmailing demands. They hit back. On 13 April 1607

Sir Henry Montague Recorder of the City of London came and declared to this Company that there is a Bill preferred to the Parliament House touching the assurance of the lands and tenements belonging to the several companies of this City. Certain rents issuing out of which said lands and tenements limited to superstitious uses were purchased by the . . . Companies of King Edward VI in the fourth year of his reign.

The judges and great lawyers of this land then being of the opinion that only the rents employed or limited to superstitious uses were the King's but not the lands where out those rents were issuing: yet in those times the very lands have been and yet are in question.

And certain Patentees in the time of the late Queen have gone about and yet do to enable the . . . late Queen and the King's Majesty that now is to the said lands and tenements [only for their private gain] as lands concealed from the Crown and not caring whether they bereave a number of poor people in this City and elsewhere . . . of their best and chiefest remedy and maintenance . . . By means of those patents they have drawn from the . . . Companies many great sums of money for composition with the Patentees of the said lands, the rents whereof they had formerly purchased of the said King Edward VI.

And so the said Company having paid first to the King, and, after, compounded with the said Patentees . . . in spite of all the money they have departed with have at this moment [of assurance] neither rents nor lands.

The Recorder went on to show what an advantage this Bill would prove to the City and he asked the Clothworkers if they would share the general expense of getting the Bill on to the Statute Book. They replied that, although they knew their lands to be as free from question as any other company in London 'they were ready to join in any measure for the common good'.

As a result of these corporate measures the Bill was passed; the Company paid £120 towards its costs and hoped sourly that 'from henceforth . . . all these lands shall be free for ever from all titles of concealment and superstitious uses'.

*   *

*

In view of the King's attitude towards the City as a kind of milch-cow for nourishing his feeble personal economy, there is a delicious irony to be extracted from an account of the lavish way in which James I was entertained by the Company during the Mayorality of Sir William Stone, the Master. The hall and the parlour were decorated with green birch boughs and flowers. Herbs were strewn about the floor and the tables were covered with woollen cloths. A picture of the King had been brought to the hall from Sir Leonard Halliday's house and an 'image or statue of Mr. Lambe'* had also been set up. A walnut chair covered with green velvet and cloth of gold with the arms of the Company embroidered upon it was provided for the greater dignity of His Majesty who, it must be admitted, was not in himself a figure of great dignity.

The King dined with his nobles at the house of Sir John Watts, the Lord Mayor, where 'they were joyfully received and nobly feasted' After the banquet the Lord Mayor presented His Majesty with a purse of gold, which James

Royal Entertainment

accepted of as a sure Evidence of the sincere love and hearty Affections of the Citizens towards him and his Family; wherefore he assured them of his paternal Love and Care for the interests of the City. Whereupon the Mayor humbly entreated that he would be graciously pleased to accept of the Freedom of their Company, which His Majesty accepting of, he called for Sir [William] Stone, the Master, whom he took by the Hand and said 'Now we are bretheren "Clothworkers" ' and being presented by the Earls of Shrewsbury and Cumberland with Bread and Wine, he took the Cup and drank Prosperity to the Society . . . Praying God to bless all good Clothworkers and all good Clothwearers. And as a farther proof of his Affection towards the Company gave them yearly for ever two Brace of Bucks to regale themselves on the anniversary

* See Appendixes D and F.

73

Election of Master and Wardens. Whereupon the said Lord Mayor Sir William Stone and the rest of the Company in token of their great joy and thankfulness kissed His Majesty's Royal Hands. [6]

That this gift was less liberal than might at first have seemed to the Company may be inferred from the fact that, quite apart from the way in which the gift hardly ever arrived in time for the dinner and another dinner had to be held to dispose of the venison, the actual cost to the Company of every such gift of four Buck was £6 13s 4d.*

* *

*

Enlargement of the Hall   Now that the King was a Freeman of the Company it was thought that the hall should be enlarged

in length one bay at the upper end, more windows for light made on the sides, a louver to be made on the top thereof and a gallery all along on the north side of the garden with a return eastwards to beautify the said Hall and garden and specially the prospect of the parlour which now by the rinnousues [?] of the houses directly opposite northwards and north east of the prospect of the parlour is very unseemly besides the discommodity of overlooking the said garden from the said houses.

Further, a picture of the King was bought for £8 10s, to hang, curtained in green taffeta, in the parlour.

Moreover, there were to be no more wardmote meetings held at the hall and the door was to be kept locked; from this and from earlier orders prohibiting weddings and dinners from being held at the hall (on one occasion when such a party was permitted there was the proviso made that any damage to windows or wainscotting must be paid for) it may be inferred that parties and meetings were apt to get out of control.

The garden was further beautified on the occasion of election dinners by the construction of arbours, the wood and wire frames of which were covered with birch and flowers.

* In spite of this discouraging precedent, an attempt was made in 1870 to revive the gift as a matter of principle. The attempt was unsuccessful.

And if the garden and hall were beautified, so too were the wardens of the Yeomanry; for Sir William Stone bought them 'four fair garlands of purple velvet with three scutcheons of the Company's Arms upon every of the said garlands, richly embroidered with gold and silver twine lined with crimson satin', and a fair box to keep them in.

The King's jester was engaged to entertain at dinner, and, in fact, in a time of scarcity and high prices, the Mayoralty and the royal membership of the Company endowed the scene, for a short while, with a glitter that it often lacked.

* *

*

It was now that the second of the great influences of early seventeenth century England – the overseas expansion of the English race – began to make itself felt in the Company's everyday life. On 4 April 1609

Colonization of Virginia

1609

a precept from the Lord Mayor directed to this Company touching the voyage and Adventure to Virginia and a copy also of a letter sent to the Lord Mayor and Aldermen by the Council and Company of the honourable plantation of Virginia was openly read to the whole assembly here present. And after the reading thereof some speeches were made by the Master, Mr. Coleby to encourage those of the Company then present to the said Adventure.

But they, thereupon, did not show any forwardness to that Adventure. Save only Humphrey Hawes who said that he had already adventured £12.10.0. And rather than the voyage should not proceed he would Adventure £12.10.0 more. And the like offer was made by Thomas Weeks whereupon because it was thought fit by the Table that the Company should have time to deliberate upon this matter ...

they were told to go away, think things over and within two days let the Master know how much they were prepared, individually, to adventure.

The response was not overwhelming. Three weeks later the Court agreed that they would make up the 'petty sums' adventured (which amounted to no more than some £30) to a total of one hundred pounds.

In December the Wardens were summoned to the Guildhall to hear the Lord Mayor demand that each Company should call the members together to know what sum of their voluntary goodwill should be adventured for the ensuing three years in Virginia. The Recorder told them that if during the next three years only £18,000 could be raised – £12,000 having already been subscribed by the magnificent efforts of the nobility and gentry, only £6,000 was now needed from the City – it was 'hoped that the country of Virginia would not only yield commodities . . . sufficient to defray the yearly charges thereof but also yield profit to the Adventurers.'

The response of the Company to this plausible prospect must have been a disappointment. 'It was thought not fit that this Company make any further Adventure towards the said Plantation.' Three years later, at the personal request of Sir Thomas Hewett, they did in fact invest another £50, but when in 1614 investment in a further lottery for Virginia was invited, the Clothworkers politely refused.

In this they were wise. The first emigrants had been attracted to the scheme by the promise of 'meat, drink and clothing, with a house, orchard and garden for the meanest family and the possession of land to them and their posterity'.[7] They were in many cases the younger sons of peasants and yeomen who could obtain no land in England or unemployed craftsmen who knew that there would be need of their skills in the new world. There were, too, many gentlemen adventurers attracted by the stories of the fabulous riches of America.[8]

All these were settlers under free enterprise – they went there of their own will. Unfortunately, the Government sent, subsequently, to join them, boat-loads of convicts and undesirables. With their arrival they spread plague and disorder. The greater part, perhaps threequarters, of the early settlers died prematurely, either as the result of disease and famine, or at the hands of hostile Indians.

The financial returns to investors were negligible: so far from being speedily self-supporting, the Colony in 1622 was forced to borrow corn for the English residents there.

Except for having to contribute towards the cost of transport of one hundred vagrant children to the Colony – an early form of Borstal treatment which perhaps leaves something to be desired – the Company heard no more of the Virginia Plantation.* They were, in any case, too greatly preoccupied with a plantation nearer home.

* *

*

Only three months after the first meeting to decide whether they should adventure any money in Virginia, it became necessary, in answer to a precept, to form a committee to consider 'the plantation intended in the North part of Ireland'. The Company decided to take no part in the plantation – a decision that was entirely unacceptable to higher authority. The members were called together again and the names of all those still refusing to contribute were taken. The great extortion had begun.

 The Irish Plantation

As a result of the rebellion in Ulster in 1595, that province had been de-populated and laid waste. Much of the land became forfeit to the Crown, and in order to resettle it and to establish a colony of Protestants there, particularly in Derry, James I made certain proposals to the Lord Mayor for colonization. As a result of the proposals and of a certain amount of high-pressure salesmanship by the Crown, the City decided to co-operate in the formation of an Irish Society.

Early in 1610 the City was taxed £20,000 to pay for the first costs of the Irish Plantation, and the Clothworkers, their early refusal ignored, were told to raise £1,130 of this amount. Such a sum was not to be raised without considerable difficulty. Only by waving the big stick of imprisonment over the heads of the Livery was the money eventually collected. But, as in all these official demands, the painful raising of £1,130 was only a beginning. In 1611 there came the first indications that they must not expect to recover their money.

 1610

 1611

* But emigration to the New World could still be a matter for free enterprise. In 1637 a member of the Court, Jeremy Norcross, was granted £10 towards the cost of his 'intended journey to New England'. That the intended journey was taken may be inferred from the fact that a few years later one Jeremy Norcross was involved in considerable litigation in Maryland.

At the Lord Mayor's order, the Company were called together. The subject for discussion was

whether you will take and accept a proportionate share of lands in the province of Ulster within the Realm of Ireland in lieu of the moneys by you already disbursed towards the plantation there and so to build the same and plant at your pleasure costs and charges according as by the printed Book of Plantation is required. Or else whether you will refer the letting of the same lands and managing of the whole business there unto the Governor and Assistants of the Company for the Plantation for the time being.

To this project the Company replied they were sorry but

owing to the taking away by God's hand of divers worthy, able and great men and the poverty of those left the Company is so weakened and so poor. And with such difficulty have payments been in part gathered and payment has been so unsavoury to everyone and with so hard a hand drawn from them

that they saw no hope of collecting any more money. In the light of previous experience of financial dealings with the Crown, it must be doubted whether the Company can really have expected that such a refusal would be accepted.

A month later the Livery and Yeomanry were called together and the same project put before them. The scheme was gone into in greater and persuasive detail. The King, it appeared, having most graciously granted to the City of London the towns of Derry and Coleraine with 7,000 acres of common ground with fishing and many other valuable rights, the City had undertaken to spend £20,000 in building houses and fortifications and freeing foreign titles. Now the King had further granted some other lands in the County of Coleraine to be developed in accordance with the printed *Book of Plantation*, and the Governor of the Plantation, it seemed, was on the point of making arrangements for letting those extra lands, to the greater benefit and glory of the City. It was quite the best time of year for starting a plantation – and, in any case, it seemed only fair that previous subscribers should have the first chance of this most advantageous offer. Surely the Clothworkers would leap at the opportunity of taking up some proportionate shares?

The Livery and Yeomanry had no doubts at all on the matter. They wanted neither land nor anything that was managed by the Government. They gave the Master and Wardens *carte blanche* to reply, in that sense, to the precept.

The Court, with a delightfully satirical touch, thanked the Lord Mayor for the opportunity. But now that they had heard the fuller details of the scheme they felt that the £20,000 (to which they had subscribed their proportion) was probably insufficient for all those buildings, fortifications, and so on. Since they were not prepared to accept any further expense, they were now prepared to sell all their existing holdings to the first buyer for no more than they gave for it. This, they implied, would be, as the Lord Mayor himself had pointed out to them in his precept, a great bargain for some fortunate purchaser.

In the meantime, a great drive was launched to collect the sums already outstanding towards the £1,130 nominally subscribed. By threats and imprisonment some of the assessments were with difficulty collected. Lord Compton, already involved in law suits with the Company over the £200 he owed them as heir to his deceased father-in-law Sir John Spencer,[*] proved especially difficult. The Mayor was asked for time to deal with him. By July, the Mayor's patience was becoming exhausted and, because the Company was still in debt, the majority of the sum outstanding being due from Lord Compton – two of the Wardens were flung into prison[9] where they remained for some months until a written promise to pay was extracted from his Lordship.

A year later the amount was still outstanding and, having no taste for further imprisonment, the Wardens undertook to pay £20 to the Town Clerk and the City Remembrancer 'if by continually following and soliciting of Lord Compton' they could induce him to hand over £200.

* It is possible that Lord Compton may have regretted the romantic moment of elopement in which Spencer's daughter had been smuggled out of her father's house in a basket.

This desperate expedient was immediately successful. Not, however, in any way successful was the Company's ingenuous attempt to dispose of their holding at a bargain price. Seeing that softly persuasive means were unavailing, the Crown showed its teeth. On 1611 23 July 1611, a further precept for £10,000 was given to the City for the first Plantation. Half the money was to be raised by 10 August. The Companies were told that they must either 'willingly' yield to the demand or else forfeit the £20,000 they had already subscribed.

The position was clearly hopeless. Hopeless, too, for the Clothworkers was any idea of raising the £565 which was their share of the levy by personal assessment – there were still some members who had not paid up the last four assessments made upon them. They decided that they would pay the money to the Chamberlain out of the corporate funds of the Company 'if of necessity it must be paid and the rest of the twelve companies which are before us have paid in their money'.

1613 When, in 1613, another precept for the Plantation in Ireland for £565 was received, it was accepted without comment. The following year the Company was forced to subscribe another £282 10s and again they raised the money from the 'Body politic' rather than by the poll tax that was so discouragingly difficult to collect.

By the end of 1613 the Company had paid altogether £3,390 towards the £50,000 subscribed by the City and a Royal Charter was issued to the Irish Society. A Committee of Clothworkers was formed to discuss with the Merchant Taylors, the Butchers, the Brown-bakers, the Upholders, the Bowyers, and the Fletchers 1615 what to do with the land the Company shared jointly with them,* and in 1615 the first results began, rather surprisingly, to show that the money was perhaps not totally lost. Applications for tenancies began to flow in.

From thenceforth the first Plantation became just one more of those administrative details of estate management with which the

* Eventually in 1620 the Company's first estates were managed and financed jointly with the Merchant Taylors.

Company were becoming increasingly occupied. Nor did the broader horizons to which the eyes of the Clothworkers were now directed lessen the managerial responsibilities of the nearer and more domestic scene.

In addition to the vast drains on the Company's funds by the first venture, there were still precepts for the provision of corn and coal and gunpowder. There were loans to be made and collected, there were the myriad tasks of maintaining the properties which had been left to the Company. There were searches to be supervised and disputes settled. The Minute Books became more and more preoccupied with these records of estate administration: the ever-increasing business minutiae of an ever-growing Corporation.

CHAPTER FIVE

THE CLOTH PROJECT

*   *
   *

1613   THEN, quite unexpectedly, there occurred in 1613 an event of quite outstanding importance, an event which was to have devastating effects not only upon the Clothworkers themselves but upon the very economy of the nation.

The first outward signs of the approaching disaster were seen when some artisan Clothworkers and Dyers, most improperly ignoring the proper procedure and 'being covetous of large employment petitioned the King and Council that there might go no more white cloths out of the Kingdom'.

For this gigantic demand they gave three reasons: firstly 'that the Hollanders making use of dressing and dying our cloth sold us our own again almost double and we impoverished'; secondly, that the poor of the Company might be employed and, lastly that dressing of cloth might be restored as an industry and, in time, 'they might have as good skill to dress the cloth as the Dutchman'.

Alderman Cockayne   Ostensibly this petition was made entirely upon the initiative of the artisans themselves, but there are grounds for believing that behind them, scheming and prompting, there stood a band of City speculators led by Alderman Cockayne, first Governor of the Irish Society and a prime mover of the idea of monopolies. Certainly it is with a suspicious alacrity, if the simple artisans were indeed the originators of the plan, that the band of wealthy capitalists sprang together to form a Company of Adventurers to carry on the trade arising from the scheme. Moreover their efficient organization bore the hallmarks of an advance planning that cannot have been ignorant of the artisans' intentions.[1]

82

A contemporary diarist[2] had little doubt that a plot was hatching and noted that 'my Lord of Rochester, my Lord of Northampton and my Lord . . . Treasurer were great agents in this business and were thought to have been promised great sums of money to accomplish it'. The Court of the Clothworkers' Company, however, seem to have been unaware of any such deep-laid plot. They were, quite simply, appalled by the immensity of the artisans' project.*

Though they had had nothing to do with the petition, had known nothing of its intended presentation, they feared 'some imputation [might] be laid upon the general body of this Company', and they sent for the Wardens of the Yeomanry to question them about it. These latter denied that they had had anything to do with the petition although, they were forced to admit, they knew something about it. They were ordered sharply that, whatever their private feelings in the matter might be, 'they would not hereafter be seen in that business'.

A few days later the Yeomanry wardens appeared and asked the Court if they might go to the Privy Council about the petition – and, later still, they asked for money to help prosecute a suit which proposed to offer 'the Crown five shillings for every cloth so dressed'. But the Court, thoroughly alarmed, refused their consent: they did not want it thought that they had anything to do with so revolutionary a project.

Yet the project, when presented, received no hint of disapproval from the Lord Treasurer (correlative evidence perhaps that, as has been suggested, he was an interested party to the scheme). On the contrary, he wrote in the most disturbing manner to the Court, touching some better government to be considered and thought upon to be established over the Artizan Clothworkers of this Company without the which his Lordship thought it would be hard to effect that great and honourable work intended to be established touching the dressing and dyeing of all manner of white woollen cloths made in this

The Lord Treasurer Intervenes

1614

---

* The enormity of the proposition will be realized when it is remembered that previously the artisans were concerned only with the dressing of one cloth in every ten.

kingdom before they be transported. To the settling whereof his honour by his Letters did offer the best furtherance and help that in him lieth.

It is only too easy to imagine the feelings of many of the Court. They were Merchants; not only did they believe the whole scheme to be impossible but also that the very foundations of the Company were being shaken. Not only did the Lord Treasurer smile upon an artisan petition – a petition forwarded first of all without the knowledge of the Court and later presented in spite of their disapproval – and call it an 'honourable work', but he also went so far as to hint that the artisans might secede from the rest of the Clothworkers' Company.*

The whole thing must have been a matter of the gravest scandal to the Court.

Upon the reading of which letters from the Treasurer procured (as it is thought) by the means of the artizan Clothworkers of this Company, of whom a good number being this day assembled it was demanded that it is which they required to be done in this business (of better government) for them by the Master Wardens and Assistants?

The answer was no less than a demand for an exclusive control over the trade, for first they required that

suits and means might be made for the reducing of all Artizan Clothworkers, as were free of the Company of Merchant Taylors as of any other Company within the City whatsoever, under the rule and government of the Master Wardens and Assistants of this Company of Clothworkers.

This was momentous enough, but it was nothing to what followed. Once, in 1566, the merchants had sought to be rid of the craftsmen. Now the position was reversed, for

Next it was required by some of . . . them that the absence rule and government of the manual artizan Clothworkers might be wholly referred to the wardens and assistants of the Yeomanry but in this point

* In this the Lord Treasurer's attitude is of interest, for it shows that the State, by suggesting a new form of government for the artisans, was thinking in terms of support for the industrial interest.

they did dissent for some (and the most part) of them were of a contrary mind.*

They were told to go away and come again before the Court when they had made up their minds. It is interesting to speculate on what would have happened in the subsequent history of the Company if this move (already suggested in 1604)[3] to secede from the Merchant body had been carried out.

The Court of the Clothworkers' Company were supported in their instinctive dislike of the Cloth Project by the practical businessmen who composed the Merchant Adventurers. From the very first time the petition was raised they had maintained their attitude against the principle that dressed cloths alone should be exported. In the face of claims from artisans that only the patentees and Merchant Adventurers gained from the export of 'whites', that the King, Realm, and Clothworkers lost treasure and honour, that if the cloth were finished in England the Crown would get eighteen pence in custom on imported dyestuffs and the Clothworkers twenty shillings on every cloth, they replied that the English white cloth which they had always exported could not stand crude English dyeing, suitable though that might be for the home market or for the new draperies. For, as the Company's scholar, Richard Hakluyt, had pointed out in a memorandum in 1579,[4] although it was acknowledged that England produced 'the best wool and cloth of the world', the English dyeing was inferior.

Continental taste, said the Merchant Adventurers, would not be satisfied. Foreigners would be driven to compete with the English in the actual manufacture of cloth. The war with Spain had already built up native manufacturers in the Peninsula, France was ready to restrict cloth imports to establish her own cloth trade. Germany and the Low Countries were in a position to produce cloth as well as, if not better than, England herself could. If such a project were to succeed then, they maintained, some other channel for exporting

---

* It was the small masters who were against the idea of seceding from the mercantile body of the Company and having to be ruled by the more irresponsible Yeomanry.

and selling finished cloths must be found, for they, the Merchant
Adventurers, could find no market for them.[5]

1614   In spite of these protests, in 1614

the Artizan Clothworkers still persisting in their suit and having such
friends to stand for them, and Alderman Cockayne, a rich merchant, to
back them [with his offer to export as many dressed cloths as they could
furnish][6] they gained what they had for so long demanded. And since
the old Merchant Adventurers still stubbornly refused to alter their
point of view that the export of nothing but dressed cloths was impracticable and would in no way co-operate, their Royal Charter was
removed from them.

They were replaced by the New Merchant Adventurers under
Alderman Cockayne.

* *
*

New   The new Adventurers got away to a somewhat shaky start. The
Merchant   Charter was theirs but they were, in fact, not quite ready to begin.
Adventurers They complained that the old Merchant Adventurers in a last
trading effort had exported more cloth than ever before to stifle the
trade of the new company.[7] They asked, therefore, that they might
be allowed to export undressed cloth until they had built up a
market, and they were granted permission for exports to be on a
sliding scale: not less than 6,000 pieces of finished cloth to be
exported in the first year of the project, 12,000 pieces in the next
year and 18,000 in the third. After this the field was to be entirely
theirs.

The project, which provided work for the native artisan who
naturally supported it whole-heartedly, was a glorious one. It was
launched in an appropriately glorious manner. Cockayne feasted
the King and entertained him with a Pageant of Clothworkers
commissioned from Ben Jonson.

For eighteen months the New Merchant Adventurers domin-
ated the Privy Council which in turn tried to manipulate the
foreign trade of the country and its principal manufacturers to suit
the wishes of the projectors.[8] The officers of the new Company
were to sit at the Custom House and no cloth was to be exported

without their seal. Middlemen were forbidden to deal in wool. In the country, Justices of the Peace were to act as state agencies for the collection of textiles. No foreign ship was allowed to unload its cargo without taking aboard English goods (preferably, of course, dyed cloth) in exchange. Foreign commerce became possible only by exceptions to the rules and each application for an exception to be made had to be considered by the Privy Council and decided upon its own merits.

The amount of extra work for the Council was enormous, the results were disappointing. The Dutch, for example, with a perverseness that seemed incredible, actually encouraged their merchants to 'make a Monopoly or unlawful confederacy whereby they bound themselves not to buy any cloth that was finished'. The first results of this little adventure in state control were that the price of cloth went down, half the looms in the West Country stopped, unemployment swelled, and the Crown lost £10,000 a year in customs duty.

The Privy Council began to show signs of impatience. Bacon wrote to the King suggesting that the whole idea should be abandoned, not because he disapproved of the idea in theory, but because he thought that, in practice, the New Merchant Adventurers were incapable of carrying it out.[9] He suggested that fresh contacts be made with the old original Company, and, as a result, the old Merchant Adventurers were authorized to hold a meeting to discuss the whole affair.[10]

The meeting was held and it is not difficult to visualize the quiet 1616 satisfaction of business men who knew they had been right, had stuck to their guns, and were now seeing the interlopers sinking slowly but surely into the mire of which they had been warned.

They did not alter their opinions in the least but, as a concession, they were prepared to make an experiment with a few – a very few – finished cloths.[11] The concession was not accepted, and for the moment the new Company was allowed to continue on condition that it bought up an unlimited number of Gloucester cloths, in spite of the fact that these were highly inferior in both finish and material.

But all too soon complaints began to pour in about the cessation of trade. Arbitrary sumptuary laws – such as one that those at Court must wear clothes of blue home-spun material – were proposed to provide a home market for cloth. Trade was in confusion. Cockayne was summoned before the Council and told to find some way of disposing of the glut of cloth 'whereof it behoved them to have a care at their uttermost peril'. He was told to consider whether he would continue with the scheme for dyeing and dressing[12].

The Cloth
Project
Collapses

The Project was now in the last stages of disintegration. The Alderman who had been so lavish a host to the King was called before his royal guest to explain just what had gone wrong: he was forced to admit that without foreign sales the New Merchant Adventurers could no longer buy cloths for export. He hoped, however, that they might be able to hold out for a little longer. How much longer he was unable to say, but he agreed that the position was serious.

In an attempt to bolster up the dying venture, plans were formulated for compelling – by imprisonment – individual Merchant Adventurers to buy cloth even though they could not sell it again, for compelling all Londoners worth £10,000 to buy £1,000 worth of cloth. The Dutch, it was agreed, should be punished: their fisheries must be stopped, the import of their cheeses halted, the market for their butter and their hops closed. Eventually,

a certain number of white cloths were suffered to be transported as well to give content to the Hollander as satisfaction and employment to some young merchants who had entered into this trade by which means those clamours were a little stayed, yet nevertheless great impression of envy is between these two Companies.

But before the New Year the great Cloth Project had died. The New Merchant Adventurers had surrendered their Charter and the old Merchant Adventurers ruled once again in their accustomed place.[13]

* *
*

Whatever may be said of the virtues of the system of monopolies for encouraging trade – and as a method of taxation it was certainly not ineffective – it failed disastrously in the rudimentary form of State socialism which was the Cloth Project.

The evil effects of the experiment, the upsetting of the old trade rhythms was felt until the end of the reign.

For not only was the Dutch weaving industry now established but other countries in retaliation joined in the competition. Foreign lands not only achieved a position of mercantile advantage but they retained the industries they had newly set up. The Low Countries disorganized international trade by confiscating as 'interlopers' at the Staple at Middleburg 'whites' belonging to the New Merchant Adventurers.

Meanwhile, the failure of the New Merchant Adventurers to find the markets they needed led to great unemployment in the City and tumultuous scenes took place at Clothworkers' Hall.

Revolt of the Yeomanry

The trouble began with the Wardens of the Yeomanry who, in 1616, suddenly refused to give security for the proper rendering of their accounts. For this reason they were forbidden to collect quarterage and their account book was taken away from them. They still remained in office, however, and the following year obstinately refused to hand over £20 they had already collected in quarterage. For this contempt of Court they were sent to jail.

Their attitude was symptomatic of the unrest that was sweeping through the artisans of many of the City Companies. At one protest meeting held at the Hall 'the whole multitude cried out . . . with such confused noise as struck terror and amazement to the Master, Wardens and Assistants here assembled in general'.

1617

The Yeomanry, now organized almost completely on the same lines as their superiors in the Livery, were thoroughly out of hand. Not only did their wardens still refuse to hand over the £20 in their hands but also combined 'with many other refractory members of this Company against the Master, Wardens and Assistants whereby the said Master and Wardens were driven to resort to the Lord Mayor for his Lordship's aid and authority to reduce them to conformity'.

Worse was to come.

At a time . . . appointed for hearing and determining the matter in difference, namely the 18th December 1616, they brought foreign counsel to speak for them . . . before the Lord Mayor . . . the Master and Wardens having then and there no counsel at all. At which time and place they brought a copy of the Company's Charter, acquainted foreign Counsel with the Company's secrets and very unjustly and un-truly taxed and charged the Master, Wardens and Assistants with the mis-spending of £1,500 of the Company's treasure which (as they affirmed) ought to have been put into the chest called the Yeoman's chest.

The Lord Mayor ordered the rebellious wardens to pay over the money and to make their humble submission at the next Court meeting of the Company. Riot was not so easily quelled. The Wardens in due course paid over the money but 'did utterly deny and refuse to make their submission . . . saying they would not betray their own innocency'.

They were again flung into prison for a month – over Christmas, just to point the lesson – but even after that, having asked to be let out and having gone before the Lord Mayor, they

stood at the first rather upon their justification than in any way acknow-ledging their errors: with [this] their obstinate carriage in such a time of dispersing dangerous libels and factious spirits breaking forth into dangerous discontentment could not be deemed to be other than great contempt and unseemly misdemeanour in them and worthy of sharp reprehension.

At last, however, they submitted themselves humbly to the Court and were dismissed. New Wardens were appointed and the Yeomanry account books handed over. They were promised all the help the Court could give them if they had any difficulty in collecting the quarterage.

The revolt was over. For another thirty years there was to be no such trial of strength in the Company.

This struggle was indicative of a new re-grouping of the differ-ent sections of the Company. The Journeymen, who had at one

time become, as has been shown, no more than an appendage of the
Yeomanry, were now beginning to hold the controlling interest
in that body. And, although the Company procured if they did not
actually promote the Act of Common Council in 1618 to protect
the status of the small Master (whose support was needed to
prevent the export of unfinished cloth), as the seventeenth century
wore on, the small Masters were increasingly overshadowed by
the Journeymen.[14]

By the time of the Civil War, when the grievances of the industrial section had become more fully formulated, the specific
aims of the small Masters had quite disappeared from view.

The social development of the Clothworkers' Company was
entirely typical of the new organizations that had replaced the old
craft-guilds. Where the Company differed from other Companies
was in the unusual equilibrium that existed between the two
interests – the commercial and the industrial. By means of a compromise that is generally regarded as 'peculiarly English' protection
of labour was, in the Company, combined with freedom of Trade:
the commercial interests were held in check by the fact that the
Drapers and Merchant Adventurers were in command of the
trade, and the industrial interests were held in check (as they were
not in the provinces) by the general commercial character of
London.

The revolt of the Wardens of the Yeomanry had been the outward sign of the clash of interests that was taking place. The
uneasiness felt by the Court at the unruliness of the Yeomanry no
doubt tempered their decisions. There does, in fact, thereafter,
seem to be a slightly more tolerant approach to the Yeomanry
petitions. Besides, the merchants had scored for the moment a
moral victory. The Court had been right – the Cloth Project had
been the wild impracticable scheme that they had always known it
would be. Their old friends, and indeed colleagues, were back in
business with the old Merchant Adventurers. They could afford, as
was prudent, to be reasonable.

A month after the revolt of the Wardens a petition came from
the Yeomanry:

to have some of the Wardens or some of the Assistants of this Company to go with them to the Merchant Adventurers' Court to make request for and on behalf of the poor artizan clothworkers of this Company that the said company of Merchant Adventurers would take compassion upon them and employ them in labour being brought into great extremity and want for lack of employment.

The Court agreed that this should be done. The same day certain Yeomanry gave notice.

that divers strangers and foreigners being of late come to inhabit in the skirts of this City and places near adjoining without the liberties as namely at Lambeth, Bermondsey House, East Smithfield, Shoreditch and Stratford at Bow ... are employed in rowing and shearing of woollen cloths to the great hindrance of the poor artizan clothworkers of this Company whose livings depend upon the like labour.

The Court agreed to have a great search of such persons for workmanship, for the number of servants they kept, what store of work they had, and so on.

The Yeomanry next asked for money to pursue a suit to the Privy Council for more work.* The Court told them to bring in an account of their expenses and they would see what could be done.

Next the Wardens of the Yeomanry asked the Court to join in a suit to the Privy Council 'for labour to relieve the great necessities of the Artizan Clothworkers of this Company'. The Court agreed, provided they could first see the petition in writing: finally they allowed them their expenses in the petition.

Only a week later, taking advantage perhaps of this new spirit of conciliation and agreement, the Yeomanry petitioned the Court to enforce the ordinances made jointly with the Merchant Taylors concerning the number of apprentices, the creation of partner-

* There are signs that the Privy Council were getting tired of these constant suits. A long dispute throughout 1617 between Merchant Adventurers and Clothworkers who demanded that every tenth cloth should be dressed at the cost of 1s for the relief of the Clothworkers ended with the Privy Council announcing that they would no longer interfere in the trade in Whites: in future Clothworkers and Merchant Adventurers must cease troubling the Council with their disputes. 15

ships, and the setting up of house without first being viewed by their Wardens.

Both these points were agreed but the Court did, in fact, refuse to carry out the ordinances concerning the searcher at the water-side – it was, they thought, useless on account of the King having granted to the Earl of Cumberland* a licence which the Merchant Adventurers were using as a convenient cover for evading the law.

This harmonious balance between the merchants and the workers of the Company came at a time when the Clothworkers had quite clearly undergone a dramatic reversal of their financial fortunes. In 1611 they had been complaining of the poverty in which they found themselves; there had been all the extortions for the Irish Estate, for 'a gratuity' to the King 'for the better supply of His Majesty's wants'; there had been all the usual expenses – now greatly increased with the cost of living – for providing coal, corn, and gunpowder; and even so they were now in the position of having the cash available to lend the Merchant Adventurers £1,000 at the usual rate of 9 per cent.

That they were financially sound is shown, too, from the fact   Prosperity that the old idea of even attempting to raise by poll tax money demanded by precept was now entirely abandoned in favour of a tax upon the body-politic. The body-politic must, therefore, have been in a position to meet such demands. What was more, the Company had grown in size as well as in influence. In 1615 it was noted that the corporate body was 'as great in number, or rather greater than in any former time it hath been': now in 1618 it was 'thought to be little inferior in number to the liveries of any of the 12 companies'.

The feasts were restored to their former splendour. There were to be many ladies invited 'and the diet to be provided in as good proportion as in former times it hath been'.

Moreover, it was decided that the Company in their new pros-perous condition should have a barge perpetually reserved for them instead of hiring one on each occasion. Not all the hired ones had been successes, sometimes there had been none of sufficient

* Free of the Company 1591.

size available for hire, and those on the Barge had to put up with miserably cramped quarters while two wherries carried the overflow.

One William Foster, a Brother of this Company, by trade a Lighterman, came and made offer to the Master, Wardens and Assistants present at this Court, at his own proper costs and charges to build a new barge for th'use and service of this Company, decent and convenient for the carriage of 60 men. And the barge so builded to have in a readiness upon a day's warning for any service of this Company upon any occasion.

The Court agreed that

for every such day, well furnished with five pairs of Oars and so many able men to row the same, with a sufficient steersman and all other necessaries whatsoever, so as this Company be not put to charges for watermen's wages or rewards, meat or drink for the watermen, rushes for the barge or any other thing,

a fee of £5 would be paid.

They would, moreover, buy and have embroidered 'a western azure woollen cloth to make a comely and convenient' covering for the Barge. The Company were flourishing in the grand manner.

CHAPTER SIX

THE REIGN OF CHARLES I

* *
*

FLOURISHING the times may have been; dull they certainly were. Trevelyan has spoken of the reign of the Stuarts up to the outbreak of the Revolution as being 'an uneventful prolongation of the Elizabethan era', and again: 'No industrial, agricultural or social change of importance took place in England during the forty years when the Parliamentary and Puritan revolution was germinating beneath the soil of an apparently stable and settled society.'

This slow and uneventful atmosphere is clearly to be seen in the Company's minute books which are filled with the record of leases granted; repairs carried out; pensions bestowed; money collected; and lawsuits or petitions begun, ended, or merely swallowed up and lost in the infinite delays of the seventeenth-century law.

Particularly did the members of the Company busy themselves with lawsuits and petitions. It was no doubt all a part of the striving by opposing interests to consolidate their various positions, to secure legal support for interests hitherto insufficiently secured.

One of the many petitions concerned the control of apprentices, and by a happy chance there appears a single brilliant ray of light illuminating the commodity to be controlled. For a moment the Minutes' impersonal and pedestrian pages sparkle with a genuine touch of life – the life of a refractory apprentice.

A Refractory
Apprentice

John Nicholson, the apprentice of Mr. Thomas Amys now Master of this Company, was complained of by his said Master for misbehaviour, stubbornness and disobedience as namely; being commanded on the

1618

Sabbath Day to brush his master's cloak, made answer that it was as fit
for the maidservant and the younger apprentice as for himself to brush
it and therefore refused to do it. And being commanded to fetch a Cloth
from a Tenter refused to fetch it saying that there were younger apprentices which might be sent for it as well as he.

And moreover being charged for going out and tarrying out of his
master's house at unlawful hours and for wilfully tearing his doublet,
confessed and could not deny but that he had tarried forth out of his
master's house until half an hour after nine of the clock at night. And for
tearing his doublet he made answer that his master gave him the outside
but the inside he paid for himself and therefore tore it.

He was ordered to 'suffer correction by the whip as in like case
hath been used to be done in this place to sturdy unruly and dis-
obedient apprentices of this Company'.

There the matter might have ended but for a postscript that was
added to the tale at the Court meeting the following week when
Robert Powell, the apprentice of Thomas Barton, was complained of

for unseemly usage towards Mr. Amys, Master of this Company, namely
for that as he passed by the said Mr. Amys and John Nicholson his servant ... said to the said John Nicholson in scoffing manner: 'Sirrah,
were you not the last day whipped at the Hall?' And the same word
'whipped' did reiterate in scorn and derision of the exemplary punishment which was inflicted upon the said John Nicholson for his offence.

Litigation   Time, money, energy, all were poured into Parliamentary
petitions and actions – actions of which nothing more is heard,
actions which perhaps, in fact, never reached decision.

1627   In 1627 the Yeomanry, weary of these vain petitions to Parliament to enforce the export laws, decided upon novel tactics: they
asked the Court for permission – and for money – to bring a lawsuit against some of the Merchant Adventurers under the Act of
1567 'for depriving the poor Artizan Clothworkers of this City
and other places of this Kingdom many years together of the labour
due to them by the said Statute'. To invoke the protection of the
lawcourts seemed their sole remaining remedy. In that suit lay
their only hope: by that suit would they stand or fall.

They said that, if the Court would agree to this course of action, they would promise 'never more to trouble this Table for any matter or charges of suit in this kind'.

After some hesitation the Court decided that action might be taken in any of the King's Courts at Westminster in the name of the Company against any of the Merchant Adventurers contravening the Statute. The Company would pay £20 towards the costs – or forty marks at the outside.

So far so good.

The suit was begun against the Merchant Adventurers in the King's Bench and the course it ran gives some inkling of the fate of many such seventeenth-century legal processes. A later statement reported that it

dependeth in the said Court undetermined. And the said wardens of the Yeomanry considering that the proceedings in the suits formerly commenced have been stopped by some special command of the King and State upon the solicitation of the said Merchant Adventurers, being strong in purse and friends, have bethought themselves of a way or mean to prevent the said Merchants from the like.

And to that purpose have dealt with a Gentleman named Mr. George Kirke, of King's Majesty's Bedchamber, very gracious with His Majesty who for a fourth part of this moiety and all penalties and forfeitures which shall be obtained and gotten upon any recovery to be had against any of the said Merchant Adventurers . . . to do his best and to use all the credit and means he can to His Majesty that there be no stop or stay in course of law for the solicitations or procurement of the said Merchants. . . .

It was an ingenious and subtle move: the Court agreed to it instantly.

But three years later, in 1630, the suit was still pending for, as had been earlier feared, the Merchant Adventurers had procured an order from the Privy Council for the staying of the suit. The Order, dated 24 October 1627, read:

This day the Company of Merchant Adventurers informed the Board of a great trouble unto Trade and the venting of the Cloth of the Kingdom occasioned by suits and molestations done them by the Master

97

and Wardens of the Company of the Clothworkers or some busy members of that Company in the name of the Master and Wardens of the Clothworkers for that they had in the Court of Kings Bench commenced sundry suits against divers of the said Company of Merchants for transporting out of the realm white cloths undressed, contrary to the Statute of Elizabeth against which suits the Petitioners humbly sought to be relieved by order of this Board.

The Privy Council recalled that for weighty reasons it had been decided from time to time to dispense with the provisions of that Statute by means of Letters Patent, the latest of which (to the late Duke of Richmond) was still in force. The Council ruled that the Merchants could go on exporting as they had been doing and the Clothworkers must stay and withdraw all pending suits and not bring any fresh ones on the Statute until further orders of the Board – at their uttermost peril.

In spite of this the Yeomanry wardens still lived in hope: 'There is a Gentleman who for a half part of this Moiety will procure the King's Majesty's letter for revising of the said order', they pleaded. The Court again agreed to the step being taken: from that moment the case is never heard of again.*

*　　*
*

With the accession of Charles I there comes another of those curious lulls in the Company's history – seventeen years of comparative calm during which few sounds of the struggle of Parliament and people to maintain their constitutional liberties against the extravagance of the King and his favourites penetrate the stillness which ended for the Company in the Civil War.

1627　　Of the King's attempt to rule without Parliament there is evidence in 1627 of the Forced Loan which was levied throughout the country.

* The Crown had until 1601 refused to permit any lawsuit to be made which would bring its prerogative into dispute. After 1601, although such cases were theoretically permissible, they were frequently stopped. Since this case would undoubtedly have centred round the Crown's grant of Licences to the Merchant Adventurers to export undressed cloths, this was, no doubt, the reason for its suppression.[1]

The City was assessed at £120,000 – of which the Company's share amounted to £3,390, a share which 'in regard to the present want of His Majesty and the difficulty which would be found in levying of the same by poll' it was decided should be raised out of the Company's funds invested in the East India Company: anything lacking after the sale of this stock was to be borrowed.

This levy reversed, almost overnight, the favourable financial position which the Company, over so long a period, had built up. The Stock of the Company – both in the East India Company and in surpluses in the Wardens' accounts amounted to £1,900: faced with this loan and since 'the inevitable necessity being upon this Company to perform the same and no way could be thought upon or imagined how to escape and go from under this heavy Burden', two Aldermen borrowed £1,500 from Sir Paul Bayling. The Aldermen were indemnified on the security of the Company's Plate.

But apart from this and, as will be later seen, demands for Ship Money, the great events of a reign which was to end most understandably in Civil War pass almost unnoticed. Only one hint of the rising temper of the people at the excesses of the King (a rage which focused itself particularly upon the King's corrupt favourite, the Duke of Buckingham) is contained in the record of £56 10s paid towards a fine of £1,000 due from the City for not having apprehended the 'Murtherers' of John Lambe, astrologer to the Duke.

*   *
*

The attentions of the Clothworkers during this time were mainly directed towards putting their house in order. The Irish lands were giving them trouble. In the first place, they had neglected some of the conditions under which the Irish Plantation had been granted. These conditions included the erection both of a fort on every Company's lands, to which the tenantry could rally in case of a rebellion amongst the displaced Irish, and a church through which Protestantism might be preached to a people strongly disinclined towards that form of religion. A castle, or stone house, had in fact been built at the Clothworkers' expense upon the ruins of the old castle at Coleraine, but no church had been built, and, as a makeshift, the Company were compelled hastily to patch up the old church at Dunboe even though it was in a place remote from the main centre of population.

But apart from this (which was to be held against them at a later date) they were having continual trouble with their principal tenant, Sir Robert McClelland. Perpetually in arrears with his rents, he gave the Company nothing but the most facile and 1624 plausible excuses. In 1624 the Company had determined to be firm with him: he had involuntarily paid £150 – attached on some money he had left in the hands of Alderman Parkhurst – towards his arrears, but now action was to be started against him to recover the £1,387 that was still outstanding.

To the news of this action there came an immediate response. Sir Robert maintained that, in the first place, he had been deceived as to the extent of the land, thinking the measurements of them to be Irish measurements whereas in fact they were English. He had had enormous expenses in bringing over 'out of Scotland so many British of his own nation into Ireland to furnish and settle the Plantation there'. He had caused to be built at great cost three stone houses, at least thirty houses of timber, and a watermill. Now he had run up against a local law in Coleraine by which he could not use his own artificers. In view of all this, he requested the Company to reduce his rent *ab initio*.

A compromise was reached: his debts were indeed reduced but still Sir Robert owed some £300 for which he made the rather feeble excuse that it was 'the result of being disappointed of a great sum of money which the King's Majesty oweth him. But maketh yet promise of payment thereof in a short time.' But in 1632, in spite of eviction orders, Sir Robert McClelland, now Lord Kircudbright, was still promising to pay next week.

Despite such unfulfilled promises, however, the Irish lands were beginning to show the Company a small profit when, quite suddenly, the Crown stepped in and confiscated them. The reasons given for this high-handed and unjust action were typical of the Stuart regime. The conveyances of the Irish lands had been made to the Companies in 1617, and, when Charles I came to the throne, his agent, Sir Thomas Phillips, launched a virulent attack upon the City Companies, accusing them of not having carried out their obligations under the Charter of Plantations. As has been seen above, there was some small degree of truth in this, but the series of informations that led to the sequestration of the Irish lands in 1632 was a deliberate attempt to exploit once again the City Companies. In 1637 a writ of *Scire Facias* was brought against the Companies and the City Corporation; and, although in 1641, dining in the City after his return from Scotland, Charles professed to be troubled about this writ and promised to restore the City to its former position, the Rebellion supervened. It was left to Parliament to rule that the whole situation was unjust and in 1641 to restore to the City its estates.

In 1654 and 1656 further restorations of the Company were made, and new conveyances were granted in 1658. Finally, the newly-restored Monarch, in 1662, granted them a new Charter and the sorry tale was at an end.

But all this is to anticipate.

* *

*

In the meantime and nearer home, a Committee was at work for enlarging the Hall. To a surveyor's first report showing that it could only be lengthened and not broadened, the reaction was one of *laissez-faire*, but in 1633, since 'the walls of the said Hall are much defective and cracked, the windows unfashionable and the whole frame uncomely and without ornament', it was decided to rebuild entirely and enlarge. Rebuilding in the time of Charles I can have met with few obstacles: the Hall was completed even to the weather vane upon its lantern roof within the year.

As a pattern for the wainscotting a room at the Antwerp Tavern was copied. At the upper end of the Hall were erected two statues by the carver, Nicholas Stone, at a cost of £50. There is no record of these statues but it is fairly safe, in the light of subsequent events, to presume that they were of James I and Charles I. With the Hall new-built and two Clothworker Lords Mayor, the years 1633 and

Rebuilding the Hall

1633

1634 must have been, in spite of the unsettled state of the country, a time of some splendour in the Company. Mr Christmas,* the carver, was consulted about the pageants for the Lord Mayor's Show of 1633, and Zachary Taylor† for the Show of 1634; on the Pageant House were set up the two carved griffins of the Clothworkers.

*   *

*

Dispute with Merchant Taylors

The splendour was only slightly marred by disputations. There was a little trouble with some of the Yeomanry over the question of service upon the Lord Mayor as Bachelors in Foynes and Budge, but that was soon smoothed over.

There was more than a little trouble with the Merchant Taylors and the observation of the ordinances regulating search and apprenticeship. A Committee charged with investigating the trouble found out that 'Many are using the occupation of being free of other Companies – especially free of the Merchant Taylors who are now so numerous as seriously to prejudice the handycraft of our Company'.

Furthermore, it seemed that faulty cloths taken in search from the Merchant Taylors (either by our searchers or by theirs) were being sent to Merchant Taylors' Hall and, so it was reported, restored to the offenders without action being taken.

The feeling of the Committee was that all cloths taken in searches, either from Clothworkers or Merchant Taylors, should be brought to Clothworkers' Hall.

The only ascertainable result of this suggestion was that at the next search the Merchant Taylors not only failed to take part but refused to pay their usual share of the expenses. The Clothworkers resolved therefore, after repeated requests to the Merchant Taylors, that in future they should go their own way without informing the

---

* Presumably Gerard Christmas (d. 1635), the carver of the Statue of James I on Aldersgate and father of John and Mathias Christmas, the ship carver.[2] The two pageants performed were, in 1633, *London Mercator* by T. Haywood and, in 1634, *The Triumphs of Fame and Honour* by John Taylor, the 'water-poet'.[3]

† Zachary Taylor, carver and surveyor employed by the Office of Works, 1631–2.[4]

Merchant Taylors, accompanied only by some representatives of the Lord Mayor, and searching both Taylors and Clothworkers, and that in future they would carry away all faulty cloths to their own Hall.

At the upper end of the social scale there was a little trouble too with some of the Court who

while the Court have been busy and employed in weighty affairs and business of this Company have gone forth into the great Hall and called such of their acquaintance as upon their own occasions attended there and brought them into the Court whilst other business has been in agitation. So that the Court have been troubled with two or three businesses of different nature at one and the same time.

It was a practice that must at once cease.

But these minor troubles scarcely even stirred the surface of the still waters of the Company. Without demur the Clothworkers paid the £440 that was their share of the £12,000 demanded by the King for 'passing the books and Patent under the great Seal of England'.*

Calmly and without disturbance they fetched out from the Long Parlour beneath the Hall the stands and rails which they lined – those of them who were not in the train bands – in dutiful loyalty and honour as the Queen's Mother, the Queen of France, and the unpopular King (with whom in so short a time they were to be at war) passed slowly by.

But it was now, at the moment when the long reign of tyranny was nearing its end, that the Company suddenly and unexpectedly revolted against the Royal will. On 3 July 1640

Signs of Revolt 1640

whereas the Lord Mayor of this City hath been very Urgent to the Master and Wardens of this Company for 20 pounds taxed on this Company for Ship money and requireth their present answer therein whether they will pay the same or no this board hath thought fit and so ordered that the Wardens of this Company do forthwith signify unto

---

* This was quite apart from the £110 5s 11d they had paid for a confirmation of their Charter in 1632 – a Charter which contained a licence of Mortmain to purchase lands as a Corporation.

His Lordship that the Master of this Company hath purposely called this Court to know the minds of the Assistants therein. Who humbly desire His Lordship's favour that they may consider hereof until the Eleven Precedent Companies of this City have made known their minds unto His Lordship touching the same. This Company being the last in Number and not willing to be made a precedent unto others.

Then came a precept for a loan of £3,200 to the King. 'After consideration and much debate had about the same this Board concluded that this Company for the present was not able to raise such a sum.' A fortnight later there came a precept for £2,750, but 'since a great number of Assistants were absent the matter was at first deferred'.

Such obstinacy and such delaying tactics while the King was still in power were, of course, ultimately fruitless and the revolt petered out; a decision was taken, since the corporate funds were insufficient, to borrow the money from individual members.

1641   In 1641, the Lord Mayor – Sir Richard Gurney – being a Cloth-worker, twenty-five members of the Company wearing chains of gold★ rode out with him to meet the King on his return from Scotland. With them rode the Clerk of the Company, Maurice Blount, carrying 'the pendant', his hat with a fine new feather and a sarsenet scarf about him – both provided by the Company. The Beadle was riding in front as marshal to clear the way for the riders, and on foot were thirty men in Kentish grey cassocks and hose, trimmed with black statute-lace and with black and white ribbands, wearing black hats with black and white bands and carrying black and white truncheons and staff torches.

Before they set out, 'messes of meat' were provided for the riders at the Mermaid Tavern, and after their return through the streets, where the rest of the Company were lining the rails, three members attended the King at dinner in their gowns faced with foynes and their Livery hoods.†

★ The chains of gold used on all such occasions were, it is interesting to note always hired for the occasion from an outfitter.

† Sir Richard Gurney entertained the King with a banquet of 500 dishes. He was fined £5,000 for refusing to publish the Act of dethronement, and, in default of payment, was imprisoned until his death seven years later.

This royal occasion was the last that any of them were to see for a long and anxious time. Many of them would never see another such. The sombre, almost funereal, colours of the Company were attending the death of an era.

*　　*
*

The year 1642 was a time of warlike preparations and of war itself. The rebellion or massacre in Ireland, was greeted by King Charles with relief, for he hoped that it might not only divert the people from their warlike schemes at home but provide him with the army he totally lacked. The Company provided for the defence of Londonderry 'one piece of Artillery called a "Sacar" with the carriage and the other appurtenances'. On it was engraved ' "The Clothworkers of London 1642" as well to distinguish it from others and to be known to be the proper goods and chattels of this Company'.*

1642
Troubles in
Ireland

There came, too, a precept to raise £5,500 out of a total demanded from the City of £100,000 for the relief of the 'pressing Necessity in Ireland'. But with the country within one month of Civil War there was even more difficulty in collecting the money than usual. On 8 June it was arranged that the Common Seal of the Company should not be given as an indemnity for the money to be raised. The lenders were to rely upon an Ordinance of the Parliament that was now in control of the Government of the country.

After a rather contradictory appearance by the Master to argue before the House that it had never been agreed to lend the £5,000, the Beadle was sent around the Members to collect the money that had been promised. Repayment, together with that of the earlier loan in 1640, was to be made with 8 per cent interest out of the monies that should come in upon the bill of £400,000 which was to be assessed on various Counties. But eight years later – in 1650 – only a fraction of the money had been recovered. Of the

---

* This 'sacar' – a gun slightly larger than a demi-culverin – was shipped to Londonderry in the *Charity*, of London. It was a cannon weighing 22½ cwts and cost £15 3s. The carriage and appurtenances cost an additional £11 11s.

money that should have been brought in by the Act for raising £400,000 there was a shortage of £166,677 13s 11¼d and 'the said arrears have grown by reason that divers Collectors and other keep in their hands sums of money which should have been brought in to the Treasurers. And Likewise that in divers Counties no Assessment hath been made of such part of the said £400,000 as was by the said Act laid upon them.'

There is no record that the money owed to the Clothworkers was at any time recovered.

CHAPTER SEVEN

THE TIMES OF TROUBLE

*   *
*

CIVIL War broke out in the summer of 1642. The City stood Civil War on the side of Parliament against the King, and the Company 1642 stood with the City. The first call for their support was for a loan to Parliament: 'for their present use forty Muskets and twenty Pikes with twenty Corselettes and Threescore Swords, forty pair of Bandolier and forty rests. To be delivered to the Guildhall.'

Next came a demand for £10 a week towards the payment of £10,000 a week assessed on the whole of Tower Ward and 'charged on the City by an Ordinance of Parliament for the maintenance of the Army'.

Other lands outside Tower Ward were also due for assessment, but the Clothworkers' support for the Roundhead cause was not so highly idealistic that they did not argue that all their lands should be assessed together – and at a lower amount than £10. There were four 'fifteens'* levied for the erecting of 'several courts of Guard in and about the City for the more safeguard and defence of the same'. The defence of the City was a matter of some urgency.

The cry from Parliament was constantly for arms. By an Act of 1643 Common Council of 27 April 1643 the Companies were 're- quested to lend such arms as they have for the better securing of this City in this time of imminent danger' – and here again the fires of idealism seem to have been burning somewhat less brightly than with a pure white flame, for the Court cautiously asked 'how and in what manner the said Arms shall be restored to them again or a valuable consideration of the same'.

* A system of rating.

Being assured that the Company would get their arms back or be compensated, the Court agreed to lend everything left in the armoury – namely nineteen corselettes, nineteen pikes, thirty-eight swords, nineteen muskets, nineteen rests, and nineteen bandoliers.

The total value, for the record, amounted to £64 12s. At the same time there came an appeal for the poor Protestants in Ireland: they had to be content with more rudimentary weapons – one dozen spades, one dozen shovels, one dozen pickaxes, two barrels of Gunpowder, and one cwt of metal. The armoury was now empty. Empty too was the Company's purse. A fitting wartime austerity was imposed: election day was to be held 'in a private manner without either sermon or feast. Only a preparation to be made of wine and cakes and such other things as the Master and Wardens shall think fit.'

The Bargehouse at Vauxhall, built on land shared with the Mercers and Fishmongers, was to be let. But far worse was to follow.

Sale of the Plate

On 7 September 1643, the Court,

taking into their sad and serious considerations the many great pressing and urgent occasions which they have for money as well for the payment of their debts as otherwise and considering the danger this City is in by reason of the great distractions and Civil Wars of this Kingdom have thought fit and ordered that the stock of Plate which this Company hath shall be forthwith sold at the best rate that will be given for the same. And to this end it is ordered . . . to take the said Plate and to expose the same to sale at the best rate (except only such particular parcels thereof as in their discretion shall seem meet to be reserved for the necessary use of this Company) And that before the same be sold they cause a particular to be made in writing particularly of all the said parcels of plate to be sold with the fashion, the weight and the several donors' names to the end that the same may be repaired and made good in status quo when God shall enable this Company so to do. The which this Court doth commend to posterity as the Act which they earnestly desire may be done.

Only nineteen years earlier that same plate had been modernized – as it was the periodical habit to do – destroying for the sake of modishness the medieval treasures: 'Such plate as is broken and out of fashion . . . to change away and instead thereof to buy and provice such parcels of plate now in fashion, cups for Wine and Beer and spoons as they . . . shall think most useful.'

Now it was to be flung into the scales, if not entirely for the Parliamentary cause, at any rate to alleviate the distress into which Civil War had brought the Company. 2,068 oz. of Plate were sold*– not quite two-thirds of the total stock (of which 1,239½ oz. now remained unsold) – and a total of £520 1s 8d was raised 'which sale was very well approved of, allowed and confirmed'. But 'inasmuch as the sum for which the same was sold was not enough to satisfy and pay the £600 with interest owing by this Company to Mr. Hough and Mr. Austin as was intended by this former order', it left outstanding to Mr Hough £100 and the interest.†

On top of this came a shattering precept for £2,750, 'being the Company's proportion, according to the Corn Rate, towards the raising of £50,000 for the necessary defence of this City and Kingdom'. From the Parliamentary Committee sitting at Weavers' Hall‡ came the order to pay the money directly to the Treasurer at the Guildhall:

This Court taking into consideration the many and great debts that they owe and their inability to pay them, much less to raise such a sum as is now required to be lent, have thought fit and so ordered in this great exigence (though not to be drawn into precedent *di futuro*) to call to their advice the Livery of this Company and the Assistants of the Yeomanry. . . .

---

* 1,159 oz. of gilt at 5s 2d oz.   £299 8s 2d
   242 oz. of parcel gilt at 4s 11d oz.   59 9s 8d
   667 oz. of white at 4s 10d oz.   161 3s 10d
† See page 99.
‡ Many of the City Companies' Halls had been requisitioned by Government Departments. Clothworkers' Hall became the Office of Sequestration. For this there was a precedent, of a kind, in 1626. On 7 December some ships had arrived in the Downs short of victuals. It was thought that unless money and provisions were not speedily forthcoming, the sailors would 'commit outrages', and on 8 December an Order in Council was made that, as money was ready for any one ship, so it was to be paid off at Clothworkers' Hall.[1]

At eight o'clock in the morning they met to discuss the Company's plight: the decision was taken to raise £1,000 by borrowing and to pay it into Guildhall as a first instalment.

Directions for payment came alternately from the Weavers' and Haberdashers' Halls (presumably the Committee of Lords and Commons for Advance of Money and Other Necessities for the Army had alternate meeting places) and from Haberdashers' Hall came a sinister demand for a list of the Members of the Company. The Masters and Wardens were authorized to produce such a list but there were strict instructions that there was 'no offer to be made . . . unto the said Committee to assess the £2,750 allotted on this Company by the poll'. Should any member be assessed separately, he was to receive the Company's seal for the sum and to be given 7 per cent on his money.

A list of 113 names, headed by Sir Richard Gurney, was submitted. On 17 October 1645 from Weavers' Hall came a summons for the Master and Wardens to appear and give information why the remainder of the money had not been paid. They were 'very urgent and pressing to bring in the said money' and twelve members of the Company offered to subscribe £20 a head (for six months at 7 per cent per annum) towards the immediate payment of £500.

£2,000 was still owing. Now it was from Haberdashers' Hall that the Committee became very pressing. The Master and Wardens, early in 1645, asked the Court helplessly what they were to do. Everyone was asked if he could lend anything but the answer was inevitably 'that this Company had done as much as they could and being very far in debt they were unable to do no more'.

It was an answer that did not satisfy the Committee. A precept was delivered to the Company for an immediate payment of £500, a precept which, this time, nominated individual members who were to raise the money. The Court decided to consult with the Fishmongers to see if there were no way out of the impasse – a consultation the result of which is unrecorded. On 7 June 1645 a payment of £200 was somehow raised out of the Company's stock* and paid to the Commissioners for the Receipt of Money and Plate at Guildhall.

One week later, with the Battle of Naseby, came the last shattering of the Royalist forces. As far as the Clothworkers were concerned – for no further reference appears in the Minutes and only passing references in the accounts to thanksgiving days for victories at Lamport, Torrington, Cardiff, and Abingdon (together with an assessment of £4 10s a month for the Scottish Army) – the Civil War was ended.

Now, freed from distractions, they could proceed with an entirely fresh dispute that had broken out with their old enemies, the Merchant Taylors.

*　　*
*

In 1645 the full results of their refusal to join in searches with the Clothworkers (which has been noted elsewhere) struck home to the Merchant Taylors.

Their brethren complained that they were 'oppressed by the members of this Society taking away their Cloths in their searches without just cause and compelling them to pay fines for the same contrary to an Act of Common Council'.

The Wardens of the Merchant Taylors suggested that there might be a meeting to talk things over – a suggestion to which the Court of the Clothworkers, 'well knowing that the members of this Society have done nothing in their Searches but what they may lawfully do and being willing to keep all fair correspondency with the said Company', wholeheartedly agreed.

A legal discussion took place at very considerable length; in essence it gave the whole history of the long rivalry between the two Companies. The Merchant Taylors now desired to join with the Clothworkers as formerly, and demanded that such defective cloths as were found, belonging to members of their

---

* Possibly as a result of a decree of the Commissioners for Preventing the Misapplication of Money bequeathed for Charitable Uses that 'Sir George Sandys should pay the sum of £2,500 to the Company being the legacy left them in 1634 by Ralph Freeman Esqre. . . . and also £900 for having detained the said legacy 9 years and £10 in part payment of costs. . . '.[2]

Company, should be carried to their Hall and there viewed and fined. Or if Merchant Taylors' cloths were brought to Clothworkers' Hall and fined 'that the same fine should go to the poor of their Company'. And if the charges of £10 per annum for this joint search were too little, they were ready to pay more.

Here was a concession indeed. But the Clothworkers, strong in their sense of legal right, were imperious in their demands. If the Merchant Taylors agreed to pay half the cost of the search dinners and to permit all defective cloths to be brought to Clothworkers' Hall and there to be fined for the benefit of the Clothworkers' poor, then and then only would they be 'content' to permit the Merchant Taylors to join in the search of their own artisans: on no account could Merchant Taylors join in the search of Clothworker artisans.

There, for the moment, the matter rested. The Clothworkers hurried about their business with the warm, comfortable glow of those who have scored a palpable hit. The informers, officially appointed by the Company, hurried about their business too, searching and inspecting. The Minutes contain three consecutive pages of cases where householders were caught keeping too many apprentices or too few journeymen. The fines on this occasion amounted to £3 8s 2d and, as a reward, there was 'given to the Six Informers 1/od a piece'. But this bustling complacency was to receive a rude and sudden shock.

There was a new and important spirit abroad in England – or perhaps it would be truer to say that there came the sudden expression of a long-pent-up emotion: the spirit of industrial democracy. In at least six City Companies this spirit manifested itself in a way of which the Clothworker Minutes give a typical example. The matter is one not only of great constitutional importance in the history of the Company, but of a general importance in the history of industrial relations.

In 1641 the Yeomanry had asked that they might have a copy of the new Charter to compare with the old and a copy of the new book of Ordinances drawn up in 1639 so that they might 'know how to conform themselves hereunto'.

Now that the Civil War was ended and they had had the time **1648**
and opportunity to study the Charter and the Ordinances, the
Yeomanry in 1648 announced that they had 'certain propositions'
to make.

There was clearly a sinister ring in the words. To settle the matter
amicably 'for the conservation of peace and unity in the whole
body of the Company' six members of the Court and six of the
Yeomanry met in Committee, 'the matter in question being
whether the Election of the Master and Wardens were not in the
Master Wardens *and Commonalty* according to the letter of the
Charter'.

In this very delicate matter of a wider electoral system for the
Company Officers, the Court relied upon the Case of Corporations
reported by Sir Edward Coke, 'whereby it appeared as an adjudged
case in law that for the avoiding of popular confusion such
elections were thought fit to be made by a selected number'. But
the Yeomanry were not satisfied; they decided to take Counsel's
opinion on the matter of whether they were not entitled to join in
the election of Master and Wardens.

A little while later, although they

Rights of
Election

presented the opinion of two Counsellors, viz. Nathaniel Hale and
William Whiting that the Election of the Master and Wardens and all
other officers was in the Master the Wardens *and Commonalty* . . . it
appeared that they had not stated their case right neither informed them
of the ancient custom of this Company in their elections. So there was
nothing more done but the matter left as at first.

There may have been nothing more done at that Committee
meeting, but the Court went into action fast. It was quickly ordered
that a preamble should be drawn up to the book of Ordinances,
setting out that all members of the Company agreed to be ruled
and governed 'according to the Contents and true meaning of the
said Ordinances'.

Everybody was to sign this agreement. But any hope that the
affair could be settled so simply was to ignore the feeling of revolt
that had so suddenly flared up again.

At the next Committee meeting the Yeomanry presented 'a protestation made by the Commonalty of this Company against the Ordinances of this Company and declared them to be invalid and no further to bind them'.

This was serious indeed. On 28 February two of the Yeomanry who had dared to sign so infamous a protestation were called before the whole Court and the offending document was read over to them 'and they did not repent themselves of anything that they had done therein'.

Moreover with considerable inconsistency the same signatories 'did then and there [cause] six of the Ordinances of this Company (against which, inter alia, they have protested) to be read and desired they might be put into execution'.

There was nothing to be done but to refer the matter to the Lord Mayor. By April it had been decided that a firm hand was what was needed – a firm hand but a reasonable one. The Yeomanry were told that

we have a Master and Wardens duly elected and sworn in their several places according to the Ordinances of this Company and that we cannot and will not give way to any such election as they may desire. And that we know our Ordinances are legally made and confirmed. Yet to show how willing this Court is to settle peace in the Company this Court is contented to suspend the examination of such of the said Ordinances as upon good grounds shall be thought fit so to be by the Lord Mayor and Court of Aldermen and the City Counsel until time permit have other Ordinances confirmed according to law.

Which in the Vacancy of the Lord Keeper, the Lord Treasurer and the Lord Chief Justice of either bench cannot be.

For a short time the affair was pushed into the background – once it was out of the hands of the Company there was an infinite opportunity for delay and suppression.

1650   Then, in December, some of the Yeomanry took this and other matters before Parliament in a petition subsequently referred to the Council of Trade. This petition alleged that they had for 'a long and tedious time been distressed and impoverished not only through the misgoverning of our Company but also through the full manufacturing of Woollen and native commodities'. They said that

through the unjust usurpation continuation and partial proceedings of Court of Assistants so called, the major part whereof are no manual Clothworkers but other Trades and callings in disposing the principal offices of the Company without the consent of the Commonalty or any regard had to ability in point of workmanship hath been utterly neglected whereby dressing and workmanship of those commodities have been so falsified as hath very much abated the esteem of them in the parts beyond the seas and not only occasioned the increase of Clothing in those parts but hath really lost to the Nation at least Ten pounds upon every Hundred Pounds worth of goods transported for these many years. . . .

The petitioners contrasted this situation with that which might have prevailed if search and control of the Company were only in the hands of those whose livelihood depended on their good workmanship and their knowledge of the trade. Moreover, they maintained that

this Company and the Nation in general have been deprived and even robbed of the essential benefit of the manufactures in dyeing and dressing of at the least Twenty or Thirty Thousand cloths yearly and to the value of forty or fifty thousand [pounds] yearly in Bays stuffs and Kerseys transported into foreign parts undyed and undressed to the enriching of the workmen in other Nations whilst thousands of our poor bretheren both Clothworkers and Dyers for want of work have been necessitated to turn porters and waterbearers and some to beg their bread and more are daily falling into the like sad condition.

Now forasmuch as this said usurpation in our Company of Clothworkers and the transportation of so great quantities of unmanufactured goods tended to the enriching only of a few or rather to the humouring of a few for they might gain as much or more by these goods fully manufactured but to the impoverishing of thousands which as our present worthy Lord General Cromwell lately intimated is manifest contrary to the nature of a Commonwealth we trust this honourable Council will concur with his Excellency in judgement herein.

Petition was therefore made:

That this honourable Council will be pleased to use your most effectual means that the Manual Clothworkers according to the right intention of their first and second Incorporation may have the choice of all their Officers from amongst and within themselves according to their Charter, and full possession given to them of their Hall with the books deeds goods and lands thereunto belonging and be freed from the encumbrance of any person in Office that shall not exercise the Manual Trade of Clothworking in one kind or other that so we may be at liberty and be encouraged to take such care of the true making and dressing of all these Manufacturers as by our Charter and by the law of the land shall be entrusted to us.

That there be strict prohibition under great penalties against the exportation of all undressed and undyed manufactures woollen or other but that all and every kind thereof may first receive their full and complete workmanship whereby thousands of people now in misery and beggary will be enabled to live comfortably and be serviceable to the Commonwealth.

That there may be the most exact course that may be to restrain the exportation of wool and fullers earth without which so great quantities of Cloth as are could not [have] been made in our neighbour Countries to the extreme prejudice of this Nation.

That for the ease of Clothiers the burdensome, useless employment of Allengers [sic] may be wholly taken away. . . .

Instead they suggested that the manufacturers should be made to affix a water seal, giving the proper length and breadth together with his name and address, with a fine of 40s per half yard of every broad cloth unstamped.

Later in the year, in December 1650, a further and similar petition to the Council of Trade was made presenting 'the Reasons why the Government of the Company of Clothworkers should be by Artizan Clothworkers and not by Drapers, Mercers, Cheese-mongers, Smiths, etc.'.

The first reason, they claimed, was that the Manual Clothworkers were the body incorporated by the Charter and having the power to elect their Master and Wardens. And as long as they did so it was a flourishing society. The whole purpose of incorporation, they said, was to control the cloth trade. Moreover, we humbly conceive that Cheesemongers, Wharfingers, Smiths etc. are not capable to govern the Artizan Clothworkers because it is a Mistery they understand not neither indeed can they because they were never bred to it nor instructed in it . . . so likewise we say they are not sensible of governing our Mistery for they cannot be touched with our necessities. For if it goes ill with us it hurts not them and if [it] goes well with us they gain nothing. And therefore not being engaged in our well or woe we humbly conceive it is unreasonable we should have such Governors enforced upon us for the ruin of our Corporation, the destroying of our Trade and the prejudice of the Commonwealth.

The Master Wardens and Assistants did make a book of Ordinances containing many Articles which in the 14th year of the late King they carried up to the two Chief Justices in the name of this Commonalty though without the view knowledge or consent of the said Commonalty which they got to be confirmed for £80 which Ordinances are point blank against our Charter and the public good of our Society.

These are some of the many reasons why the Government of our Company might be by Artizan Clothworkers. . . .

On the face of it these were weighty charges and on 3 January 1651 the Council of Trade called for an answer to them.

In their reply the Court recalled that this matter of popular elections had been brought up three years earlier and that when the case was at last heard, in August 1649, 'the Petitioners then pretended an unreadiness and fail of Council and so put off the hearing which case is depending before the . . . Committee unto this day.'

As far as the present petition was concerned the Court stated that 'most of the Agitators in the former proceedings are the same . . .'. They affirmed that the elections were carried on as they had been in the City from time immemorial and that not only were searches carried on as diligently as ever they had been – and by artisans at that – but they further alleged 'that upon such Searches we find resistance by none so much as by the Petitioners for which there are Suits at Law depending against them at this present'. The Court further stated

that Artizan Clothworkers might be as often Master and Wardens as any others if they refuse not to come upon the Clothing or Livery of the

Company when called as some of the Petitioners and many others of the said Artizan Clothworkers have done, and that, of the Masters for the space of eight years last past 6 of them have been Artizan Clothworkers.

The Court also professed that they had done their utmost to prevent the illegal export of undressed cloths until they were prevented from doing so by the Privy Council: there were actually suits still pending in the matter. They agreed entirely with the petitioners that all cloths should be dressed before export and that there should be a prohibition on the export of wool and fullers' earth. As for the complaint about aulnagers, they would not presume to question the wisdom of earlier legislation on the subject. The reasons the petitioners gave in their case were 'immature'.

They added as a general comment on the petition that this matter of bringing in the diffusive body of the Company into elections had always been attempted by discontented members of the City Companies and had always been

exploded upon solemn consideration of the Sages of the Law and others, the Governors of this Nation, as a way tending to much confusion, which cannot be otherwise conceived to be in so numerous a company as ours is, consisting of two united Corporations . . . both very numerous and we are heartily sorry that they should express so much violence of spirit against the body of which some of them are Members: neither would we have believed that they would have been so bold to have demanded possession of all, as if our Charters and Corporation itself had already been condemned and adjusted forfeit by the Parliament of the Common Law of this Realm.

The Court had, as it happened, as early as 1616 taken the opinion of Sir Harry Yelverton* for the Company's Charter from Henry VIII. He had been of the opinion that

the Master, Four Wardens with their Assistants be Master, Wardens and Commonalty without the Yeomanry or any part of them and that the Master and Wardens of the Livery be likewise the Commonalty for they may make Ordinances lawful and break them again at their pleasure

* 'This Yelverton is a Knight and a great Lawyer, the King's Solicitor. He had a Jacobus for his fee for this present.'

without Contradiction and the Yeomanry must still be obedient to the same. It is now made a case by Custom. Look in my Lord Cooke his cases and divers others.

The Court in fact had the great advantage in this dispute of knowing exactly what their own intentions were in the matter.

The Yeomanry, on the other hand, had the disadvantage not only of being in a state of mental confusion but also of being divided amongst themselves. There was a considerable body of the employing class amongst the Yeomanry who, much as they might dislike and regret the exclusiveness of the Court of Assistants, realized that they had far more to fear than to gain from a revolutionary movement among the rank and file, who had proved themselves largely incapable of constructive thought. The Yeomanry's own Wardens, too, though representatives of the popular movement, were against it. On 19 December they and some of the assistants of the Yeomanry declared themselves against the proposal that a Common Hall should be called for the election of Master and Wardens.

The hands of the Court were considerably strengthened by such a declaration: they announced that 'the Company has been governed in the way it has for many years according to Ordinances which they were empowered to draw up and which were passed by Parliament'. They were sorry that they had no power to elect Officers at a Common Hall.

That this answer satisfied the rank and file may be doubted: the Court themselves were in no doubt about the popular feeling. A Court Committee was hastily formed to take Counsel's opinion as to 'what course is best to be taken for the prevention of such act or order as some of the Yeomanry of this Company do now endeavour to get and obtain for the rule and governance of this Company at their will and pleasure'. The Company also agreed to canvass as many of the Yeomanry as they could 'to subscribe their consent and assent to the present Ordinances which are confirmed for the rule and government of this Company'. Subsequently, it was alleged that 360 of the most able artisans and others had consented to be governed by the existing constitution and ordinances.

To assist this canvass and in the interests of propaganda, there emerged into the light of day what must be one of the most delightful pamphlets ever to be produced in defence of Privilege.*

A Curious Pamphlet

'Compiled by a Member of the Court', it begins as it intends to go on:

Sir,

We doubt not to say That God in the beginning did not only give a resemblance of Political power when the light created on the first, was on the fourth day contracted in those two great Rulers of the World.

But that he did it according to Ordinances; for the Psalmist speaking of Heaven and Earth, saith,

'They continue this day according to thy Ordinances' (Psalm 119).

Working, apparently with a Biblical concordance at his elbow, the anonymous member of the Court goes on to quote from Kings, Hebrews, Exodus, and Jeremiah – from any source where the word 'Ordinance' is found.

And, having thus established a good precedent for rule by Ordinance, he delivers a stirring passage which places the members of the Court on a high plane:

As God in the 2 Kings 17 complaineth that they neither feared God, nor did after their Ordinances nor after their Customs: So (and not without just cause) do the present Governors complain at this present of our dissenting bretheren . . .

A highly ingenious piece of casuistry follows: so ingenious, indeed, is it that with its extensive and complete documentation it must have been entirely above those muddled minds that were striving to create an industrial democracy. But the pamphlet is interesting not only because it includes a historical survey of the Company but also because it examines fearlessly – and lucidly – one of the chief grievances brought by the artisans before Parliament:

Objection: But the Corporation was at first founded for the good of the handy trade; what skill have Mercers or Cheesemongers to govern the handy trade?

* Undated, but presumably in 1650–51.

Response: We answer, all the Charters in express words admit others to be of the fraternity or guild as well as Artizans.

The Master and Wardens constituted by the Charter of Elizabeth were all but one of other trades, no Artizans. Let the Master and Wardens be never so ignorant yet they have always the most judicious and skilful Artizans their Assistants whose livelihood depends upon the manufactury. The present Master is, and 5 or 6 of the handytrade have successively been, Masters.

Ten of the Assistants whereof any twelve make a Court are at present of the handy trade.

These are assisted by twenty-four Artizans of the Yeomanry [and] many Artizans of the Livery of known ability, skill and judgement. All tied by oath to assist the Master and Wardens on all occasions.

The Search view and review is made always by able, skilful workmen of the handytrade, both Fullers and Shearmen.

'And' says the member of the Court, with a turn in the argument not entirely complimentary to the wealthier element of the handytrade, 'it is most for the good of the handytrade that others have a part in the Government for else the rich would oppress the poor.'

The pamphlet ends with the sneer: 'if ... *Ignobile Vulgus* be admitted to govern or choose the Governors *Tum tua res agitur paries cum proximus ardet, de te fabula narratur.*' Faced with this formidable, and to them largely incomprehensible argument, the artisans could answer nothing. Divided as they were, their cause no longer held any hopes for the future.

The argument dragged itself one-sidedly along for a short while. And although in 1651, the artisans did gain certain concessions from the Council of Trade – they might have the disposition of any monies in the Yeomanry funds, they might elect their own officers, the Beadle and the Informer, when next the posts fell vacant – these were not the concessions of universal suffrage which they had sought.

In case there should be any further trouble from the workers, the Court, privily, made transcriptions of Orders by Lord Mayors in the reigns of Henry VIII and Edward VI that might subsequently prove useful – orders which talked of 'the sundry Sinister Arts and

Attempts daily perpetrated, practised and done by divers and sundry froward and [ill] disposed persons being Citizens and Freemen of this City' and disenfranchised unruly Haberdashers and Waxchandlers.

Modern industrial democracy was, in fact, having a hard struggle to be born. In at least six other Companies the same struggle was being waged, the same democratic crisis had been reached. But in the City it was very nearly the last flash in the pan of a moribund cause. Backed as it had been by Puritan sympathies, there was no place for it in the days of the Restoration: new attempts at incorporation by artisan bodies were rejected by the City Council. Although in future there might be industrial disputes, unlawful assemblies, strikes among the artisans, there would be no more fear of popular universal suffrage in the City Companies.

On a flyleaf of the volume of Minutes recording these labour pains, a contemporary hand, grimly biblical to the end, has written: 'Many are called but few are chosen.'

*　*
*

Victory was to the strong. In their strength they could afford to give a show of magnanimity.

1652　In 1652 assistance was given to the Yeomanry 'to suppress the Kentish Clothiers from rowing and shearing their cloths in Kent and to do what they could either in that or anything else that the poor Clothworkers here might be set at work'. In addition, 'one or two suits' – there is a pleasing vagueness about it – were to be brought against the Merchant Adventurers for the transportation of cloth undressed. Alas,

when the said Actions were ready for Trial the Merchant Adventurers obtained another order from the Council of State, wherein is expressed that whereas the said Causes were ready to come to Trial and by the letter of the law the Merchant Adventurers apprehended they should be overthrown, etc. They should proceed to Trial; but if so it proved the Clothworkers should forbear to take out Judgement and Execution for the space of one whole year unless they had leave from the Council for so doing: And that after the expiration of that year they should likewise forbear in case by that time the Trade be brought to a Settlement.

The greatest dispute of all with the Merchant Adventurers was coming to a head. On 18 December 1656, the petition of the Clothworkers at last got a hearing. As Burton wrote in his diary:[3] 'Sat till after eight upon the business of the Clothworkers' against the Merchant Adventurers but we came to no resolution.'

The case presented to Parliament by the Clothworkers, and stripped of all but the essentials, was this. There had been from time to time throughout the centuries of their existence Statutes made for the restraint of export of undressed woollen cloths.*

The Merchant Adventurers, transporting contrary to these Statutes, and several suits being commenced against them by the Clothworkers have almost these thirty years last part had recourse to the Council Table: where (although they have there acknowledged the Clothworkers' right yet) they procured Injunctions to restrain them from reaping any benefit from the said suits.

The occasion of these illegal injunctions were grounded upon former Letters Patents granted by King James and the late King Charles unto the Duke of Lennox to transport all manner of unwrought woollen cloths without restraint of number or price. The last whereof the Merchant Adventurers set forth in their Answer does yet continue under which they still claim to transport contrary to the Statutes although it was expired at Michaelmas 1655.

1. The Clothworkers pray That they may have some benefit of their forfeiture given them by the Statute of 8 Eliz. from Mich. 1655 without any further law suits. . . .
2. That according to the said Statute of 7 Ed. IV no woollen Cloth be henceforth transported unwrought etc.
3. That free licence be granted to all persons (as well as to the said Merchant Adventurers who have not any peculiar privileges herein more than other) to transport all Cloths wrought and dyed as it was formerly granted in the time of King James.

*7 Ed. IV cap. 3; 3 Hen. VII cap. 11; 3 Hen. VIII cap. 7; 5 Hen. VIII cap. 3; 27 Hen. VIII cap. 13; 33 Hen. VIII cap. 19; and 8 Eliz. cap. 6.

The petition ended with the comment:

As King Edward the Third began and settled the manufacture of Clothing in England, by inviting over the Flemish Cloth workers with their whole Families and investing them with many privileges and immunities; so contrariwise since these monopolizing Licences of transporting unwrought Cloths, many of our English cloth workers with their families, wanting employment here, have settled themselves in Flanders and the Low Countries, etc.

1657   Coming to no resolution at this first hearing, the matter was adjourned for five days, when Burton notes:

After long debate we were outvoted by the Merchant Adventurers' party, though it was clear to me the vote was hard to the Clothworkers and the general wealth of the nation. So that unless we recover it on Thursday next in the business of free-trade the poor Clothworkers may turn tankard bearers, etc.

The great debate on free trade, attacking the monopoly of the Merchant Adventurers, took place on 6 January 1657.

Sir Christopher Peck who is a Master of the Merchant Adventurers' company turned in the debate like a horse and answered every man. I believe he spoke at least thirty times.

In spite of this, only about six or seven out of the thirty-three members of the Committee voted for the Merchant Adventurers.

In future, free trade was to be allowed to Germany and the Netherlands 'without prejudice to the marts at Dort and other places in Holland'. The free traders were jubilant.

They tell us it will so advance the woollen manufacturers of this nation that both the clothiers and the wool merchants will be much enriched by it as that the price of wool will rise two or three or four shillings in a stone. I wish it be not too specious.

1660
Complaints
of Bad
Workman-
ship
   Burton's cautious lack of optimism proved not unjustified. Four years later, in 1660, the cloth trade was in one of its periodical doldrums and the Committee for the Advance of Trade wrote to the Company on 12 February 1660:

Taking into consideration the many Complaints that have been lately made unto them of the great decay of Trade by reason of the importation of fine Dutch Cloth especially of blacks and whites And of the great abuses used in English Manufacture. And being very desirous that the true cause of these evils may be found out.

To these queries the Clothworkers replied that the import of Dutch cloth would mean the ruin of the home market. They sought, therefore, a complete ban on the import or sale of such foreign cloth and the right of the Company to search for foreign cloth. They sought also the levying of a fine on the master of any ship bringing in foreign cloth and on any Merchant or factor handling it.

We further present and humbly conceive that black and scarlet cloth is better dressed in England than in any other parts beyond the seas. And for proof thereof we humbly present that fine Black Cloth imported is for the most part redressed here in England which will be made good to your honours.

Lastly tradesmen do find that the Nation is of late most addicted to fancy foreign rather than Native commodities and that we conceive to be the only reason why the Dutch fine cloths (especially blacks and scarlets) do outsell those of our own manufacture ours being really better as we are able to prove.

This was, in fact, no kind of answer to the accusations of abuse in workmanship and, though they might patriotically protest that English blacks and scarlets were second to none, it is clear that there was considerable reason for complaints, for later in the year there were put forward:

> The Proposals of the Company of Clothworkers in London
> what are the Grievances and Defects in the Woollen
> Manufacture of this Nation and their Reasons
> for Remedy of the said Abuses.

The first grievance was that Suffolk and Essex cloths for export contained many defects in the spinning owing to the unskilled nature of many of the workers – a state of affairs that could only be remedied by employing none but skilled workers.

The next complaint told of defects in weaving, such as not putting sufficient threads in the warp to make it the full breadth of the loom, of defects of a technical nature in milling and dressing, of neglect of searching and sealing in various towns: 'The Sealers and Searchers are generally persons of no repute who do only what is required of them by the Clothiers who are often left to apply their own Seals.'

There followed a long technical list of faults and remedies for cloths made in Gloucestershire, Wiltshire, and Oxfordshire, in Worcestershire, in Kent, and in Yorkshire, which make it clear that the abuses were widespread.

* *
*

For the further annals of the Commonwealth, reference must be made to other histories than that of the Clothworkers' Company. Never noticeably prone to reflect the outside world, the Minutes bear hardly a mark of the Puritan regime. Not even through the Company's estates in Ireland does there come the slightest whisper of the disastrously successful reign of terror in that country.

The reign of the Army and of the Protectorate remains, as far as the Company are concerned, a void as drab as the spirit of the times that, in 1652, resulted in a precept from the Lord Mayor that, in view of what had been taking place in some of the Halls and other public places of the City, the Company were 'straightly charged that there be no Dancing, Maskings, Plays or any other unlawful meetings'.

Even the Beadle's affairs were called into account: 'For many years past too much beer hath been drank or spent by the late Beadle of this Company and his family' – a new system of providing his beer was to be worked out. Only in the case of the barge did the Clothworkers seem to let themselves go. In 1655 they decided at last to build a barge of their very own. They bought a barge-house for £120, had the Clothworkers' Stairs repaired and, in 1656, took delivery from Alexander Saward, the shipwright, of a fine new barge at a cost of £115.

The
Company's
Barge
A blue half-cloth was bought to enlarge the old barge cloth and make it fit the new barge; Anthony Earl agreed to be barge-master for no payment other than the provision of a free house and garden,

and, in 1657, all was ready in time for it to be lent, manned by 'Anthony Earl and his fellows, for the accompanying of such as go to fetch up the funeral corpse of General Blake, late deceased'.

It was all ready, too, for the splendours of the Restoration which, suddenly and without warning, break into the little obscure world of the minute-writer.

CHAPTER EIGHT

THE HAPPY RETURN

*   *

*

1660   IN February 1660 the hated rule of the Army over Parliament and Country had at last been broken. And, wasting no time in conforming to the new regime, on 28 February, the Clothworkers' Company decided 'that the Lord General Monk and all his field officers shall be invited to dine at this Hall on any day after Tuesday next that his Honour shall please to appoint'.

Entertain-
ment of
General
Monk

Whatever the real feelings of the Court may have been to the sudden *volte face*, they were making no mistakes about the organization of the Livery dinner. The preparations for it were more detailed than any before or after. There was an air of excitement, a 'lets-have-a-party' spirit about it, that after the Puritan austerity was doubly welcome.

Eight stewards – instead of the normal three – were to make the dinner, and any costs over £200 the Company undertook to pay.* The invitations to the General, his lady, and her attendants, to the field officers (whose names were obtained from the General's Secretary) were delivered personally by the Master, Alderman Sir William Peake, five Assistants, and the Clerk, who drove to St James's in two coaches. For the dinner itself, the Lord Mayor's officer, Mr Cliff, and nineteen other officers were in attendance as well as the Company's butler and fourteen other Wardens.

Two marshals were posted at the Hall gate. Two more were posted at Ludgate Hill 'to keep the hill clear from stops of Coaches

---

* Normally, the expenses of banqueting fell on the various members of the Court and Livery in turn.

128

and Carts'. Four more went to Temple Bar to receive the General and conduct him to the Hall.

At a rail inside the Hall the Clerk stood collecting tickets and filing them: no wives, children, servants, or friends of the Court were admitted. The dinner committee had been at the Hall at eight in the morning supervising the arrangements. At last it was announced that the General and his lady had arrived. The stewards who had provided the dinner marched before the Master, Wardens, and Assistants, from the Hall to the Hall gate with white staves in their hands.

Between the two gates the procession opened to right and left. As the General got out of his coach they faced about 'two and two together bareheaded before him to the Stairs' foot', where Mr Cliff was ready to conduct him with the Master, Aldermen, Esquires, and such of the Assistants as pleased to follow into the lady's chamber: the others went to the parlour to entertain the other guests – in particular the Field Officers.

Meanwhile, the General's underlings were not neglected. His coachman and footman were not only entertained at a nearby house but they were given £1 between them into the bargain: the General's Life Guards (there being no room anywhere to fit them in) had £5 given to their Captain for their entertainment.

In the Hall, 'while the Meat was serving and setting upon the Table the Musick played with their wind music and when the second course came in they came down into the Hall to play and sing'. At the high table wine was set out and the glasses replenished out of the butteries by the butler; the other tables had 'bottles set to every Mess and . . . supplied, as occasion might require by the Stewards and Butlers'.

All this while, the Livery attending the dinner, for want of room in the Hall, were waiting at Fenchurch. As soon as the first two tables had been 'served and set and the third a-serving' the Beadle of the Livery fetched them to the Hall and conducted them to the parlour where it was arranged that they should dine. But for them the dinner was a shortened affair. They had to be finished by the time the second course came into the Hall 'and then to rise and walk up the Hall and make their obeisance to the General and his Lady and the rest of his guests and so depart from the Hall'.

The second course being set upon the Table the Clerk presented the Great Cup unto the Master of the Company. And upon his reception one of the Committee spake these works as follows: 'My Lord and Master, in the name of himself and the Company of Clothworkers, in a friendly cup present their service unto your Excellencey and your honoured Lady and bids you a hearty welcome and the rest of your Honoured Company', after which a speech was made to the General by one of the Musicianers. . . .*

As an unprincipled mixture of flattery and self exculpation, the speech may well be unsurpassed:

Nay then let me come, too with my *Addresse*
Why mayn't a *Rustic* promise, or professe
His good Affection t'you? why not declare
His wants? How many and how great they are?
And how you may supply them? Since you may
See our Hearts mourn, although our Clothes be *gray* [sic]

Great Hero of three Nations! Whose Bloud springs
From *pious* and from *pow'rful Grandsire Kings*,
With whose *Bloud-Royal* you've enriched your *veynes*
And by continued *Policy* and *Pains*
Have equalled all their *Glory*: So that now
Three *Kingless Sceptres* to your Feet do bow
And court *Protection* and *Allyance* too.
And what Great men still *reached* at *stoups* to you.

But you're too truly *Noble* to aspire
By Fraud or *Force* to *Greatness*: or t'acquire
Sceptres and *Crowns* by Robbery, or base
And wilful breach of *Trusts*, and *Oaths*, nor place
Your Happiness in *avished* [sic] Dominion
Whos Glory's only founded in *opinion*;
Attended still with danger fear and doubt
And fears *within*, worse than all those *without*
You must still *watch* and *fear* and *think* and must
Lose all *content* to *gratifie* one Lust.

* According to Hazlitt, the speech was written by Thomas Jordan.

Should you invade the *Throne* or aym at *Pelf*
Throw *down* three Nations to *set* up your self,
Kings are but royal *Slaves*, and Prisoners too
They always *toyl* and always *guarded* go.

You are for making *Princes* and can find
No work proportioned to your *Pow'r* and *mind*
But Atlas-like to bear the *World* and be
The great *Restorer* of the Liberty
Of three long captiv'd *Kingdoms* who were thrown
By others strong *Delusions* and their own
Misguided zeal to *do* and *suffer* what
Their very Soul now *grieve* and *tremble* at.

Debauched by those they thought would *teach* and *rule* 'um
Who now they find did *ruine* and befool 'um
Our *meanings* still were *honest*, for *alas*!
We never dream't of what since came to pass:
'Twas never our *intent* to *violate*
The settled *Orders* of the *Church* or *State*
To throw down *Rulers* from their lawful Seat
Merely to make ambitious *small-things* great,
Or to *subvert* the *Laws*; but we thought then
The *Laws* were *good* if manag'd by *good* men;
And so we do think still, and find it true
Old Laws did more good, and less harm then *New*
And 't'was the *Plague* of Countries and of Cities
When that *great-belly'd* House did spawn *Committees*.

We fought not for *Religion*, for t'is known
Poor men have *little* and some great Ones *none*;
Those few that *love* it truly, do well know
None can take't from us, where we *will* or no
Nor did we fight for *Laws*, nor had we need,
For if we had but Gold enough to feed
Our taking *Lawyers* we had *Laws* enough
Without addressing to the *Sword* or *Buff*
Nor yet for *Liberties* for those are things
Have cost us more in *Keepers* than in *Kings*

Nor yet for *Peace*; for if we had done so
The *Souldiers* would have beat us long ago:

Yet we did *fight*, and now we see for what,
To *shuffle* men's Estates; those *Owners* that
Before these wars could call *Estates* their own
Are beaten out by others that had *none*.
Both *Law* and *Gospel* overthrown together
By those who ne'er *believed* in, or *lov'd* either.
Our *truth*, our *trade*, our *peace*, our *Wealth*, our *freedom*
And our full *Parliaments* that did *get* and *breed* 'um
Are all *devour'd* and by a *Monster* fell,
Whom none, but you, could *satisfie* or *quell*.

You're *great*, you're *good*, you're *valiant*, you're *wise*
You have *Briarius'* hands and *Argus'* eyes★
You are the *English* Champion, you're the true
St. George for *England*, and for *Scotland* too
And though his *Storie's* questioned much by some
Where true or false this *Age* and those to come
Shall for the future find it so far true
That all was but a *Prophecy* of you
And all his great and high *Atchievements* be
Explained by you in this *Mythologie*

Herein you've far outdone him, he did fight
But with one single *Dragon*; but by your might
A Legion have been tamed and made to serve
The People, whom they meant t'*undo* and *starve*
In this you may do high, and make fame
Immortalize your *celebrated* name
This Age's *glory*, *wonder* of all after
If you would free the *Son*, as he the Daughter.†

★ There is a contemporary preoccupation with 'Briarius' hands and Argus' eyes'.
Montrose's verses on the execution of Charles I, set to music by Pepys, contain the
same phrase. Briarius and Argus were two legendary figures, one with a hundred
hands and the other with a hundred eyes.

† The General was compelled to sit through other and similar panegyrics, rustic
dialogues, anagrams, and the like at the Halls of the Drapers, Skinners, Goldsmiths,
Vintners, and Fishmongers. Lady Monk suffered additional panegyrics at Fishers'
Folly and Bedlam.

When Dinner was done then the Countryman and the soldier did discourse by way of dialogue and in the close the Countryman danced alone and so went away.[1]

Tobacco and pipes were then provided and white wax candles, and a little while later

the General with his Lady guest and other attendants were conducted up to the banqueting room to a standing banquet by the Gentlemen Ushers, our Master, two Aldermen and some other of the Assistants. The banquet being ended they were conducted to their coaches at the Hall gate. . . .

The party was over.

What the bluff General, to say nothing of his Field Officers, had thought of the musicianer's speech is not recorded. It is just possible that there had come to his notice or his memory that under the Mastership of Sir John Ireton (the brother of Cromwell's son-in-law) – all too soon to be plain Mr Ireton again – the Company had given a lavish display at the funeral of Cromwell. 'The worshipful Company found all the taffeta and fringe that was used', and what with shields, banners, and standards, and all the painting done, had spent £164 on the occasion.[2]

Now in a very short time the order was received for the Commonwealth Arms to be removed and the Royal Arms erected in their place. The pictures and statues of the Kings which had, by an order in 1650, been taken down and a certificate submitted to say that the iconoclasm had been carried out, were replaced. *Restoration of Charles II*

There came, too, an order to pay £660 as the Company's share of 'a present to the King's Most Excellent Majesty as a Testimony of the sense this Court and the whole City have of his gracious letter and declaration to them'. The King was coming into his own again. On 25 May he 'landed at Dover and made his way amidst the shouts of a great multitude to Whitehall.'[3]

The welcome, though no doubt genuine, had been carefully staged. The precept had come to the Company that the King 'be received and entertained with the greatest demonstration and manifestation of our and all our fellow Citizens' most bounden duties, hearty affections and joys for His Majesty's happy return'. To this end, 'Twenty-four persons of the most Graceful, Tall and comely personages of your said Company, every of them to be well horsed and in their best array of furniture of Velvet, Plush or Satin and Chains of Gold', and attended by one footman each 'in decent habits', were ordered to meet the King. The Company were also to 'have in readiness the Rails, Standing Cloths, Banners, Streamers and other Ornaments of Triumph belonging to the Company'.

The banner with the Commonwealth Arms was hastily converted to the King's Arms. Lackeys were rigged out in light grey coats, breeches, and stocking with three yards of black and white ribbons at each knee and nine yards of similar ribbon for trimming their coats. They wore false sleeves of white fustian and their hats were of rough black felt lined with calico and decked with hat bands of white tinsey with knots of black and white ribbon.

Since the time of the King's visitation was not known but he was likely to pass 'very suddenly', the Company were ordered to have their horsemen, their stands, rails and ornaments of Triumph – the rails hung with blue cloth – at a state of one hour's readiness. The rest of the Company had, compulsorily, to line the rails in their finest attire, without any women or children being present. After the King had gone by to the Guildhall they were allowed to 're-fresh themselves' as long as they were back in their places by 3 o'clock to cheer the Royal return to Whitehall.

For the King's entertainment at the Guildhall, the Company lent their 'Trumpeter Mr. Steps and his three fellows', six more handsome, tall, able, and sufficient men as meat servers, and £165 towards the cost of the Banquet – a Banquet calling for so many cooks and such a quantity of provisions that the City Companies were forbidden to make any solemn feasts simultaneously at their own Halls.

The King was restored and for the City Companies their financial troubles and struggles were all to do again.

*   *
*

The taxed contribution that the Clothworkers' Company were expected to make towards the costs of the Coronation amounted to £330, 'to express so far as can be uttered the unspeakable joy, love and loyalty of this City, His Majesty's Royal Chamber, to His Sacred Person and Government'. This was but the beginning of the old story again. Next comes a precept 'forthwith to pay into the Exchequer Chamber for the use of the King's Majesty the sum of £200 as a free voluntary present of this Company according to an Act of Parliament lately made'. Government Levies

There was a pressing demand for corn money, which, so it was alleged, the Company had failed to provide, a state of affairs which 'by reason of the present scarcity and dearness of corn may prove to the offence of His Majesty and prejudice of this City'.

In 1664 the City was to lend the King £100,000, of which the Clothworkers' share was £2,000, 'for his present great Affairs wherein the prosperous and happy estate of the City is especially concerned'. There were pressing demands for ship money, for which the subscriptions had fallen far behind. Eventually the Company raised £400 towards the building of 'Loyal London'.

Financially, the routine of the Company was falling into its old pattern of Government levies so heavy as to make membership of the Company a burden rather than the blessing it had originally been. In other ways, too, there were some familiar problems. Firstly, a fresh attempt was made, in 1661, to ban the export of undressed cloths by a petition from the Master and Wardens of the Clothworkers to the new King, a petition which pointed out that non-observation of the laws had driven many families to emigrate to get employment overseas. Export of Cloth

Secondly, the old case of the Merchant Taylors and their dispute over the rights of search suddenly appeared again. Now it was referred to a Committee of Aldermen who, though they found it most difficult to decide the merits of the case, eventually ruled: Dispute with the Merchant Taylors

That both the Companies of Merchant Taylors and Clothworkers go friendly together (and not the Clothworkers' alone) in search of all Clothworkers free of the Merchant Taylor's Company. And that the Merchant Taylors do first enter and lead the way into the house, workhouse or shop of every such Clothworker of their own Company. And that all defective workmanship found in such search be brought to the Merchant Taylors' Hall and the offenders punished by sentence of the Master and Wardens of the Company of Merchant Taylors only.

To this ruling the Clothworkers observed sourly: 'Upon a reading of this order it is conceived it is not drawn up so fully and plainly as it might have been yet nevertheless it is ordered that it be entered into our Court Book. . . .' They added that if any defective workmanship, either in rowing or shearing, were found hanging on a tenter in the field, Merchant Taylors' cloth or not, it would be taken, as they would take the cloths of their own Company, to the Clothworkers' Hall for judgement there.

But clearly they were not satisfied with this ruling: they would take Council's opinion 'about the strength of this Company's Charter in order to search for good workmanship in rowing and shearing of Cloth'. They would also ask the Recorder of London how far the order of the Court of Aldermen was binding upon the Charter.

But, apart from these reminders that there was trouble lurking for the Company, the Restoration tale is for the most part one of feasting and pageantry. When the Company were not themselves taking part in pageants they were prepared to lend their stage properties: 'The two Griffins and the Lambs belonging to this Company to be delivered to Mr. Jarman', or 'the green men's shapes, periwigs and beards belonging to this Company shall be lent to the Company of Grocers'.

Pageantry

In 1662 there was a precept to attend in their barge the coming by water of the King and Queen from Hampton Court to Whitehall, since the King 'expects such demonstration of affection from this City as hath been usual upon so great and solemn occasion'. The marshalling of the Companies upon the water was left to Mr Water Bailiff. Two anchors were to be provided to moor the barge 'at head and stern – being to lie at anchor during their Majesty's passage'.

1662

Great and solemn the occasion might be but cheerfulness kept breaking in: the Clothworkers prudently provided themselves

with 'three dozen bottles of Lambeth Ale for the better accommodation of the gentlemen of the Assistants and Livery of this
Company in their said Barge when they shall attend the said
Solemnity'. There were also to be five trumpeters and – so long as
it did not cost more than £3 – a consort of string music. And, as a
later precept ordered, there was to be 'besides Standards, Streamers,
Colours and other usual ornaments . . . something of Pageantry
relating to your Mistery or of such other signification as to you
shall seem meet'.

In 1662, the occasion for feasting was heightened by Sir John 1662
Robinson,* one of those who had helped in the Restoration of
Charles II, first keeping his Mayoralty at the Hall, and, the follow-
ing year, entertaining there the King, the Queen Consort, the
Queen Mother, and the Duke and Duchess of York[4].

And somehow the Company got involved in paying for 'a
Pageant erected, representing and attending to St. Paul's Church,
by order of the said Sir John Robinson without any consent of this
Company'.

But all this feasting was not without its attendant dangers: the Alderman
story of Alderman Sir William Cooper who, collapsing at a Cloth- and Lady
worker Banquet on St Thomas's Eve, was hastened into eternity by Cooper
being dosed with brandy instead of – as Lady Cooper indignantly
bewailed the following morning – being plied with Hollands gin,
his usual remedy, indicates that the pleasures of the table could be
over-exaggerated.†

*   *
*

Death, that struck singly that December day, was to strike at 1665
thousands only a few months later. 'All public feastings and Plague

* According to Samuel Pepys, 'a talking, bragging, buffle-headed fellow . . . that
would be thought to have led all the City in the great business of bringing in the
King . . . as very a coxcomb as I could have thought had been in the City . . . nor
hath he brains to outwit any ordinary tradesman'.

† Though no confirmation of this event has yet been forthcoming, the custom of
serving brandy and gin in the middle of Clothworkers' dinners with the query 'Do
you dine, Sir, with Alderman or Lady Cooper?' is of considerable antiquity. It is
said that Lady Cooper made a gift to the Clothworkers' Company to provide
Hollands gin in perpetuity.

common dancings . . . ' were 'forbidden and wholly laid aside.' The plague, that constantly recurring menace to English existence, had again seized the country.

The Clothworkers, as was usual in time of plague, refrained from having meetings of the Company at the Hall and, 'considering the great multitudes of poor people which by reason of the said infection have their houses shut up and are restrained from their daily trades and labours whereby to maintain themselves and families and by means of . . . the utter cessation of trade endure great wants and extremities . . . ', the Court decided that one-third of the sum that would have been spent on feasting should go to the relief of the infected.

1666   The Lord Mayor asked for a certificate of what had been laid out in the similar circumstances of 1625. He was told that the Company laid out £30 at a time when they 'were in a better Capacity and Condition'. However, to 'show their willingness to so good a work' they would pay the same amount on this occasion.

But there were other things as well to be done for the poor. A precept from the Lord Mayor alleged that the Company had not laid in its corn as they were supposed to do. They were to buy immediately 550 quarters of well-conditioned wheat and, said the message warningly, '. . . depend not upon Chandlers, Bakers or any others to make your provisions nor compound with any of them to furnish and provide the same in your Stead'.

The plague was followed closely (so closely that many felt it to be a Divine judgement) by a catastrophe so great as to be unparalleled in all the ancient history of London.

Fire   The Great Fire of 1666 'raged for five days and destroyed the whole City proper between the Tower and the Temple'[5]. Thirteen thousand houses and ninety churches were destroyed.[6] Starting in Pudding Lane on the night of 1–2 September, it very soon, as Pepys observed, reached the Steelyard. The activity at Clothworkers' Stairs was chaotic.

Everybody endeavouring to remove their goods and flinging into the river, or bringing them into lighters that lay off; poor people staying in their houses as long as till the very fire touched them, and then running into boats or clambering from one pair of stairs by the waterside to another . . . as the wind mighty high and driving it into the City.

It was not long before it had reached Clothworkers' Hall. Being of brick the Hall was not instantly consumed as were the houses of lath and plaster. In fact it burned like the wick of a lamp: Pepys commenting on the strangeness of seeing it '. . . on fire these three days and nights in one body of flame, it being the cellar full of oil'.

With Clothworkers' Hall were burned large numbers of the Company's properties. The Court

upon consideration of the great loss . . . sustained by the late sad and dreadful fire that happened in this City many of their houses being burnt to the ground to the value of 540 pounds per annum. And whereby disabled of the performing the Charity they were heretofore accustomed and enjoined to pay out of the rent of the said houses. It is ordered that for the present no money or annuity to be paid to any person whatsoever by this Company without further order of this Court.

Something had been salved from the wreckage. It had been possible to rescue some of the Company's deeds and writings which were carried away into Drury Lane. Pepys speaks of the streets and highways being 'crowded with people running and riding and getting of carts, at any rate, to fetch away things'. There is evidence that cartage was indeed at a premium, for the papers which had cost £4 7s 6d to remove to Drury Lane cost no more than 4s 1d to return.

The administrative problems were immense. Immediately after the Fire the Court met first at the house of Mr Nicholas Penning★ to consult about the affairs of the Company, and, later at Mr Dennis Gawden's.† A committee for rebuilding the Hall met at various taverns: 'The Ship' in Fenchurch Street, 'The Bull' in Bishopsgate, and 'The Castle' in Broad Street.

Cellars, presumbly for storing the Company's goods, were viewed in Bow Lane. Such plate as had been salvaged was taken to Mr Boylston's house where it was viewed by a committee. Later it was taken to the house of the Master, Mr Phillip Chetwind, and

★ Master 1664.　　　　　　† Master 1667.

139

weighed before being handed over to Gray, the goldsmith in Bishopsgate Street: any that was repairable was mended and burnished and the Company's Ceremonial Staff, which had escaped comparatively unharmed, was repaired.

Then there was the clearing-up to be done. It was

ordered that the Iron, Brick and Rubbish and other materials of building belonging to this Company, which are now remaining upon the Company's ground and in the Cellars on which their Common Hall and houses adjacent lately stood, be forthwith cleared and secured in the backyard, and vault thereunto belonging to this Company.

One hundred and sixty-five loads of rubbish were carted away from the site. Five men were employed collecting 'the iron together that lay loose about the Hall'. Two more men dug up the remains of the pewter from the Charcoal Cellar. A fence of deal boards, lent by the Master, was built around the site to keep out looters, and for greater safety the old iron and pewter was bricked up in a vault. Watchmen were employed for long periods, and evidently there were other guardians too:

Item: Paid for a Dog to keep the Hall secure   16/–
       Another for the same Purpose   5/–
       Collars and Chains for the two Dogs   4/10d

And then, later and most significantly:

Item: for another Chain for the Great Dog   5/–

Later still, it was found necessary to provide a 'maistiff dogg' for the Company's use: lead thieves* were particularly busy and although, surrounded by dogs as the Hall site now was, no lead was stolen from the ruins, there (even though the fencing was twice blown down by the great gales that added to the City's difficulties), yet at William Lambe's Chapel, profiting by the attention of the citizens being elsewhere, thieves nearly got away with part of the lead from a roof largely unharmed by the Fire, 'but being discovered made their escape and left the lead behind them which was since secured by the Constable and Sexton of Cripplegate Parish'.

* Lead thieves continued for several centuries – certainly lead was an essential currency in the criminal economics of the mid-twentieth century.

The Court hired watchmen from the Constable to watch over the lead where it lay, for they had decided that

for the time to come the meetings of this Company for the despatch of their affairs and business shall be held at Lambe's Chapel near Cripplegate, part of which is standing and to that end the Carpenter employed by this Company is ordered forthwith to enclose the end of it, which lies open to the air, with deal boards.

The Company's tenants, too, were having their difficulties.

Mrs Moore, Tenant for two houses at St. James in the Wall, desired that the Company would be pleased to take the care and charge of the Timber and other Materials of Building belonging to those houses and which were lately blown up for the prevention of the raging and increasing of the fire in these parts. . . .

The Court, with enough on their hands already, refused to 'meddle' in that affair: it was, they said, her responsibility.

Gradually order was restored. Mr Gawden, in his house on Tower Hill, promised 'the Company the conveniency of a room or two twice a week, Wednesdays and Thursdays in the morning, to consider of the state and condition of the Company as now it is'. As a result of these meetings the Committee that met there decided on a policy. 'Such monies as hath been borrowed and are owing by this Company on their Common Seal should be first paid, or at Least the interest money, for the said money debit, as it becomes due'. Annuities payable out of houses still standing should be paid but annuities payable out of houses destroyed were, for the time being, to cease.

It was, in fact, quite the very worst possible moment for Captain Jackson in Ireland to ask for money to rebuild the church at Dunboe – preferably somewhere more central, at Ardacleave for instance – which was falling down. The British in Coleraine, he thought, would subscribe £20, and he himself was prepared to lay out £10. If the Company could see their way to a gift of £50. . . . The Bishop of Londonderry himself added his testimonial for the scheme: 'I pray God open your hearts and hands to the encouraging and effecting of this pious work which (I doubt not) will bring a multiplied blessing upon you, your Corporation and families. So that you will have occasion to bless me for the opportunity of your obtaining that blessing. . . . '

It was a blessing that the Clothworkers, unfortunately, could not at that moment afford: they had lost so much in the Fire that their whole preoccupation lay in raising the money to rebuild their own properties.

Rebuilding A Committee of Parliament was sitting to discuss the rebuilding of the City as a whole and, in due course, the representatives of the Company were summoned before it. Arrangements had been made for the rebuilding of the Hall when there came

the Incomparable proposition of that never-to-be-forgotten benefactor Squire Gawden, [who] out of the Tender respect and kindness which he hath for this Company since the late dreadful Fire was pleased to declare that if the Company would leave it wholly to him he would at his own Charge and trouble undertake to built up the Company's Parlour and Kitchen (so far as the ovens extend) with the rooms over them and when it was done he would give the Company an account of the Charge. Whereupon the Court returned their hearty thanks to the said Mr. Gawden for so high and extraordinary a favour – And promised to pay the Charges he should be at in the performance of the same when required.

This offer did, at any rate, ease the Company of the immediate necessity of finding quite so much ready money for the rebuilding. Throughout the City as a whole reconstruction went forward at a 'pace that astonished the world'.[7] The Parlour (and probably the Hall itself) was in use by the end of 1668 for the Fishmongers, Drapers, and the Honourable Artillery Company were by then meeting there for Court business.

The new Hall that was built has been described by Maitland as

a lofty Room, adorned with Wainscot to the Ceiling, where is curious Fret-work. The Screen at the South End is of Oak, adorned with four Pilasters, their Entablature and Compass Pediment is of the Corinthian Order enriched with their Arms and Palm Branches. The West end is adorned with the Figures of King James I and King Charles I, richly carved* as big as the Life in their Robes, with Regalia, all gilt with Gold,

* These were by Bumstead, the carver. They were not put up until 1679.

where is a spacious Window of stained Glass. . . . The Outside is adorned with curious Brick fluted Columns with Corinthian Capitals of Stone.

The spacious window of stained glass in 1668 included the coats-of-arms of Sir William Peake, Alderman Francis Chaplin, Mr (now Sir) Dennis Gawden, and Sir J. Robinson.*

Effigies of William Lambe, John Lute, Samuel Middlemore, John Heath, Lady Anne Packington, and other benefactors, if they could be procured, were to be hung in the new Hall. And, locking the door well after the horse had disappeared down the road, the Court of Common Council then set out an Act for the Prevention of Fire in London.†

* *
*

The results of the Fire, coupled with the Second Dutch war, were disastrous for the cloth trade. The capital was the great cloth repository of the Kingdom. Many clothiers had lost thousands of pounds worth of cloth and had gone out of business altogether.[8] Another result of the Fire had been to break down the opposition to the employment of 'foreigners' or non-freemen in the City. The vast amount of rebuilding to be done had, inevitably, involved the use of 'foreigners' and, once the principle had been established, the restrictive practices and the closed shop of the guild freemen were on a slippery slope.

In 1675, the 'Journeymen Clothworkers' petitioned the Court and informed them that

* That Sir J. Robinson, the Lieutenant of the Tower, may well have been the buffle-headed fellow that Pepys alleged might be inferred from a letter from him to the Master:

'Sir: When I was to go to my Lord Mayor the Beadle acquainted me, but not having with me a Ticket I forgot it. And last night finding a Ticket to dine with the Sheriff I was pre-arranged to dine with my Lord Ashby and Lord of Exeter whom I met at Whitehall yesterday. Therefore excuse me to the Sheriff. I have sent five pieces enclosed. And since I was Lord Mayor had never one hundred pounds beforehand. But the first hundred pounds I have shall go towards the rebuilding of your Hall . . .'

† There is a report in the Art Journal to the effect that parts of the building are thought to have been by Inigo Jones. Inigo Jones's father was a Clothworker, but there is no evidence that either he or his son took the Freedom of the Company or had any hand in their Hall.

several members of this Company do employ altogether foreigners so that the poor freemen with their wives and children are like to perish. They most humbly desired this Court to take it into their serious considerations. Whereupon the Court returned them this Answer that they could not force any person that lives out of the freedom to employ freemen. But however the Court desired the Gentlemen that do employ foreigners to make use of freemen if they will work for the same wages and be constant to their masters.

So slack were the times, in fact, that the year after the Fire, 'in respect of the deadness of Trade and the small quantity of work that is now amongst the Artizan Clothworkers of this Company in and about London', it was ordered that no Search Day should be held.

New Economic Theories

There was, moreover, a new feeling in the country against the restraints on internal trade and industry. A group of Restoration writers had violently attacked the economic dogmas. The idea that 'no man ought to live and trade in a corporation that is not a freeman of the place' was denounced by Child,[9] corporations were castigated by Roger Coke as obstacles to the progress of trade. The author of *Brittania Languens* complained that 'most of our ancient corporations and guilds are become oppressive oligarchies'. By exacting arbitrary fines for admission, he said,

beginners in manufacture and other trades, being 'foreigners' and having but small stocks, can never obtain freedom, and without it are burthened and plagued with by-laws, penalties, distresses and seizures. Nay, if a man be exquisite in his trade he shall hardly get a freedom for money in a corporation where there are more free of the same trade, for then he is looked on as a dangerous person and likely to eat the bread out of their mouths, as they phrase it.

The trend of judicial decisions was now towards industrial freedom, and judges were particularly active in undermining the legal position of the craft guilds.

In future nothing was to stand in the way of the *entrepreneur*: he was left by Parliament to make his own dispositions as to wages, length of service and quality of labour.[10] And, since there was no longer any legal obligation on employers to keep their men at work in time of depression, the workers were thrown upon their own resources: they formed benefit clubs which were 'one of the links in the chain that led to trade unionism'.[11]

The Court of the Clothworkers' Company were sensitive to these new trends. In 1671 'several Artizan Clothworkers of the Livery and Yeomanry of this Company proposed to this Court that there might be some restraint or prohibition upon the Cloth-workers in and about London not to dress any of the Dutch black cloths that come from Holland and if the Company would countenance them herein it would add much to the good of the handytrade'.* Counsel's opinion was taken over the 'prohibiting of planing, pressing and mending of Country dressed Black Cloth after it came to London', and it was the opinion of both the Counsel consulted that 'it would be accepted and accounted a combination and would be liable thereon to lose their Charter and advised the Company noways to Meddle with it'.

In view of this decision – a very different attitude to that prevail-ing in the old days of the Company – the Court decided not to involve the Company in its corporate capacity, 'but if any member of the handycraft in and about London act therein amongst them-selves at their own peril, so be it'.

There was evidence, too, that the attitude of the Company was changing in other ways, that the conception of the Mastership was altering.

In 1676, a complete outsider, not even a member of the Com-pany, Sir Joseph Williamson, a Member of the Privy Council, the Principal Secretary of State,† was chosen to be Master. In the absence of any evidence or contemporary comment in the records it is almost impossible to guess the reasons for this innovation.‡

1671

---

* The trade in Dutch black cloths was a direct legacy of the fatal Cloth Project (*q.v. supra*) which had given a permanent stimulus to the woollen industry abroad.

† 'A pretty knowing man and a scholar, but, it may be, thinks himself to be too much so,' commented Pepys.

‡ The innovation was, however, a lawful one. A fairly new Ordinance (No. 35) of 15 April 1639, empowered the Court without other consultation to admit by composition and redemption any who should seem 'meet and convenient to be a brother or freeman'.

Certainly, it cannot have been for any insufficiency among the existing members of the Court who included Sir Thomas Beckford and many Assistants of long standing.

It is just possible that some faint feelings of the King's attitude to the City Companies, which was to culminate in the enquiry of *Quo Warranto*, led to a desire to cultivate those in high places. It was a policy, certainly, that paid dividends in prestige and in more tangible assets too.

Sir Joseph Williamson presented the Company 'with a Noble present of Wine and Plate viz. One Basin and Ewer, One Standing Bowl and Cover and one Salt, all of them being very fair and large and richly gilt with his and the Company's Coats of Arms en-

1676   graven upon them . . . '. A modest letter accompanied the gift:

Brother Beckford,

Not being able to wait upon the Company myself as I could have wished to have done, I must beg of you or who else of my bretheren does me the favour to supply my place today that you will please to present two or three small pieces of Plate in my name to the Company as an expression of my sense and thankfulness for the many obligations and respects they are pleased to place on me.

I have taken leave to send two or three dozen of my own Moselle to pledge me the Company's health and prosperity which I drink and wish with all my heart. And I pray you in a fit time of dinner see it go about in the bowl. And I (I can desire for ever) to be remembered by the Company, Brother Beckford, I pray that health may be appointed to be drunk in that bowl for the future.*

The following year, 1677, saw the same policy of introducing strangers to the highest offices in the Company continued with the

Samuel   election of one whose name shines perhaps most brightly among

Pepys   all other names in the history of the Company. On 7 August 1677, 'the Honourable Samuel Pepys Esq.re Secretary to the right Honourable the Lord Commissioners of the Admiralty was elected and chosen Master of this worshipful Company for the year ensuring'.

His connexion with the Company is not entirely clear. It seems unlikely to have been a family one, though there was, it is true, a

* More than 250 years later the bowl was still in use.

146

SAMUEL PEPYS

Richard Pepys who was tenant of a yard belonging to the Company in Cornhill; he was probably the cousin of whom Samuel Pepys wrote in 1665: 'With my cousin Richard Pepys upon the 'Change about supplying us with Bewpers'* from Norwich, which I should be glad of if cheap'. But he was an unsatisfactory tenant, continually asking for – and failing to get – reductions in his rent, and in constant action against a Mr Drope whom he accused, as the Court thought unreasonably, of encroachment.

It is more likely that the connexion came through Sir Dennis Gawden – the 'never-to-be-forgotten benefactor'.

Sir Dennis Gawden was Victualler to the Navy and, as such, was in constant touch with Pepys. He occurs frequently in the Diary and it is clear that his business relations with the diarist were such that, normal as they were in an age in which bribery was no matter for comment, they might in a more particular age cause a faint raising of the eyebrows. But, such relationship apart, the two were obviously friends. From Gawden Pepys received Christmas presents, in 1660 and again in 1662 of 'a great chine of beef and half a dozen of tongues'. With Gawden at 'The Dolphin', Pepys discussed financial matters. At Gawden's house at Clapham, Pepys kissed Gawden's daughter ('a buxom lass'), walking and reading in the gardens there until it grew dark, after which there came supper and music and bed 'in the best chamber, like a prince' – all this is evidence of Pepys's close social relationship with the Clothworker. It seems fairly safe, then, to suppose that it was through Sir Dennis Gawden's influence that Pepys became Master of the Company and that 'little Sir Francis Chaplin',† who had once been Gawden's servant, supported him.

At the time of his election he was not even a member of the Company, but that was adjusted the following day – 8 August 1677 – when 'Mr. Samuel Peepyt' – the Minute Clerk had some slight difficulty with the name – 'was pleased first to take the Oath of his Admission into this Court of Assistants and afterwards the Oath of Master of this Company for the year ensuing.' 'This day also ... he was pleased to make choice of William Edwards

* Probably 'beaupers': pieces of cloth containing 25 yards.   † Master 1668.

Esqre' (Master two years earlier) 'to officiate in his room as Deputy Master for the year ensuing.'

Two months later came a vote of thanks to Esquire Pepys for his 'great favour in presenting them with one large standard, having the Company's Arms with their supporters, and their Patron and Crest, and a Griffin supporting their Arms, and the Dragon supporting the City Arms, the trail very richly gilt with fine gold. And also one fair Banner of his own particular Coat of Arms both amounting to the sum of £26.10.0.'*

After a year of office in which not more than five appearances at the Hall are recorded, Samuel Pepys disappears almost completely from the records for six years, a period during which no more than one appearance, in August 1682, has been reported.

It is a period that coincides, first, with his committal to the Tower on an accusation of Papistry, and then with his subsequent fall from office. But in 1684 – the year that he was again appointed Secretary to the Admiralty – Pepys came back for a long period of service with the Company.

It was he who was one of those who, as will later appear, carried the Petition of the Company against a writ of *Quo Warranto* to Hampton Court. It was he who was one of those who successfully pleaded with the King for the restoration to office of the Clerk, Edward Gurney, who had been removed against the will of the Company in 1686. He was on the Committee that investigated the setting up of the Machinery known as 'Labady's Patent'.

In 1688 he was asked to 'take upon him the trouble of setting up Esquire Hewer's Arms in one of this Company's windows in their Common Hall' and 'also that he would be pleased to take the like Trouble upon him in putting the Table of this Company's Benefactors in a right method'.

There was, too, that occasion which, with its sudden conjunction of great figures, stirs the imagination strongly. The Clothworkers' Company had begged leave of His Majesty in 1684 'to erect and set up the statue or Effigies of his Royal Grandfather King

* More munificent still, was his gift of Loving-cup, Rosewater Dish, and Ewer.

James in the vacancy next adjoining to that of his Royal Father on the Royal Exchange' – a suggestion originally put forward by Sir Thomas Beckford – 'hoping that this their Act would be a precedent and encouragement to other Companies of this City to set up the rest of the former Kings as they stood before the late dreadful fire of London.'

To this His Majesty 'graciously' agreed, and a Committee for the Erecting and Setting up of the Effigy of King James in one of the Vacancies in the Royal Exchange, which included Mr Secretary Pepys, 'to take care of the management of this affair', decided that it should be made of Portland stone and by the best hand that they could procure.

In accordance with this objective, they reported on 30 May 1684 that:

The following agreement was made with Mr. Gibbons, His Majesty's Artist in Carving:

That he should perform it with his best skill and make it with good Portland stone, 7 feet high, with a table or pedestal of Marble and such inscription upon it as the Committee shall think fit and also any device or Emblem that may be thought proper by this Committee to be put up with this King and when it was finished and set up they would Order him fifty pounds to be paid to him for the same; and withall they desired him to draw a model of it and bring it to them that they might consider of the habit. To all which proposals Mr. Gibbons assented and promised to bring the Model in a few days and to finish the Effigy in three months from this date.

On 9 December 1684, the Court

desired the favour of Mr. Secretary Pepys and Mr. Bridgeman that they would oblige Sir Christopher Wren (with them) to take a View of the Statue of King James, lately set up by Mr. Gibbons on the Royal Exchange by order and at the charge of this Company. And to make their report to this Court (if faulty) what their dislikes are and withall that they would be pleased to order Mr. Gibbons to attend them on the view. And that he may have their directions for the emendment where it is amiss and that they should be pleased to take Sir Christopher Wren's opinion for the most convenient place for the inscription.

This meeting of the giants took place apparently on Boxing Day 1684. Mr Bridgeman, Sir Christopher Wren, and Samuel Pepys viewed the sculpture set up by Grinling Gibbons and presumably passed it without adverse comment: the carver was eventually paid £50 for his pains. A Tavern Bill on the occasion of the outing, for the four of them, amounted to £1 4s 9d.

On 13 September 1687, Pepys was mentioned again when a Committee was discussing streamers as decorations for the Barge: 'It was the opinion of the Committee that the King's Arms may be over the Master's Chair in the Barge . . . to take Esquire Pepys direction for the Subscription on the Master's Arms.' But this last sentence is then deleted.

Again, on 24 October, 'it was decided to consult with Mr. Secretary Pepys for the inscription' under William Hewer's Arms in the Hall Window.

In 1688, the year before his final retirement, after a charge of selling information to France, Pepys suddenly disappeared again from the records for more than six years, turning up again in 1694. His last personal appearance at a Court meeting was on Election Day, 18 August 1696; his last mention in the contemporary records came in 1700 when the Court ordered that Mr Gurney – the Clerk he had saved from the King's dismissal – or Mr Chase 'should attend Mr. Pepys for the Catalogue of this Company's benefactors which were left in his hands some time since to be transcribed by one of his Clerks'.

On 26 May 1703 death came to the old Clothworker – for surely he had by now earned that title – in the house of the faithful William Hewer, his former clerk, now, like himself, a past-master of the Clothworkers' Company. It was the house where once Pepys had kissed a buxom lass and, after an evening of music, had gone to bed in the best chamber like a prince. For the great house at Clapham that had once been intended for a Bishop's Palace had been bought by William Hewer after the ultimate ruin of that incomparable benefactor, Sir Dennis Gawden.

* *
*

But to leap forward into the new century and to the death of A Call for Economy 1682 Samuel Pepys is to anticipate. There was still a most difficult passage of the seventeenth century to navigate. In 1682 there came a sudden call for economy, although what prompted this call is not apparent for there had lately been no record of forced loans or undue financial outgoings, nor had there been the usual rising scale of complaint about the distressed condition of the Company. Be that as it may, the Company were in debt, were perhaps still in debt from the disastrous days of the Fire, for, although rebuilding had been speedy, there had been 'many businesses depending before the judges between the Company and its tenants since the Fire'.

In 1682 the Economy Committee produced its proposals for austerity. Not more than sixpence per head was to be spent at meetings; not more than two gallons of burnt wine to be drunk on St Luke's Day; nothing more than burnt wine and cakes to be provided for the St Stephen's Day visit to William Lambe's Chapel; dinner on view days was not to cost more than £10; no allowance would be given for dining with the Lord Mayor; travelling expenses were to be cut – the whole list had a depressing ring to it. One or two of the economy moves led, as it happened, to better service. 'The Music of Waits might do as well as a noise of Trumpets in the Company's barge on the Lord Mayor's Day and also to play before the Company from their landing all the way to the Hall because the Company are generally ill-served with trumpets on the day and the waits may be procured for half the money.' It was, however, thought 'convenient' that the drum be continued in the barge as long as it did not cost more than five or six shillings a day.

Apart from the economy, there were other problems which had Industrial Unrest to be solved. In 1686 there was, for example, a Labour Dispute in which

several of the Masters of the working Trade appeared before this Court with several of their journeymen whom they had summoned in. They objected against them that they had deserted their services now when a shipping was upon them and refused to work under 12/– per week.

The Journeymen, in answer, complained that their Masters used them only for a small time in the year and, when winter came, turned them off and employed 'foreigners at under wages'.

The Court proposed that the masters should give their workmen 10s a week and agree to employ no foreigners. 'But the journeymen stood upon higher wages. And so departed.' Here is clear evidence of the change in attitude that accompanied the Restoration. No longer was there any firm injunction against the employment of 'foreigners', no longer was there any form of wages regulation. Where once the Court had ruled in these matters, they now proposed. They were arbitrators and not wholly effective arbitrators at that: the confirmed twentieth-century habit of complying with arbitration only so long as the arbitration was an agreeable one was finding its first expression.

There was another problem that had first arisen the year previous, when in 1681 some country-dressed cloths had been seized from Mr George Boddington* for ill-workmanship and he had been fined 6s 8d a cloth. There had been some dispute whether the Company were, in fact, empowered to deal with country-dressed cloths, 'and in regards that the shipping for Turkey was then in haste and the Court had not leisure to examine the Company's power . . . they were then contented to deliver him the said cloths and to remit the one half of the said fine to him'. Now they had consulted their charters and they were satisfied that their power allowed them to seize country-dressed cloths: the case of Mr Boddington was not to be taken as a precedent.

That they were already entitled to do so was apparent in the charter of Charles I, which specifically gave them the power over cloth 'brought from whatsoever parts of this our Realm of England or parts beyond the seas or elsewhere . . . to our said City or the suburbs thereof or within three miles distant on all sides from the said City.

Quo Warranto But, quite suddenly, the Charters became valueless to them, 'a herefacies or quo warranto being brought against the Company just as the Court were rising . . .'.

* Master 1705.

Charles II had, no doubt, never forgotten that the City had been ranged against the Crown during the Civil Wars. Now his enquiry into the validity of the City Charter made him Master of London and of all the Corporations in England. The Charter of the City was declared forfeit on two grounds. Firstly, for the highly doubtful reason that citizens raised toll in markets (as their Charter entitled them to do) and secondly, on the grounds that petitioning the King for redress of grievance was libellous.[12]

Directed ostensibly against the City, the mastery of the City Companies was, in fact, the most important aim. Even before the City Charter was forfeited, several City Companies, alarmed by the proceedings, surrendered their charters. The Clothworkers sent a deputation to Hampton Court – Pepys amongst their number – with a petition to the King.

That your Majesty will be graciously pleased to remit whatever occasion they may have hitherto given of Offence to Your Sacred Majesty and accept of their most humble and Entire Submission both of themselves and [their] Charter to such regulations for their future Government as in Your Royal Wisdom shall be held expedient.

Resistance was considered useless: instruments of surrender were prepared.

Know ye that considering how much it imports the Government of this City and the Companies thereof to have persons of known Loyalty and approved Integrity to bear offices of tryst therein, we the Master Wardens and Commonalty of the Freemen of the Art or Mystery of Clothworkers of the City of London, Have granted, Surrendered and yielded up ... unto our most gracious Sovereign Lord Charles the Second.... All and singular the powers, franchises, Liberties, privileges and Authorities whatsoever, howsoever granted. ... And we ... do hereby most humbly beseech His Majesty to accept of this our Surrender and do with all submission to His Majesty's pleasure implore His Grace and favour to regrant unto us ... and our successors ... the naming and choosing such officers who shall manage the governing part of the said Company. Under such restrictions, Qualifications and reservations as Your Majesty in your great wisdom shall think fit. ... [13]

The abject but inevitable surrender placed them completely in the hands of the Crown. Certainly it was alleged that the King

designed not to intermeddle or take away the rights property or privileges of any Company, nor to destroy or injure the ancient usages or franchises of their corporations, [but to have] only a regulation of the governing part so as His Majesty might for the future have in himself a moving power of any officer therein for mismanagement in the same way and method that they themselves now used and claimed to have by power derivable from the Crown. 14

But no longer had they any freedom of control over their own affairs. The revised Charter for which they humbly begged – and for the granting of which they had heavily to pay – put them entirely in the hands of the agents of the Crown.

Although they were re-incorporated in their ancient names and were granted the right of perpetual succession, their choice of wardens and clerk, who had to be Protestants, communicants, and take the prescribed oaths of allegiance and supremacy, was subject to Royal approval, and the wardens and commonalty were, further subject to the Lord Mayor and Aldermen (also duly approved by the Crown) who had also to approve all admissions to the livery.

The charter added, ironically, an affirmation of all former uses, liberties, and privileges, without any molestation from the Crown or officers of the Crown.

A few days after the surrender, there was celebrated the annual and solemn festival appointed by Act of Parliament in commemoration of 'the happy return of His Sacred and Royal Majesty Charles II, our Most Gracious King, into this Land'.

CHAPTER NINE

THE TYRANNY ENDS

* *
*

W ITHIN six months the King was dead, but if the Company   1685
had hoped that with his death would come any relief from
the stranglehold of the Crown, they were sadly mistaken. On 18   A New
February 1685 the new Charter from His late Majesty was received.   Charter
The new oaths were signed and the Company, of whom at least
fifty had been removed by the Crown, settled down uneasily to
await His Majesty's further pleasure.

Amongst other attempts to influence the City, the Lord Mayor
was told to secure a list from the Companies of 'such loyal and
worthy members as might be judged worthy and fit to be, by the
Lord Mayor and Aldermen, approved of as Liverymen to elect
members to serve for the City of London at the approaching
Parliament'. The seriousness of this threat was increased by the fact
that the most independent aldermen had already been removed
and creatures of the King put in their place.

The number of the Court and Livery had fallen from 160 to 100
when 'William Hewers Esq$^{re.}$ one of His Majesty's Commissioners of the Navy and a worthy member of the Assistants of this
Company, was elected and chosen Master for the year ensuing'.
His arms were set up in the Hall in as large a manner as those of his
old master, Samuel Pepys, and of Sir Joseph Williamson.

On 28 September 1687 came an order from Windsor, removing   State
twenty-five Members from the Court. It was followed by an   Intervention
order from the City Council that the vacant places be made up: at
the same time those members who had been removed upon the
first granting of the New Charter were to be restored to their

former places. Soon, as the names were shuffled and reshuffled, it became difficult to know who were Clothworkers and who were not. In the general confusion it is possible that some of the orders for removal were overlooked or ignored.

Certainly, in 1687, when William Hewer presented the Company with a new barge, the committee of barge-building included the names of many who had been proscribed. The attempt to remove Mr Gurney, the Clerk to the Company, was resisted, and Mr Bridgeman, Mr Pepys, and Mr Hewer were 'earnestly entreated to use their utmost endeavours with His Majesty for the continuance of their said Clerk in their Service' – endeavours which were, no doubt, successful since there is no evidence that Mr Gurney was removed, even temporarily, from the post which he held until 1703.

1688
Low State
of the
Company

By 1688 'the Livery of this Company was grown so low that there did not remain Stewards to provide dinners for the Company on the usual Festival Days in the year'. Dinners were, in future, to be held in taverns until the times improved.

In addition to the doubtful privileges of being a Member of the Company, and thereby being brought to the notice of an unpredictable and extortionate Crown, were added the high costs of being a Clothworker. A father introducing his son into the Company commented that they were 'a very chargeable Company whereas he [the son] is at present offered to be received into Another Company on much more easy terms for the present and future . . . . '.

Faced with this accusation, the Court agreed, having regard for his father's respect to the Company in introducing his son to such a 'chargeable Company', to admit the son to the freedom but to excuse him from coming on the Livery for five years, he being 'but a very young man'.

It became increasingly difficult to secure new members of the Livery. After the election of 1688, several of those chosen refused point blank to come on the Livery, and the Court had to order 'that they should have patterns of cloth sent to them as a Summons to bring in their fine this day'. Next, the Yeomanry asked to be excused altogether from coming on the Livery and so, for the present, that source of entry was suspended.

The Company were in very low water indeed when quite suddenly the tide turned as, with the Rebellion, there ended the second Stuart tyranny. A Charter of Restitution, granted on 3 October 1688 by James II to the City Companies, restored them to the state they had enjoyed before the Judgement of *Quo Warranto*.

Restoration of City Privileges

On 25 November 1688, by a happy coincidence the anniversary of the opening of this history, the instrument of surrender was by an Order in Council returned. Many members of the Court earlier removed reappeared and 'the Wardens delivered unto the Court the surrender that they received back from the Lord Chancellor which the Court ordered to be cancelled presently. But the new Charter was ordered to be preserved and laid up with the former under the Keys of the Master and Wardens.' The latter, although they had been elected before the surrender was delivered back to the Company, were to continue in office.

With the coming of William III of Orange there disappeared the last remaining vestiges of the writ of *Quo Warranto* – an act that has been described as 'the last public event of consequence in connection with the Livery Companies'.[1] Attempts were still to be made upon their existence by Royal Commissions of Enquiry but from thenceforth no attempts were made by statute to influence their freedom of action.

The affairs of the Companies began slowly but steadily to improve.

*   *

*

Meanwhile, while the last of the Stuarts still reigned, there were radical changes taking place in the structure of the textile industry. The development of the West Indies and the American Colonies had led to an ever-expanding demand for cotton materials of all kinds.

Increase in Cotton Trade

On 8 November 1686 'several of the Yeomanry petitioned this Court for some redress against a Frenchman that had set up an engine for Cottoning and Mantling of Cloth and other Woollen manufacture which if not timely prevented would prove the ruin of many families of the Working Trade'.*

The Committee of three, Mr Pepys, Mr Bridgeman, and Mr Hewer, were consulted to see what should be done: the resulting dispute continued for six years, during which Cotton versus Wool became a controversy extending even into the sphere of politics.

Labour, particularly in the cloth trade, had always been inimical to mechanization.[2] In the thirteenth century there was an agitation against the use of watermills by fullers; in the fifteenth century shearmen had been forbidden to employ any instrument other than the 'broad shears'; in the sixteenth century Parliament condemned the use of 'engines' for stretching or straining cloth and of gig mills for raising the nap.

In 1690 the matter cropped up again. This time the cottoners were to have £10 'to carry on their business against these patents that are granted for Napping and Cottoning of cloths by an Engine lately invented'. A week or two later they were granted a further £8 'to carry on their charge against the French Engine of Napping and Frizeing Woollen Manufacture in this Nation'.

No more is heard of Labady's Patent. In the meantime the cottoners had other complaints to raise. The Court were kept busy in dealing with them. It was seldom, that there was complete peace between the various interests of the Company. Hardly had the cottoners been disposed of than the journeymen were petitioning, in August 1692, 'against the Master Clothworkers who employed foreigners and refused to set them at work'. That the complaint was justified was soon seen, for the Court took immediate action; several Master Clothworkers (including the Master of the Company himself) were fined 40s each for employing foreigners in shearing and rowing and 'refusing to set on work poor freeman of this City'. The only excuse they could devise was that they were ignorant of the laws.

1692

Petition of the Journeymen

* In 1663 householders had complained to the Privy Council that 'many drapers and merchants . . . rowed with gig mills which force the cloth wrought by them longer by three or four yards in each cloth than they were from the fulling mills and hinder much labour. For one man and a boy with a gig mill could row as many cloths as eight or ten can do by labour of hand'.

It is noticeable that with the dilution of the clothworking inter-ests* in the Company the rules of employment were more strictly upheld by the Court and for a few years this insistence on the rules of employment seems to have had effect: not until the last year of the century are there more of the same complaints – complaints from which arose the Court Order that freemen should be em-ployed before foreigners, that they were not to demand more than 10s per week and that both journeymen and masters should give each other a fortnight's notice of ending employment.

Masters were summoned before the Court and ordered to employ freemen 'provided they behave themselves as they ought to do and were workmen at their Trade . . .'. Moreover, 'if any Master Clothworker should trouble the Journeymen and not employ them by reason of this complaint the Court would defend them provided they behave themselves civilly towards their said Masters'. In the phraseology of a later age there was to be 'no victimization'.

*   *
*

Now a new reign had begun. The Clothworkers, having no doubt a certain gratitude for the fact that the advent of William III had been decisive in bringing to an end the instrument of surrender, made no demur when the King made it known

that his Affairs at this instant (before the supplies which are intended can be settled in a Parliamentary way and made effectual) are very much straitened for want of money to be applied to the Navy, the reducing of Ireland and other uses of great importance to His Majesty and the Public.

They decided to lend some of the £2,000 they now had lying in the great iron chest† – such were, it is presumed, the results of the drive for economy – 'considering the 7% interest would be a

The Great
Iron Chest

---

* Among the new freemen in 1690 were seven Cheesemongers, four Merchants, one Timber Merchant or Sawyer, one Confectioner, one Scrivener, one Ship's Chandler, one Tripe Man, one Butcher, and one Grocer. The only three new freemen in any way connected with the textile trade were a Draper, a Silk Dyer, and a Salesman.

† That same iron chest, no doubt, as the one mentioned on page 20 above.

great advantage to the Company ... until a purchase could be found rather than let the money lie idle in the chest'.

The reducing of Ireland was, in any case, a work which could only be profitable to the Company. By 1692 'most of their tenants' had 'lost their lives and were plundered of all their Cattle and goods by the Irish Army so that they have made little or no rent ever since the rebellion began and are now much to seek for Tenants that are able to stock their farms ...'. Most of the houses there were 'so spoiled and demolished by Bombs and Cannon Shot during the late siege that they are no wise habitable for the approaching Winter'.

Help was needed to put up temporary dwellings and since the Irish Society had no ready cash the twelve Companies were asked to, and did, provide £100 each.

Some more money – another £200 – came out of the chest 'for raising Horse and Dragoons for the service of their Majesties against the Invasion of the French which is somewhat feared at present ...'.

In spite of these expenses on defence and in making good the desolation of war, there was still money to be spent on the sort of pageantry that had always been the happiest feature of the City Companies. In 1693, it was agreed that the barge should be repaired

The Barge

as far as needful to attend all those members of the Court of Assistants and their ladies that shall be pleased to go in her on Wednesday, 26th instant, to divert themselves and their ladies upon the water and to dine where the Master and Wardens shall think most convenient: first to meet at the Steelyard by 8 of the clock in the morning and from there to take Barge with their Ladies. And this to be done in performance of Mr. Hewer's desire when he presented them with the Barge.'

Because it was the 'first and only time that this Court performed and answered his desires by going abroad in it with their Ladies ...', the Court decided that the outing should be paid from the Quarter Wardens' account.

It is pleasant to record that the occasion must have been a triumphant success, for in August 1695 – there had been, as will be seen, the sufficient excitement of a Lord Mayor's Show in the intervening year –

the Court taking into consideration that their Barge was lately repaired and made very fine and the season of the year inviting, thought it a convenient time to go abroad in her with their Ladies as high as Putney or Barn Elms and then to return and dine at Chelsea to see the College and Physic Garden and any other diversions that were in that place. . . .

In 1694 the Lord Mayor, Sir Thomas Lane, was a Clothworker and to the Company fell the duty of providing the pageantry. The Hall was, of course, offered for the Lord Mayor's use, but for some reason he had already arranged to use Skinners' Hall. Mr Wallis, the Herald Painter, was to make seven banners with the Arms of the King, Sir Joseph Williamson, Samuel Pepys, William Hewer, the City, the Lord Mayor, and the Clothworkers' Company.

1694
A Cloth-
worker
Pageant

There were to be four pageants made by Mr Holmes, and the poet Elkanah Settle – the Minute Clerk referred to him as Mr Suttle – was paid £10 for writing the libretto. In addition, the painter and poet were given £170 to find 'Men to carry the Pageants, children and persons to ride upon them' and 'music and all things belonging to them'.

On the day of the show the whole company assembled at Clothworkers' Hall in all their finery; with banners flying and bands playing they marched through the City streets to the waterside. A fleet of barges gloriously bedecked sailed up the river to Westminster to the echoing thunder of 'peals of Ordnance in token of Love'. Then, the Lord Mayor being duly presented, all returned by river to the City.

The Lord Mayor being landed at Baynard's Castle, the Gentlemen of the Artillery Ground accommodate his Lordship with their Company . . . with Drums, Fifes, Trumpets, Colours, Silkwork, Pensioners, Gentlemen Ushers, Budge Bachelors and Foynes Bachelors all in an equipage ready to march.

Through the streets lined by the other Companies they marched to the stocks where the 'Scenes or Triumphs appear'. The Lord Mayor was greeted with a eulogistic address:

I may justly concede You this Fair Renown: viz. That the whole Grandeur of England is in a high measure owing to your worthy Society. For the Gold of our Fleece and the Wealth of our LOOM is in a manner our whole English Peru: And the back of the Sheep and not the Entrails of the Earth is our chief Mine of Riches. The Silkworm is no Spinster of ours; and our Weal and our Web, Gentlemen, are all your own.

This, as Trade, is the life-blood of the English Nation, and, indeed, the very supporter of the Crown; So the greatest Branch of the English Trade lies in the Clothworkers' Hands.

Our Floating Castles, I confess, our Naval Commerce bring us in both the Ore and the Argent and, indeed, the whole wealth of the World. They bring it in 'tis true, but when thoroughly examined, 'tis your CLOTH sends out to fetch 'em.

And thus, whilst the Imperial Britannia is so formidable to her foes, so potent to her Friends, her Strength and her Power, when duly consider'd, to the Clothworkers' Honour I may justly say 'tis Your Shuttle nerves her Arm and your Woof that enrobes her Glory.

At this moment came the first pageant, *The Seat of Sovereignty*:

A Stately Pyramid stands erected upon four Rich Columns wreathed round with Golden Laurel and other Ornaments. Round this chief Pyramid upon the Cornish of the Columns stand four smaller Pyramids, all of them hung with Trophies as being the Acquisitions of Sovereign Power.

In front of the Pageant sits Augusta representing London with three Figures, viz. Concord, Prudence and Justice. Beneath are planted Four Figures more, viz. Europe, Asia, Africa and America, the other Four, Thames, Tyber, Nile and Indus. Intimating that the whole World, by way of Trade and Commerce contributes to the Wealth and Grandeur of London. The whole Pageant is duly applied to My Lord as being the Representative of Majesty within the City of London.

Augusta speaks:

> ... Fair Virtue's Propagation is your due
> Encouraged Piety, cherished Industry
> Corrected Vice must Your great Province be.
> And whilst Your Lordship's Smiling influence
> To happy London shall its warmth dispense
> With Rosy garlands I'le adorne my Tow'rs
> I'le wear them, Sir, but you shall plant my Flow'rs.

This was the Cue for the second pageant, *The Garden of Plenty*, to be carried or wheeled before his Lordship.

On a large Stage at each end are planted four Flow'r potts richly embossed with Gold; over these arises a Rich Arbour all sumptuously deckt with Flow'rs and Fruit of Gold and out of four less Flow'r Pots more, above the Arch, these Pots likewise of Gold, issue fair Trees adorned with several fruits and Flowers, and over all is hanged a Golden Fleece. Beneath this Arbour sits Jason, as the Capital Figure with a Dragon in a large Shield, who conquer'd the Dragon to obtain the Golden Fleece. . . . Jason is attended by Three other figures representing Commerce, Navigation and Industry.

From this pageant Jason spoke.

> Jason of Old was a bold Youth of Greece
> Subdu'd a Dragon for a Golden Fleece.
> A fairer Wreath Your Lordship's Worth attends
> For here proud London's prostrate Dragon Bends.
> So just a Hand with Pow'rs Regalia graced
> Honour and Trust were never nobler placed.
> And, Sir, if great Examples could but teach
> The imitating World their heights to reach
> Your leading Virtue such deserts to Crown
> From the kind Heavens must pull those Blessings down
> Till this Blest Town shall my rich Treasures hold
> Reap both my Golden Fruit and Fleece of Gold.

The Garden of Plenty then creaked away to be replaced by *The Chariot of Apollo*:

A very Rich Chariot is drawn by two Golden Griffons* [sic] . . . in the Chariot is seated Apollo. . . . Upon the approach of My Lord, when Apollo arises to address him, a Rich Figure of the Rising Sun, of about 10 foot Diameter, not seen before, appears above his Head out of the Back of the Chariot with all his Beams display'd in Gold. On each Griffon ride triumphant figures.

Apollo then spoke and was followed by the fourth and last pageant, *The Pageant of Trade*, in which was

* They were hired, this year, from the Grocers for 30s.

the whole Art and Mistery of the Clothworkers exprest by all manner of Persons actually concerned in all Branches of the Trade as Carding, Combing, Spinning, Rowling, shearing of Wool etc. The Chief Figure is Jack of Newbury in his proper Habit upon a Rich Seat erected for him. In the Front of the Pageant is placed the Golden Ram, the Crest of the Worshipful Company.

The Pageant a very large one, being filled with several persons in Rurale and Pastoral Habits Dancing and rejoycing with their Pipes and other Country Musick suitable to their characters and also to the Solemn Joys of the Day.

Jack of Newbury having spoken, the excitements of the show ended with *A Song*:

> Come all the nine Sisters that fill the Great Quire
> For here's a Rich Theme must the Muses Inspire
> The Clothworkers' Glory
> So fair lies before ye
> So famous and antient their Honour begun
> When Adam first delved and our Mother Eve spun.
>
> For the Gold nor the Pearl old England shall lack
> You send out your Cloth and the Indies come back
> On Your fair Foundation
> The Wealth of the Nation
> Our Wool and our Web the Supporters of Crowns
> Tis Wool-Sacks found Bridges and Fleeces build Towns.
>
> Whilst thro' twelve Starry signs, as Astronomers say,
> To circle the Year, drives the great God of Day
> Thro' Aries and Taurus
> Triumphant and glorious
> Whilst the Ram in the Heavens does so splendid appear
> Tis the Clothworkers Crest begins the Fair Year.
>
> Two Griffons of Gold, your Supporters so fair
> Those compounds of Lyon and Eagle wait there
> The Lion tis true, Sirs,
> In homage to you, Sirs,
> As Lord of the Land and the Eagle of the Ayr
> To the Clothworkers' glory their Fealty bear.

The Thistle, the Clothworkers' Servant so kind
Long glit'ring in Gold in their Scutcheon has shin'd
The Thistle tis true, Sirs,
To give her her due, Sirs,
With the fair English Rose, both of Royal Renown
To the Clothworkers' Honour, the Thistle and Crown.

Since Fortune's but Whele and the great Book of Doom
With Life but a Thread is the work of the Loom
The Fates those dire Sisters
Our Destiny Twisters
Tis Clothworking all. For Living or Dead
Tis he's only blest that spins a fair Thread.

As the Lord Mayor's shows had declined in their quality as literature, so had their splendour in design increased. Sorry stuff though the versification might be, the ingenuity of the setting was now of primary importance to the spectator.

It was the last of the great shows which the Company had staged during the seventeenth century and perhaps the pageant of Apollo was truly symbolical of the Clothworkers. The days of religious persecution, of forced loans, of usurpation by the Crown, of Civil War, of Revolution, of interference by the State – all of these, for the moment at any rate, were things of the past. Before their eyes, as in the pageant, the eighteenth century – not seen before – was rising, and 'all its beams were richly bright with gold'.

CHAPTER TEN

THE CONSTITUTIONAL CRISIS

* *
*

BRIGHT though the prospects of the new century were for the Company, for the chronicler the results were at first dull and of lamentably little interest.

1702   In 1702 there was a dispute, evidently about bad workmanship, between the master workmen and the journeymen. The complaints were to be investigated and punishment meted out where punishment was due. But it was nearly the end of the Company's concern over workmanship, good or bad. The Court were even then beginning to be uncertain of their powers: the Clerk was instructed 'to investigate the Statutes in force for the good manufacture of Cloth and to find how far the Company is empowered to prevent bad workmanship'.

But, apart from this, the Company, secure and at last unmolested, settled down uneventfully to the everyday business of administering their estates. From the outside world came little to disturb the calm; a day of thanksgiving for some such occasion as 'the late signal victory over the French and Bavarians in the valley of Hochstett', the accounts of the ravages of 'a great dreadful wind' – these were almost all that break the year of carefully recorded details, of the granting of leases, the repairing of properties* and the distribution of alms.

Every now and again into the cold facts and hard figures there comes a flash of feeling that warms the heart with its humanity. On

---

* The barge was among properties repaired in 1709 and, in addition to larger repairs 'a new Horne to be put to ye Unicorne. Also a small bit of wood be put to amend the Ramms legg in the Stearne.'

18 January 1716 – in the middle of an extremely cold winter – twenty poor aged persons – ten men and ten widows, free of the Company, were admitted pensioners of 20s a year each.

This Court being afterwards moved with pity and compassion at the appearance of the great Age, Want and extreme necessity of such pensioners remaining after the above said Twenty were admitted . . . were pleased by a unanimous Vote to admit the remaining numbers of 35 poor pensioners.

This compassion that could, on the spur of the moment and at the sight of the distress of poor old derelicts who had miserably thought themselves passed over in the distribution, override the existing rules was charity in the very truest sense of the word. It was a charity that, in an England of which a German visitor of 1710 commented that Sunday observance was the only visible sign that the English were Christians at all,[1] and in a London 'of crime and turbulence and hard living',[2] tokened well of the Clothworkers' Company.

The lawlessness of the age had, in fact, crept into a sphere of the Company's interests, where perhaps it was least to be expected. Clandestine marriages had for a long time and for various reasons been a feature of the English scene – those taking place in the Fleet Prison being the most notorious. Suddenly in 1703, Mr Wild, the Reader at Lambe's Chapel, the Clothworkers' own benefice, 'was charged with Marrying persons without Licences or being asked in the Church'.

On being summoned before the Court 'he had little to say for himself' but because 'he had a Wife and a great charge of children' his offence was pardoned and he was allowed to continue in office after promising to be of good conduct and 'to keep a true and perfect register and enter all Marriages that he marries in the said chapel for the future'.

So much for the promises of the divine: in 1706 Mr Wild was again accused of marrying persons without licences or banns. Again he was permitted to continue under a bond for his good behaviour of £100. Two years later in 1708 came a letter from the Bishop of Gloucester setting forth that Mr. John Wild, this Company's reader at Lambe's Chapel takes such liberty there in Marrying as is Intolerable and that he is a Mighty Nuisance to his curates in taking their business of Marrying people of his parish of St. Giles, Cripplegate out of their hands and so wronging them of their dues and also that he marries without Banns or Licence as he pleaseth as appears by a Paper delivered to this Court which is of Mischevious Consequence. . . .

This charge was ardently brought by the Curates and there being no positive proof of the same it was left to further consideration.

In the meantime, Wild was ordered to produce the Register but, refusing to give it to the Beadle, he was summoned to produce it to the Court. On the day appointed, Mr John Wild failed to appear at all and was removed from his post.

For the time being all seemed to be well with the spiritual affairs of the Company when in 1709 there suddenly came the complaint from a Mr William Day – tenant of the Hall Cellars – that Mr Charles Badham, the new Reader at Lambe's Chapel, and George Wilson, the Clerk there, had 'married a Kinsman of his without a Licence or a Certificate of Banns Asked . . . '.

The pair duly appeared before the Court: Badham had little to say except that he had a licence that he took out at Doctors Commons after the ceremony, but, unfortunately, he was 'heartily sorry' he could not produce it, he must somewhere have mislaid it. George Wilson was content to say blankly that he knew nothing about the wedding and, in fact, was not there at the time – a defence which he stoutly maintained in spite of the fact that 'Edward Payne the person so married declared that the said Wilson came to him that morning to a public house near the Chapel and told him the Minister was ready'.

Both of them were there and then, on the spot, dismissed, and in their place was elected Reader Mr Richard Sticklethorp. For his better encouragement the Ten Commandments, the Lord's Prayer, and the Creed were set up in the Chapel.

The early rewards of his virtue were disappointingly small. The 'unlawful practice being left off there is but few Married there' in Lambe's Chapel. Whereas the former Readers had made 'their places very considerable by Marrying Clandestinely', it became necessary to increase Sticklethorp's salary by £6 13s 4d a year.

The tightening up of the laws against clandestine marriages, and their observance, was in fact symbolical of a religious revival that was taking place in the country.

'The Queen, the Duke of Marlborough, Several Army Officers. The Two Universities, Nobility, Gentry and Merchants' having given a lead, the Clothworkers gave £10 towards the erecting of an English Episcopal Church in Rotterdam, and later in 1735 came the 'Scheme to Reform the Irish'.

Under Royal Charter the Incorporated Society in Dublin for Promoting English Protestant Schools in Ireland had been formed

Scheme to Reform the Irish

as the only effectual means to convert the children of Popish Parents from the Errors of the Church of Rome by instilling into their Infant Minds the principles of our Holy Religion, likewise curing them of their Native Sloth and Idleness by inuring them early to work and labour especially in Husbandry, Gardening, improving and spreading the Linen Manufacture over the Kingdom.

To this project – which to a later age has a positively Swiftian cadence about it – the Clothworkers' subscribed £50. The Company were, in short, both spiritually and financially in a flourishing condition. Two-fifths of the whole of the British export trade consisted of cloth woven in England,[3] and the cloth trade was indeed, as Elkanah Settle had indicated, still of immense importance in the national economy.

The Company Flourish

The war against France and Spain in 1702 was largely dictated by the stern necessity of keeping the markets of the world open to English cloth. The taking of Gibraltar in 1704 was essential to maintain a free trade in the Mediterranean, for, not only was English cloth a very successful line of merchandise in that region, but also the oil used in its manufacture was brought back from southern Italy and Spain.

America and Russia were providing in the new century a growing market, and, in spite of the competition of silks from India (the only market where heavy English cloth was impossible to sell), the trade flourished and infinite pains were taken to protect it from foreign competition. This fear of foreign competition – even though the Spanish cloth industry had fallen into a decline and was now so nearly at an end that England imported Merino wool from the Peninsula and sold the finished cloth back to the Spaniards – led to such fantastic laws as the prohibition of sheep shearing within four miles of the coast lest the woollen raw material be smuggled overseas.

Smuggling wool out of the country had long been a matter of concern to the authorities. In 1695 'some persons' petitioned the Court of the Clothworkers 'to allow something towards the charge of setting out a vessel of force to suppress the Owlers* that carried away the English wool into France'. But the Court, 'conceiving it to be a national concern and therefore fit to be brought in Parliament would not intermeddle with that affair but dismissed the gentlemen.'

With the flourishing condition of trade the Company had money in its pocket both to spend and invest. The bargemaster was provided with a gold-laced hat, and, perhaps because the barge then looked a little shabby, a new barge was built at a cost of £230. In 1732 the Hall was 'repaired and Beautified' – a progress which involved taking down the bow window in the Great Parlour and pulling down the front of the Hall and rebuilding it straight with grey stock bricks, putting in sash windows and installing two 'lamp lights' at the Hall gate.

For investment the Clothworkers had chosen the South Sea South Company. By 1720, the year the bubble burst, they had £2,000 in Sea its funds; and, although they were arranging to realize £800 of Company that amount, it was not from any reasons of doubt in the soundness of the project.

Yet, in some mysterious way the Clothworkers seem to have avoided the maelstrom and ridden out the financial storm with complete unconcern: no mention is made of any losses in the South Sea Company, further investments in it are made without com-

*Owlers: persons or vessels engaged in the illegal exportation of wool or sheep from England.

LORD MAYOR'S DAY 1747

ment three times in 1723. By 1727 the Clothworkers owned £2,000 in South Sea Stock and £1,700 annuities in the same company.

As long as trade flourished, the craftsmen and artisans also flourished in a modest way. They worked long hours – fourteen hours a day was usual – and they formed the bridge between the rich and the poor of the City.[4] But the changes in industrial organization, such as the threat of the introduction of machinery into the methods of manufacture, the spread of uncontrolled entry into the labour market and the general slow decay of the guild system, kept them in a state of anxiety for the future, a state of anxiety that made them react quickly to any threats to their status and 'to combine in order to insist on their rights under Tudor industrial legislation'.

This instability was a feature which had to be reckoned with in London politics: it gave the artisans an importance which had to be recognized.

It was at the request of the Yeomanry, showing a change of attitude that was quite startling, that a Court Committee was formed and promoted an 'Act for Liberty to Export White Cloth paying a small duty of 5/- per Cloth which otherwise would be very prejudicial to trade'. Then the Yeomanry complained that Clothworkers free of the Merchant Taylors were taking off and setting cloths on the tenters on Sunday and the Court agreed to secure the punishment of the offenders.

Next the artisan clothworkers successfully asked the Court to petition Parliament against the wearing of calicoes. The Court in turn, in 1717, appointed a Committee to inspect the constitution of the Yeomanry:* the Committee reported: 'We find the Wardens and Assistants of the Yeomanry have been constituted by the

The
Usefulness
of the
Yeomanry
1717

* The Court, at the same time, took a critical look at its own affairs; attendance had been bad; 'Gentlemen have not given their constant attendance according to their several summons'. To encourage good time-keeping an allowance of 2s 6d would be paid to the Master and the first two of the four Wardens and the first twelve Assistants 'to appear in the Court Room after the hour appointed in the Summons and . . . to give their attendance the whole time the Court is sitting'. On Quarter Days and the days of Special Courts, the Master, if more than half an hour late, was to forfeit his half-crown.

Company and continued time out of mind. And have always been serviceable in promoting the Benefit and Advantage of the Working Trade.' The Committee were of the opinion 'that the Yeomanry are useful in going Searches and Collecting quarterage for which the Company have made them some allowances. And that the election of Wardens of the Yeomanry be continued in the same manner as they were by Ancient Custom.'

The Yeomanry, confirmed in office and in power, continued their searches. The results of their efforts were numerous. Mr Josiah Byfield, for instance,

being summoned at the complaint of the Yeomanry for not sending into the Hall a Cloth seized in his hands appeared and submitted to the fine. And humbly desired the Court would take into consideration and restrain the Wardens of the Yeomanry from seizing coarse Yorkshire Cloth which hath lately much damaged the City Trade and caused the work to be done in the Country. . . .

Mr Jonathan Cordingby, too, had failed to send in his cloths seized for bad workmanship but 'the Court being acquainted that the Cloths were of a low price for the Russian Trade and in haste for Shipping were pleased for this time to remit the fine, but to be no precedent . . . .'.

Imbued with this new sense of their own political importance, it was probably inevitable that a clash should come between the Journeymen and the ruling members of the Company. This clash proved to be no mere internal dispute of minor interest. In the history of the constitution of the Company it was of monumental importance. It marked the end of the medieval ranks of the Clothworkers: from it there sprang a new and reorganized Company.

1739   On 24 October 1739 the storm which for six years had been gathering broke.

Some Ordinances were read to the Yeomanry of this Company and after the same were read as usual the late Upper Warden and other persons then present were pleased to complain of the great Hardships they laboured under in regard to the expenses of serving the office of Wardens in the Yeomanry, which to redress they insisted upon having such Privileges granted to them by this Court as they before had exhibited and now reassume and insist upon which if they refused they were determined not to choose persons to present to be Elected and confirmed by this Court as usually had been done.

They were acquainted by this Court that they could not conceive that they were laid under any Hardships by this Court, that what they Term'd so were the product of Emulation that had crept in and increased gradually amongst themselves of their own making and establishing and which they might easily remedy if they were minded so to do, they having been several Times advis'd so to do by this Court; that the large Expenses they complained of were the sole and voluntary Act of their Own and no constraint put upon them by this Court and that to grant the several particulars mentioned by them this Court could not comply with. For to admit of Innovations would be attended with no Service or Credit to this Company, but on the Contrary there would be the consequence of disturbing the Peace and Welfare of this Society as well as creating a Succession of perpetual Contentions. And therefore pronounced their demands unreasonable.

Which Reply, not being Satisfactory to them, moved Several of them to Vent uncommon insulting Expressions and that they would remedy themselves elsewhere, etc. and so withdrew.

The Court upon such indecent Behaviour, repugnant to and in Breach of the Ordinances, and upon further Debate of the Matter resolved (although proper persons were ordered to be summon'd for that Purpose) not to Elect Wardens of the Yeomanry which by the Ordinance Number 19 is in their sole Power, but was pleased to suspend the choice of Wardens and Leave the further consideration thereof to some subsequent Court, and Ordered that the Clerk should receive the Quarterage of such persons as should come to Bind and make Free Apprentices etc. and he to account for the same to this Court when demanded.

Business in spite of alterations was, in fact, to go on as usual. Searches, in the absence of any Yeomanry Wardens, were to be arranged, somehow, by the Master and Wardens. In the meantime, the Court had another look at their Charter for reassurance and 'also a Case was drawn . . . to be laid before the City Recorder, Mr. Solicitor-General Strange, for his opinion thereon and also to take Councillor Green's opinion, both which Opinions to be procured against the next Court'.

The Auditors, too, had been getting to work on the late Upper Warden of the Yeomanry's Accounts. They reported that

Mr. Thomas Reynolds the said Upper Warden appeared but thought proper to come unprepared and notwithstanding Arguments used, all Persuasions proved ineffectual, resolving not to make out an Account, pleading very Trifling Reasons to the Contrary, attempting to bear down Truth and Reason by the force of a matchless Assurance, the Auditors disavowing such his obstinate Proceedings as a Breach of his Affirmation (as well as By-Laws of the Company) and thought it advisable to order that he be summoned to the next Court to answer such his Contempt and obstinate Assurance as were never attempted or heard of before in this Company. . . .

The Court indignantly summoned Reynolds before them. On the day appointed for the Meeting he 'accordingly did attend at the Hall but thought fit to depart before the Court had an Opportunity to send for him in to answer his unprecedented Contempt'. By this time the spirit of unrest had infected the Under-Beadle-Informer, Richard Lawrence, whose 'Ill Conduct and Misbehaviour and almost total Neglect of Attendance' led to his dismissal.*

For a moment it looked as if strong action might lead to the ugly dispute fizzling out. New Wardens of the Yeomanry were elected and accepted office. The Court 'were pleased to recommend unto them Peace and Union and for them to Retrench the extravagant Expenses very lately so much complained of that have of late years crept in and gradually increased amongst such of the Commalty or Yeomanry as have from time to time been chosen to serve in the said capacity or office of Wardens of the Yeomanry'.

Richard Lawrence humbly asked to be reinstated but the Court decided that 'since the late unprecedented Behaviour and Pretences

---

* The same spirit was in evidence outside the Company. On the occasion of the Lord Mayor's Show in 1741, the Company's barge was damaged by a lighter, an accident ascribed by the Bargemaster in 1742 to the fault of the Watermen, 'many of them the last year being very unruly and unfit to be in the Barge and under no command of the Bargemaster which was a great Cause of the Accident that happened by the Lighter running foul of the Barge – much more so than want of skill in the steerage thereof'.

of the Late Wardens of the Yeomanry and others in Combination with them and upon the footing they now stand are continued such Officer may be laid aside'. In future there would be no separate Under-Beadle-Informer. Instead, the Under-Butler would become Under-Butler-Under-Beadle-Informer and, because his duties were greatly increased, would get a rise in salary.

As for Mr Thomas Reynolds, still stubbornly refusing to make up his accounts, he would be sued in the King's Bench and so would the man who had stood surety for him. But Reynolds, with considerable obstinacy, fought back. He brought an action in Chancery to obtain an injunction to stay the suit that the Company had brought in the King's Bench to recover the money in his hands. Subpoenas were issued wholesale. There was a great getting-together of Lawyers. High-mindedness marched firmly with economy and, for some reason, with a certain uneasiness about undesirable publicity. At first the omens for agreement were favourable; they showed

a forward Inclination to compose and finally Determine all Matters alleged. For which purpose and to promote so good a Work the Court debated the whole Affair and to show their Inclination to blind and secrete so imprudent a Combination and unjust Prosecution contrived and entered into by persons free of this Community who should be bound as much by Duty and Interest as by Oath, and as much by Inclination as either, to support and protect the whole Body and every Member thereof and to Abhor those things that may bring a Reproach or any way tend to its Destruction or Prejudice (as much as the Gentlemen of this Court can wish or endeavour or are bound by Oath or otherwise obliged to do for without some Laws – and them observed and Obeyed – no Community can long subsist) the said Court have Condescended [and] with the Advice of Counsel and Solicitor do hereby Agree for the Honour Peace and Welfare of this Company . . . to have a Meeting or Meetings . . . in order to have the Affair compromised.

At the next Court Meeting much more was declared in the same resounding terms: the 'Torrent of so unjust and vexatious a Prosecution' must be stopped and Mr Green, the Company's counsel, must get together with Mr Capper, counsel for Thomas

Reynolds, to stop it. To achieve this the Company were prepared to make concessions, they were 'compliable' and consented 'to have no more Elections made out of the Commonalty or Yeomanry to serve the Office of Wardens' and 'if the majority of those that had already served in that Office' were prepared to sign a petition for its abolition, then the Court would do away with it as it had already been done away with in other Companies. Moreover, any ex-Wardens of the Yeomanry who asked to do so and who were prepared to pay the livery fee (now reduced from £40 to £30) would be accepted on to the livery. What was more – and this was a concession indeed – if only Thomas Reynolds would behave himself and hand over his money to his successor, then the Company would 'consent to pay all Costs at Law and in Equity (subject to Taxation)'.

From the generous, perhaps too generous, offer it must seem that the Court were most anxious that Reynolds should not go into the witness box against them. With the lapse of time it has become impossible to judge of what it was that they were uneasy. In the meantime, the Yeomanry Wardens for the year 1741–2 were elected as usual, and the meetings to arrange a compromise were prosecuted with considerable vigour.

'For the sake of Peace' the ten Complainants – Reynolds and the nine others who had joined with him – were admitted to the livery. Reynolds was to pay over the balance of his account and there would be 'no more Elections of Wardens of the Yeomanry thereby to destroy all Complaints of Expenses in providing Quarterly Dinners, etc.'. Further, the Court gave the rebels 'Preference before Others as being served in the Office of Wardens for the Yeomanry of this Company and borne some Expenses in such Service', and in consideration of these expenses a by-law would be made to secure some reduction of their livery fine.

This handsome gesture was by no means well received. Doubtless, with the arrogant confidence of men who had clearly got their opponents on the run, eight of the ten men turned up at the meeting and all either refused point blank to come upon the Livery or asked to be excused. The Court, magnanimously resolved 'not to use any Compulsion but to Accept of their Refusals and to Excuse all of them accordingly . . . '.

Flushed with victory, the complainants began their suit in Chancery. All the Company's books were sent for to be inspected by the prying eyes of the lawyers. With calculated impiety the rebels themselves turned up at the Court meeting, demanding to inspect the books, and a scene unparalleled in the whole history of the Company took place.

After the Court had been sitting for some time Word was brought into Court by the Beadle that some of the Relators in the suit now depending were without and desired to be admitted into Court. Word was sent out that they should [be admitted] but that some Business was obliged to be first despatched, which taking more Time than was Agreeable to their Patience to wait, they sent in a Paper signed by them which contained several Demands of the Court (or 'pretended Court' as they were pleased to call it). . . .

On behalf of themselves and other Freemen of the Company they demanded a sight and inspection of revenue and estate books, the deeds and writings, the books relating to the application of rents and profits for the previous six and a half years. They demanded, too, an inspection of the charity accounts. They demanded the right to take copies of any documents and to have a list of the 'pretended Court'. This paper – which indicates how very far the dispute had gone from the original complaint of the expenses of taking office – was signed by Thomas Reynolds and five others. The Court read it and considered it and ordered 'a Short Reply to be drawn up proper as a Directory to the Master to make as an Answer . . . '.

Gentlemen,

We have given you all the Liberty of inspecting Deeds, Writings and Soforth according to Lord Chancellor's Orders and while the Suit is depending we can't comply with your demands, shall take Advice of Counsel and at present can't do any Thing without my Lord Chancellor's further Order and Directions.

If it was intended as the proverbially soft answer then it failed signally to turn away the wrath of the rebels. The Clerk was ordered to go out and acquaint the relators that the Court were ready to receive and hear them but, as the Court had been informed

that Mr. Cracraft, their Solicitor, was without, that they would not permit him to come in with them, Which enraged some of the Relators to declare that he should, especially Mr. William Cooper who seemed to be the Mouth and chief Ringleader of them, violently to utter many and passionate words, and that he should come in and had as much Right as they and insisted upon it. Which the Clerk returned Answer to the Court who desired and insisted that he might remain without but all to no purpose – all Persuasions were wind to them and to him too, and in they Rushed without any regard to decency or good Manners still insisting and taking with them this their said Solicitor, behaving in a very unbecoming manner to the Court, and in a very tumultuous and riotous manner. The Court still desiring Mr. Cracraft would please to withdraw and then they would be heard and regarded and that nothing could be done without Mr. Cracraft was also acquainted that he had no business there that they knew of, and strove to persuade him to withdraw, that then they should be heard and some Answer given them but all proved ineffectual.

In the Clamour it was Sayed by the Master, but whether took notice of by the Relators or their Solicitor is doubted: That nothing could be done in regard to their Demands without an Order from the Lord Chancellor.

And after much insulting the Court with very abusive and violent Expressions in utmost Contempt to all Rules, Government or common Decency [they] clamorously withdrew in Rage, Indignation and loud Threatening what they would do and departed the Hall after much Interruption and Disturbance to the Company's Affairs.

Which indecent and insulting behaviour exciting the Court's just Abhorrence and Resentment, accounted to be without Precedent, the Court was pleased to Order that the said signed Paper of Demands left behind them, together with an account of their Behaviour, should be delivered to Mr. Councillor Green for the best Use and Purposes he can make thereof. . . .

The rebels had indeed overstepped the mark. There were such things as laws against riotous assemblies and unlawful combinations. Once cooling-time had intervened (and in the calmer atmosphere of their own homes) there was, perhaps, the feeling that they had gone too far. At any rate it was from the relators that came the next attempt at concession: Reynolds, Cooper, and another were prepared in company with their counsel, Mr Capper, to meet any three of the Court with Mr Green 'to settle all outstanding disputes at one meeting'.

The Court replied stiffly that, in view of their recent behaviour, they would have nothing to do with them except in the Court of Chancery. The tactical balance had suddenly shifted on to the side of the Court. As a result of their unconstitutional behaviour the rebels suddenly found themselves, although technically the complainants, now on the defensive. There was considerable legal coming and going, an injunction of some kind was obtained against Reynolds, who was now offering 'to speed the Cause and bring no Writ of Error and to execute a Release of Errors'. But then the usual delays of the Law supervened: through 1743, 1744, and 1745 the case dragged on, the subject of a maze of legal ingenuity.

In 1745 there came a sudden dangerous turn to the case: an amended Bill of Information was put into the Law Court 'in particular in regard to the Management of Mr. Samuel Middlemore's Charity'. The Clothworkers were, however, not unduly dismayed since they 'apprehended [it] to have been justly performed by the Company although not to the express tenor of his will in regard to purchasing'.

And then, quite suddenly, the case collapsed; Thomas Reynolds made a stay of proceedings. He turned up one day at a Court meeting and said that the whole affair had gone on much longer than he had wished – he was prepared, at long last, to pay what was owing on his Warden's account. The Court agreed to settle the case. £47 10s was paid over. The books were to be returned, the costs of the case were to be settled at a later date. Thomas Reynolds went quietly away.

A very short while later he returned again with some of the other relators. Their submission was complete and absolute. They acknowledged their 'ill-advised' proceedings and submitted the question of costs and all other matters to the decision and final determination of the Court. All of them 'acknowledged their mistake and had for a long time been inclined and now more than ever disposed to suppress and put a Period to so ill-conceived and bad-advised a Prosecution'. The whole proceedings they added had been 'managed contrary to their inclination' and they asked, therefore, for clemency in the matter of costs. The costs were, indeed considerable. The rebels had involved themselves in an expenditure of £307, and the Company had run up a bill of £350. Reynolds, it was known, was a man of substance, but such an expenditure may well have contributed towards his decision to abandon proceedings which, after more than three years, still showed no signs of settlement.

Towards the costs of the case the rebels offered to pay £20. The Court refused so trifling an offer. The rebels offered £40. The Court made a counter-proposal of £100 to be paid into the Hall and 'all their papers to be delivered up to be kept as a Memorial For After Ages'. This was, in fact, the Court's minimum demand. To a repeated offer of £40 they again gave refusal, being quite determined to make Reynolds pay the £100 they were demanding.

At the next Court Thomas Reynolds handed in to the Hall his promissary note for £100. The revolt was over. Once again business could go on as usual: the first item on the agenda was a request from Thomas Reynolds for a gratuity in respect of a search for bad workmanship he had carried out, way back in 1739, when he had been Upper Warden of the Yeomanry – a gratuity that the Court, in their wisdom, were pleased to grant.

Whether this sudden collapse of the most serious revolt in the history of the Company was due to a lack of finance on the rebel side cannot be determined. Since that great and tumultuous scene in the Hall and the chilling reflections which must have followed it, the case had lost its drive. The first exhilarating rush of mob-passion ended – and how essentially ugly the scene had been – it was only the lawyers who could hope to benefit by dragging out a case in which many of the instigators had lost both heart and interest.

Yeomanry
Wardens
Abolished

In 1754 there came the culminating results of the momentous constitutional struggle: the Court took into their serious con-

sideration the necessity and utility of choosing four persons to be
Wardens for the Yeomanry or Freemen of this Company and
after

debating the matter and it not appearing to be essentially necessary to go
to any Election of such Wardens and thereby to avoid all pretensions of
Complaint of Attendances, Burthen and Charges in serving such Offices
(and for other reasons alleged) it is agreed and ordered that the Election
of Members to serve in such offices as Wardens of the Yeomanry be
discontinued.

* *
*

Towards the end of this crisis in the Company's affairs there had
come in 1745 a threat to the stability of the nation itself, a threat
which possibly helped to close the divided ranks of the Clothworkers, 'when a considerable number of traitorous and rebellious
persons in Arms have presumed in violation of our Laws to
assemble in the North West of Scotland and set up a Standard in the
name of the Pretender'. Members of the Company were warned
that they would be expected to sign 'a loyal and dutiful Association
for the Support of His Majesty and the Security of this Kingdom
against the Wicked Attempts of the Pretender and any foreign
Invasion'.

The response to this appeal was regrettably tepid: only half the
Company turned up to signify their loyalty. The Beadle was
hastily sent around to find out the reason for this state of affairs and
the Company subscribed £212 10s to a Winter Relief Fund for the
Army. Defeat of the invaders followed with a gratifying speed. The
Highlands were utterly conquered and gradually became a
picturesque wilderness. Though taxes were dangerously high, the
Company, their own private war satisfactorily concluded, settled
down with a balance of £453 in cash and £3,642 1s 7d in Bank and
South Sea Stock to cultivate their garden – and, incidentally, to
install at the lower end of it a new-fangled water seat in the necessary houses – and to administer their considerable estates.

CHAPTER ELEVEN

DOMESTIC INTERLUDES

*   *

*

THE years 1740–80, as Trevelyan points out,[1] were a brief interlude of peace 'between the religious fanaticisms of the past and the fanaticisms of class and race that were speedily to arise and dominate time to come. In England it was an age of aristocracy and liberty; of the rule of law and the absence of reform; of individual initiative and institutional decay...'. And although, materially speaking, the institution that was the Clothworkers' Company could not be said to decay – for it was more prosperous than ever – yet, with the abolition of the Yeomanry Wardens the end of its existence as a trade guild was very close at hand.* Soon the Company would have dissolved imperceptibly into a vestigial state, powerful and wealthy certainly, but no longer anything more than an organization which administered charities and estates and met on social occasions that but faintly reflected the glories of the past. There is, inevitably, a consequent lessening of the 'human interest' in the Company, a concentration upon the purely legal side of the business. What the Clothworkers gained in administrative ability, they lost in picturesqueness.

Trade Controls Weaken

But even though, with the improvements in communications that led to an increasingly effective competition from country workmen who were outside the guild system of organized labour and wages, the control over the trade was draining away from the

---

* Even the apprenticeship system was breaking down. Boys in 1773 were being bound to Masters without any intention of serving a proper apprenticeship but merely to qualify for admission to the freedom of Company and City. It was a state of affairs that must be stopped, ordered the Court. It was, they said, 'a growing evil'.

City Companies, the mid-eighteenth century saw many attempts to keep workers within the membership of the guilds that nominally represented them. In 1757, the Butchers' Company entered three *caveats* against Freemen Clothworkers to prevent them from taking the freedom of the City so long as they remained in the Clothworkers' Company. The three Freemen appealed to the Court: they did not wish to be translated to the Butchers' even though that was the trade in which they were engaged. 1757

The Court was of the opinion 'that there is much Greater Strength of Reason now to conceive what was the Opinion of their predecessors in 1657 that the Acts of Common Council then lately made against Binding and making free of other Handicrafts [members] of this Company, should not be repealed and made void as being contrary to the fundamental Laws of this Nation . . .'. They petitioned the Lord Mayor, therefore, that the three butchers should not 'be made free of the City in any other Company by Compulsion and Illegality'. Membership Problems

Of this case there remains no further trace. But in 1760 this constitutional issue occurred again and its implications were taken most seriously by the Company. The situation was the same. A butcher named William Cope, free of the Clothworkers' Company, asked to become free of the City of London. Acting 'upon pretence of a Custom not warranted or set out, or else by Virtue of a By-Law or Act of Common Council made in 1754 (and if not supported by Custom the same deemed a void By-Law)', the Butchers' Company entered a *caveat* against him doing so. This action, argued the Clothworkers' Company, would have the effect of depriving the man of the rights he had obtained by servitude to the Company in which he was bound after serving his apprenticeship' pursuant to Act of Parliament (and not of Common Council)'.

William Cope petitioned the Common Council but his petition was rejected and the Company decided to issue a writ of *mandamus* to get the matter heard in the King's Bench.

The Court being of the opinion for the future Peace and Quiet of this Company not to be continually disturbed by persons entitled to their Freedoms in this Company who by Trades may be Butchers, Cooks,

Upholsterers etc. and to put a stop to so modern a power and growing Evil of making (in restraint of Trade) such By-Laws lately made in favour of several inferior Companies (to the prejudice and Damage of the Twelve Chief and other Companies) of London besides this Company of Butchers; as Cooks, Bakers, Upholsterers, Cutlers, etc. that there appears to be inevitably an immediate necessity for this Case to be Argued in the King's Bench for the same to be adjudged.

Unfortunately for the peace and quiet, the King's Bench, when three years later, in 1763, the case came before its notice, decided that the Butchers' answer to the writ of *mandamus* was good and sufficient in law without any trial being held.

* *
*

Peace and quiet were, in the great outside world, also at a slight discount. There were wars and rumours of wars. One hundred pounds was voted towards clothing the Soldiers in Germany. Three hundred pounds was subscribed 'to support a just and necessary War undertaken in defence of the Rights and Privileges of His Majesty's Crown and for the Security of the Colonies, the Trade and Navigation of Great Britain'.

But, although the eventual loss of the American Colonies was to lead to a considerable disruption of trade, it no longer had the power to influence greatly the uneventful stream of the Company's existence, concerned as it was much more deeply with such matters as the Clothworkers' rights of Advowson in Derry – rights on which they insisted at Dunboe and Killowen, but which after years of litigation (during which the Bishop of Londonderry who opposed them behaved in the most exemplary and Christian manner by preventing them on several occasions from committing costly errors that would have inevitably there and then ended their case) concluded in an inconclusive but friendly compromise with both sides paying their own legal costs.

Decline in Feasting   Nearer home than Ireland times were changing. Although the eighteenth century has always been regarded as the hey-day of John Bull, whose familiar bucolic appearance was such a feature of contemporary caricature, there are signs that in the Clothworkers'

Company, at least, there was a falling-off from the gargantuan appetite that had built up that gross and complacent figure. In 1764, the Court ordered that

The Roast Beef and Mutton and Broth that have from time Immemorial been provided for as breakfasts for the Gentlemen of the Court of Assistants on the four Quarterly day Courts shall be laid aside and not continued any longer as superfluous and unnecessary and that only Coffee and Tea be provided which hath been found more acceptable and pleasing to a majority of the Court.*

In future, too, there was to be no further entertaining of the Court and their ladies with dinner and dancing on election days, but instead a dinner only for the Court and Livery.

Yet, out of Regard and Respect to the Ladys it is referred to the Master and Wardens to consider of some method and ways to effect and make things more agreeable to the Ladys, conceiving it may be so, for the Assistants and Ladys to have a Day of Pleasure in the Barge at a proper season in lieu of the Election Day, which became incommoding and very disagreeable by the Hall being crowded with strangers and others that had no Right to be admitted and for other reasons for laying aside as hath been prudently done in some of the other superior Companys.

This complaint of strangers invading the Hall was one of very long standing. For at least 150 years the Company had been trying at frequent intervals to limit entry to the Hall at a time of feasting and entertainment. In 1612 there had been trouble with 'unnecessary people' coming to the Hall: the porters were warned that

Strangers in the Hall

---

* Changes in diet were accompanied by changes in fashions. In 1764 it had been decided that the garments distributed to the poor in the charitable bequests should be improved. In future the old men were to go to the tailor to be measured for a surtout coat for which three yards of material were to be used. There were 106 men and the cost of making each coat was 7s 6d, quite apart from the cost of the material at 6s a yard. Each of the 106 old women was to be given 3s towards making her own gown with the fourteen yards of Cathinance to be supplied to her by the mercer at 1s 6d per yard of twenty inches width. But within only two years the Company decided that surtouts were an outmoded form of clothing even for poor old men. In future they were to be fitted out with close-bodied coats and waistcoats. Any ingrate caught selling these charitable gifts would be barred from future distributions.

they must do their job better. In particular the Beadle had been told not to bring his friends and neighbours to the Hall at times of assemblies. The rule had been made that, on election days, there should be no guests 'for the preventing of . . . pestering in the House with people unknown'.

In 1634, 'consideration being had of the great disorder used to be by the admission and letting in of Young men into the Hall to wait and attend upon their masters at feasts and dinners . . . ', a rule was made that no one except those who had been Wardens (or fined for wardenship) should have their servants to wait upon them.

In 1661 it was sourly reported that 'there hath been much abuse and disorder in this Hall on festival days by several persons that have been admitted into this Hall under pretence of being the Company's servants'. There should be closer control over tickets, the Court decided: but by 1697 no lasting solution had been found and a Committee was formed 'to consider of a way for the admission of persons into the Hall thereby to prevent a disorderly intrusion of any person that hath no right to come there on these (festive) Days'.

In 1731 the Hall was still crowded 'with Strangers and others with no right to be admitted on Election Days. In future every member of the Court should have a single ticket' to the entertainment of dancing only at 6 o'clock in the evening. But still the abuse continued and, even after the latest example in 1764, which caused the abandonment of the Ladies' Dinner, it was to occur again.

Restrictions on Liquor The 'other reasons for laying aside' the Ladies' Dinner, as had 'been prudently done in some of the other superior Companies', may only be guessed at. In that drunken age, it is possible that the scenes at Company Halls, thronged with strangers at time of entertainment, were sufficiently displeasing. Certainly, about this time, there appear to be attempts to restrict and certainly to control drinking. Regulations were made that included a complete ban on giving drink to the waiters at dinner. Even the sobersides on the Court found themselves the victims of a self-denying ordinance that, in future, 'before Court sits no wine to be dranked'. As for the Livery, in 1781 it became necessary to order 'that no Claret or Hock shall in future be drunk at Livery Dinners except by the Master, Wardens and Assistants in the Binding Room after Dinner; and no Madeira but at the Court Table at Dinner and afterwards in the Binding Room'. Of excursions in the Barge it was noted that 'the Distribution of Wine (according to the present Mode) ... is attended with considerable Inconvenience'. In future 'a pint of Lisbon [would] be given to every Liveryman who shall be in the Barge and that no other sort of Wine be had therein'.

The following year there was to be no Claret or Hock at or after Livery dinners, the Court were to retire to the Court Room and not to the Binding Room: reading between the lines, it may well be that the Liverymen of the Company were lacking in the elements of decorum which were, generally speaking, to distinguish them in the twentieth century, and for this reason the ladies of the Company had begun to find dinners at the Hall lacking in enjoyment.

With the general standard of behaviour in Hall somewhat irresponsible, it is hardly surprising that the Court began to worry about the risks of fire to their premises, the chimneys of which were continually catching alight in an alarming way. The Hall, certainly, was insured with the Hand-in-Hand Insurance Office. But after a member of the Court had lost everything in a great fire, in 1765, in Cornhill and Bishopsgate, and had been temporarily accommodated in part of the Hall, the Court, with this pitiful example before them, began to worry about finding a safe place for the charters and documents, the plate and the valuables. The advisability was discussed of having 'a large Cistern or Reservoir upon some part of the Hall which it [was] apprehended would prove of great benefit in case of Fire'. *Precautions Against Fire*

With such thoughts in mind, the refusal to subscribe to the sufferers from a great fire in Barbados may have seemed to some members to be asking for a visitation upon them: at any rate, they gave next year £100 to the sufferers from fire in Antigua, £50 to the sufferers from fire in Basterre, St Christopher's, and – at the request of Barlow Trecothick – £50 for the sufferers from fire in St George, Granada.

The Hall, in any case, was not as commodious as it might have
been. In both 1768 and 1773 considerable rebuilding and re-
decorating took place. New furniture for the Hall was to be
supplied by Liveryman Francis Pyner and while the alterations
were taking place the Company dined at the London Tavern.

In such pleasant domestic pursuits did the Court pass their time.
There was a moment in 1771 when the Company found themselves momentarily in financial low water. Their money was all in
'the funds' and in South Sea Stock. These were standing at such a
low figure that to sell any stock to meet their immediate needs
would have meant a severe loss. For this reason, then, they
borrowed £700 from the Master and asked the Merchant Taylors
to accept their share of the dividends from the Irish estates in instalments. But this setback was short-lasted. Within a few months
their stocks had risen to what they had paid for them and they sold
£1,400 of 'the funds' to settle the Merchant Taylors' Irish accounts
without more ado.

Irish Lands   The Irish problem was to the fore again: once more, as a result
of the poverty of the Irish, the tenant, Jackson, was having difficulties in raising his rent for the Company. The Clothworkers were
sympathetic but, replied that as Trustees, they were afraid they
could not be of much help to him. However they bid him be of
good heart for, no doubt, things would mend in a few months.
To this cheerful letter of encouragement, Jackson replied in
tones of the deepest gloom: he saw no likelihood of things improving and added the sinister warning that he feared 'there is
something deeper and more alarming in it than they are aware of'.

The following year he wrote to say that really it was impossible
to make a success of the estates in Ireland. He sent the Court a copy
of his rent roll for their inspection. If the Company could not see
their way to do anything about his proposals, which were lengthy
and involved, then he would be forced, reluctantly, to give up his
lease. If Jackson thought that this threat would be a powerful one,
he had misjudged the temper of the Court: after taking counsel's
opinion, they wrote him a 'spirited letter', refusing his proposals
and demanding arrears of rent. Greatly nonplussed and, indeed,

alarmed by the turn of events, Jackson hurried over to London to see the Court – a gesture which paid him the considerable dividend of gaining a reduction of the amount due from him and thereby saving him 'from utter ruin and Gaol'.

In such ways, with skill and good judgement and in a great calm, the daily business of the Company – and not even requests from the Lord Mayor for money to defray 'the expenses of the late Tumults' could disturb them – was conducted and flourished.

In 1781, however, a matter arose that, while of no great national importance, could not be tolerated by an efficient administration. It was a matter, too, that seemed almost incapable of solution. 1781

The Company had sent down to Sutton Valence in Kent a party of visitors to inspect the Free Grammar School there, the school administered by the Company under the terms of the will of William Lambe for some two hundred years. The visitors were Sutton Valence

sorry to inform the Court that the 'foresaid school, one of the earliest Institutions of its kind in this Kingdom, founded and endowed in the dawn of Reformation for the sole purpose of removing the Ignorance of those Times and bestowing a liberal Education on the then and future rising generation and which has by a later Donation had the benefit of sending two Scholars to St. John's College in Cambridge with Exhibitions of £10 a Year, to be paid to them by the said College, no longer answers the public spirited Intention of its worthy founder, there being no boys now sent to it to receive such Education as he had planned for them, and that there were nine Boys now in the School and they only instructed in reading English, in writing and in the first and most common Rules of Arithmetic so that the School has become a mere Sinecure to the Master, the Business of it, such as it is, being transferred to the Usher and he of very Inferior Abilities. That notwithstanding such true Account of the low State the School is now in they (the Committee) were of the Opinion that during the Life of the present Master, who is very infirm, nothing could be done to put Things on a better footing or making such a Reformation as is greatly wanted and much to be wished; tho' it would likely be impossible ever to bring the School again to answer the design of Mr. Lambe, so many nurseries of Education everywhere now abounding throughout the Kingdom.

However, when a fair opportunity should offer they recommended to the Company to take the Matter into serious consideration and to do all in their power to make the School more Beneficial to the Neighbourhood and, as far as possible, still a Credit to its worthy founder and his Trustees. . . .

And here it may be convenient to take a swift backward glance at the history of the School as the Clothworkers' Company had seen it.

*   *

*

It is fairly safe to hazard that, when Mr William Lambe of his beneficence humbly besought Queen Elizabeth in 1576 to 'vouchsafe to be erected and established a Grammar School for the good education and instruction of boys and youths in Sutton Valence', no thought crossed his mind – nor the minds of the Court – of the chequered events that were to follow the gift. Founded perhaps under some sort of mischievous omen that led the charter clerk to describe those who were to be Governors of the School, after the death of the worthy founder, as the 'Master and Wardens . . . of the Art or Mystery of Slothworkers', the School since its inception had provided its Trustees with an endless succession of incidents both undignified and unseemly.

Schoolmasters were appointed and dismissed with a disheartening regularity. The reasons for their departure were many and varied. Of Robert Sharpe the townsfolk of Sutton Valence complained, in 1591, that not only did he continually absent himself from the School but that he haunted taverns. But his eventual dismissal in 1608 was 'from want of sight and other infirmities'.

No reason was recorded for the sudden dismissal in 1622 of Job Davenport, but his successor Edward Pensax was, in 1640, charged

with neglect of his duty in the due execution of his place whereby the School is out of request and the County disheartened to bring their children thither to be taught. He confessed that there had been a necessitated but not a voluntary neglect and that the same was occasioned by reason of his present poverty, He being much in debt. And that he was now minded to bend his studies and endeavours to some other way.

Thomas Philpot, who followed him, faced a scene of hopeless decay with which he was quite incapable of coping. In 1644 came the inevitable complaints that he did not 'demean himself as he ought'. He had, it appeared, 'broken the heads of one or more of his Scholars which hath caused the Parishioners to keep their children from School'.

The end, for Thomas Philpot came, the next year when it was reported of him that he

is so drunken and in his drink so silly and so simple in his carriage and conversation that those few scholars that he hath jeer him to his face and may sooner learn anything than what they ought. And that is the only cause why the school is not frequented and that the inhabitants are forced to send their children elsewhere. And that of late the said Philpot hath carried himself very ill towards the inhabitants, railing on them because they will not set their hands on his behalf. That he hath very little attended the School of late and hath shut up the School doors and excluded both the Usher and the Scholars.

In between outgoing and incoming schoolmasters the Clerk would 'ride down into Sutton Valence, take possession, lock up the doors of the said School and Schoolhouse and bring the key thereof to this Board until such time as they shall make some choice of some other to execute the said place'. The School would remain shuttered and closed. Soon it became a matter of difficulty to find a qualified schoolmaster ready to take over the reformation of the School. Henry Bradshaw, for example, found that he could not 'take upon him the said place without incurring the displeasure of some of his best friends'. His successor, Thomas Carter, finding the inhabitants of Sutton Valence 'unwilling to have their children taught in the Latin tongue it did much discourage him to spend his labour there', after one short year resigned.

In 1658 the next schoolmaster, Samuel Garrard, was dismissed because 'of the decay of the School and discontent of the Inhabitants'. There followed a period of comparative calm which ended with the dismissal, in 1677, of Richard Nichols for a rather novel reason. Not only was he accused of being negligent in his duties and scandalous in his behaviour but he had appointed an Usher who practises the Law as an Attorney, setting the neighbours at variance, one with the other, by encouraging the differences amongst them which will undoubtedly bring them all to beggary by which means the reputation of the School is lost, no person in the County being willing to send their children to board either at the School or in the Town as formerly they have done.

The run of ill fortune with the schoolmasters of Sutton Valence seemed endless. When after much deliberation and checking of references John Peveril was appointed by the Court to succeed Nichols it was found that he 'had presented them with a Certificate of his Marriage which, since their return home, they had found to be false and counterfeit'.

So the sad tale continued. If the schoolmaster was found to be sufficient it was the inhabitants who then were lacking in co-operation. So continuously did they complain that the teaching of Latin was superfluous that, in 1685, the Court agreed rather disparagingly that, 'the Inhabitants being for the most part mean people and not able to breed their children to be Scholars', English should be taught so that children 'may be fitted for Trade and other Civil Employs'.

From thenceforth the School settled down to a period of peace between inhabitants and schoolmaster. If there was no great degree of success attendant upon the venture there was, at any rate, no great scandal either. But all through the uneventful years there must have been the same neglect from within, and lack of support from the townsfolk without, gnawing away at the foundations of the school's prosperity.

In 1736 for example the Reverend Culpeper Savage, accused of 'Neglect of instructing the Scholars' complained that the 'Parents were very negligent in keeping their Children constant to School'.

A further succession of schoolmasters came and went until with the appointment in 1746 of the Reverend Joseph Hardy the Clothworkers' troubles seemed to be at an end. For twenty years no breath of scandal was heard from the censorious inhabitants of Sutton Valence. There were a few complaints about the usher but nothing came of them and – except for a surprise visit in 1767 when a committee of visitors had found only sixteen boys at work (though all of a tender age, they were very promising), the rest being out haymaking for their parents or kept away by the small-pox – there was nothing to prepare the Court for the blow which had now, in 1781, after two hundred years of an existence that could hardly be held to have justified the pious generosity of Mr William Lambe, again fallen unexpectedly upon them.

*   *
*

Those who thought at this moment that the Free Grammar School at Sutton Valence was for ever finished were reckoning without the stubborn determination of its trustees. They acted slowly but they acted surely. In 1784 another visitation descended upon the School to make a report. Upon their arrival the visitors were told by the Reverend Joseph Hardy that there were fifteen boys in the School upon the Foundation but, upon their proceeding to take an account of such boys, he and the usher together could only furnish them with the names of eleven. 'And upon inspecting the writing Books of such as were taught to write, they found two Books of Boys who were then absent, one of which they had not been writ in for above three months past and the other since the year 1781.' What was more,

Instead of finding the School room kept in cleanly Order and make a decent Appearance the visitors were not a little surprised to see it made, and that without the least Necessity, a Thoroughfare to the Master's House; and one side of it nearly filled with Faggots belonging to the Usher and other Lumber – improprieties which it is scarcely necessary to limn should be immediately rectified.

The Company, it seemed, were spending £65 a year – more than £30 in excess of the Founder's provision – on having ten or twelve little boys 'from 7 to 14 years of age, taught by the Usher only, reading English, writing and the first Rules in Arithmetic; and those Boys, few in Number as they be, are suffered to be absent from the School as much as they please'. This state of affairs had been going on for thirty-seven years. The usher, the visitors noted without surprise or disapproval, 'previous to his Appointment by Mr. Hardy, followed the Trade of Shoemaker'. But, they added, he 'writes a tolerable good hand, appears to be pretty well qualified to teach such boys as now attend the School . . . and is well spoken of by the Inhabitants of the Town'.

What was to be done? The visitors concluded reluctantly that 'the Age, Infirmities and Habits of the Present Master totally exclude the idea of his co-operating in any Plan of Regulation', but that, after he had been disposed of great reforms could be made.

The excellent Situation of the School in a Healthy and Pleasant part of the Country – a commodious Dwelling House for the Master, well adapted to the reception of Boarders and contiguous to and communi-cating with the School which is a large and spacious Room – A most delightful hanging Garden behind the School – the Privilege of sending two Boys . . . to St. John's College with Exhibitions of £10 per year are collectively taken circumstances and Things which clearly bespeak the practicability of re-establishing a reputable and respectable Seminary of Classical and useful Learning.

1787   A visitation in 1787 reported that under the Headmastership of the Reverend John Griffin they had

the pleasing satisfaction to see that ancient Seminary of Classical Learn-ing rapidly emerging from the deplorable Obscurity into which for a considerable time past it had been unfortunately sunk and wearing an Aspect quite the reverse to what had been seen before.

The School had a respectable appearance, the two dozen boys upon the Foundation were getting on fast, 'it was with pleasure found that the Principal Farmers and Tradespeople in the Neigh-bourhood, sensible of the Alteration . . . were become anxious of having their Sons admitted to the Foundation'. So pleased were the Court at this report that they gave to Mr Griffin a gratuity of £100 as a 'Testimony of the Court's Approbation of his Conduct and to enable him the better to Support his Credit during the Infancy of his Undertaking'.

The disillusion that followed was all the more bitter for this first wave of enthusiasm. Five hundred pounds had been spent on repairs to the School when Mr Griffin asked for a loan of £150 to enable him to discharge his debts. Taking into consideration the heavy expenses they had had with the School and finding 'that upon some Inquiries having recently been made concerning the state of the School there appeared no prospect of Mr. Griffin's succeeding in it', they refused his request.

The Reverend John Griffin resigned and, tired perhaps of an endless succession of unsatisfactory clergymen, the Court elected as his successor a gentleman, John Bridgland. But even here they were unlucky in their choice: within a few months of taking office he died.

The whole thing was a great disappointment to the Cloth-workers and it is little wonder that there came a slight falling-off in their enthusiasm for and belief in the prospects of eventually completing the reformation of the Free Grammar School of William Lambe.

* *
*

Revolutionary Influences

The last years of the eighteenth century were years in which the influences of the French Revolution made a profound and lasting impact upon British political thought. There was now no longer any doubt in the minds of anyone 'as to the strength of the middle and lower classes and their capacity to achieve political dictatorship by violent and revolutionary methods'.[2] And, had the Clothworkers' Company now retained any semblance of control over the working elements of the trade, it is certain that there would have been scenes even more distasteful than those recorded in the early political struggles within the Company. But the Company had now to all intents and purposes totally lost the character of a trade society. Since 1754 – a date by which it had, in any case, become no more than a formality – the appointment of searchers had been abandoned.

Arbitration, too, had ceased for there was no longer the power to enforce arbitration and, as has elsewhere been noted, arbitration was already only accepted by the party to whom it was agreeable.*

Reform was everywhere in the air and with it enthusiasm for the purification of the institutions of government. In *The Rights of Man* Thomas Paine had proclaimed the necessity for universal suffrage and the sovereignty of the people, a doctrine received with much popular enthusiasm. This enthusiasm took the form, in the Clothworkers' Company, of the sudden serving in 1784 of a writ of *Quo Warranto* upon Samuel Knight to show by what authority he held the post of Master. Two members of the Company – John Scaber and James Andrews – were the signatories of an affidavit in support of this writ but the feeling of the majority of the Company was against them. Some of the Liverymen early in 1785 asked for a meeting 'to take into Consideration the Proceedings of some Individuals of the Company' and on 9 March a Common Hall of Liverymen took place. It was there resolved by a large majority in each case that proceedings had been taken without approval of the Livery, that although the action purported to be one in support of the rights and liberties of the Company it was, in fact inimical to them, and that the current method of electing the officers of the Company conformed to the ancient usage.

Clearly, then, the attempt was – as it had been in 1614 – one to widen the scope of the elections within the Company. This time, however, there was no need to refute heresy by quotations from Holy Writ. The Livery, as a whole, were determined to support the Master and Court in the matter. When a written paper, which contained proposals of accommodation, was put before the Court by 'The Committee for conducting the prosecution against the present Master of the Clothworkers' Company', the Livery formed a counter-committee to help the Court to fight a case which had 'a direct tendency to destroy the ancient and approved usage and Customs of the Company'. Faced by this depressing lack of sup-

Margin notes:
1784

1785

Attempts to achieve Rights of Election

---

* Only in one respect did the Company still continue to insist on any standards of workmanship. As late as 1819 a Committee decided that to be an artisan Cloth-worker 'it is indispensably necessary . . . to wet out or damp the cloth in the Stocks, then put it over the Porch and rough it sufficiently with card or Teazle, then set it and afterward shear it by hand or frame with the Broad Shears and to finish the process by plaining or pressing it'.

port, the rebels' case fizzled damply out. No more is heard of it, and the only reminder of the attempt comes in 1800 when James Andrews resigned the Livery and became one of the Company's tackle porters.

But, all the same, there was in the land so wide-spread a spirit of revolutionary thought that, when the events in France terminated in the execution of the French King, it was thought by the Cloth-workers to be both necessary and desirable to summon a Common Hall of the Company to 'consider the Expediency of a Declaration being made by them at this critical Juncture expressive of their firm Attachment to the excellent Constitution of this Country as consisting of King, Lords and Commons'. The Common Hall

Resolved Unanimously that at this Juncture when divers evil minded Persons are industriously circulating Seditious Publications and pro-pagating Opinions with a view to alienate the Affections of the People from their Sovereign and render them disaffected to the Constitution and Government of their Country we consider it a Duty indispensably incumbent on us to make a public Declaration of our Sentiments and Intentions on such an emergent Occasion.

This loyal declaration affirmed that

We . . . animated with Loyalty to our King and inspired with a sacred veneration for the Constitution of this Country as it was acknowledged and confirmed at the glorious Revolution of 1688 and holding in detestation and abhorrence the nefarious attempts which are being made to infuse into the public mind a spirit of Discontent and Dis-loyalty and to disseminate doctrines subversive of our fundamental Laws and Liberties Do Solemnly declare we are fully convinced that in the present we enjoy a most happy Constitution of King, Lords and Commons, and that we will steadfastly persevere in our Allegiance to His Majesty and in every respect to the utmost of our Power support the established Government of this Kingdom.

There were 116 signatures.

* *
*

The country was now well launched into the wars that Pitt had so optimistically hoped to avoid. The Company, worth at the time

£17,641, busied themselves on providing money and comforts for the troops. Extra clothing was provided for the soldiers in Germany and sympathetic consideration given to the 'General United Society for Supplying the British Troops on the Continent and The Seamen in the Navy with Extra Clothing'. The course of the war was at first entirely disastrous. The very inclement weather noted in the Minutes had led to the freezing of the dykes and canals in Holland and a devastating defeat of the British forces there.

Discontent   Defeat in Europe, disaster in the West Indies, loss of markets, bad harvests at home, all led enormously to the discontent in England. Owing to the alarming scarcity of provisions, and particularly of wheat, 'all the Company's Dinners were for the time being discontinued' and one hundred guineas distributed among the poor members. In Ireland, where a rebellion was brewing – it was subsequently put down with appalling brutality – the tenant, Mr Jackson, had died leaving debts of more than £9,500; the Company were having great difficulty in recovering anything from his Executors.

Sutton   In fact, the sole bright spot in a scene of great gloom was the
Valence   school at Sutton Valence which, 'in spite of setbacks occasioned by the Reverse (as they had found to their mortification after all their fair hopes) that unfortunately took place in Griffin's conduct . . . and by the untimely death of Bridgland', was now, under the leadership of Mr John Ismay, for the moment flourishing.

1797   In 1797, however, the endless tale of defeat was dramatically broken by Admiral Duncan's victory over the Dutch at Camperdown – a victory which caused immense relief to the public. But a suggestion that one hundred guineas should be subscribed 'for the Relief of the Widows and Children of the brave Men who so nobly fought and fell in the service of their King and Country and of such as have been wounded in the glorious Action off the Coast of Holland' was not proceeded with.

England had narrowly avoided complete financial collapse by daring innovations such as the tax on incomes – the Company's
Economic   payment that first year of Income Tax was £400 – which had
Difficulties   raised the money to carry on the war more successfully. The price

of bread and other provisions was still high and a subscription had to be raised to give relief to the industrious poor. As the eighteenth century drew to its troubled end, although defeat had been staved off entirely as a result of sea power, the figure of Napoleon still darkened the horizon not less menacingly than any of the twentieth-century dictators, for 'there was nothing but half-trained half-armed Volunteers to march against the finest General and the greatest army Europe had yet seen'.[3]

This bogy was not to be finally laid for fifteen years, years during which the Company passed a life in which the ordinary everyday pursuits went on interspersed by the additional irritating demands that came inevitably from a war. The granting of a subscription of £25 to the 'General Sea Bathing Infirmary' was followed by a vote of £300 to the 'Patriotic Fund at Lloyds Coffee House'.

The preparations for the Lord Mayor's Show of 1803 – which, exclusive of wine, cost nearly £200 – was followed by two refusals to subscribe to the 'River Fencibles of the City'. Reports of a tiresome setback in the prosperity of Sutton Valence, where it was found, *inter alia*, that no progress had been made in learning (some writing books had for months not been made any use of), were interspersed in the Minutes with demands for subscriptions such as for the '9th Regiment of Loyal London Volunteers'.

Moreover the Company were going through one of those periods when money was uncomfortably short. Though there was sufficient money invested in the funds, the yearly excess of expenditure over income amounted to £150. No doubt the state of their finances somewhat affected the preparations for the Lord Mayor's Show which indicate all too clearly how that pageant had fallen away from the somewhat exotic graces it had displayed a century earlier. Forty metal shields (not to cost more than 9s each), a banner (not exceeding 14 guineas); gowns and bonnets for the band of pensioners carrying the cheap metal shields in the procession (10s); the West London Militia's band of music (sixteen pieces in their regimentals); the barge★ lent by kind permission of the Phoenix Insurance Company – no doubt it all, especially the glass coaches

Lord Mayor's Show

★ The Company's own barge, decayed and useless, had been sold in 1799.

199

for the Court, made a fine show, but it already bore upon it the imprints of the pallid hand that by the twentieth century had reduced the pageants from 'stately Representations of Poetical Deities, sitting and standing in great splendour on several Scenes in proper Shapes with pertinent speeches, jocular songs (sung by the City Musick) and Pastoral Dancing'[4] to floats representing the Women's Institute or the Land Army in khaki mackintoshes.

Certainly it was lack of money that led to orders being given that 'during the continuance of the Property Tax the Use of Hock and Claret at the Court Dinners be discontinued'. In spite of the order for Retrenchment, 'in compliance with the Wishes of several of the [Court] Members' at the next dinner the Master 'had permitted some of the Hock and Claret remaining in the Company's vault to be used: which was approved and it was ordered that the Remainder of such Wines may be used at Court Dinners'.*

But the Company, though hard up, were still able by means of their charities and their own self-denying ordinances to support exhibitioners (such as Thomas Barnes, afterwards the great editor 1808 of *The Times*) at the University, and gradually, by retrenchment and clever investment, the balance of surplus income began to grow. By 1808 there was a surplus of £650, and although this fluctuated and the Company were frequently having to sell bonds to find ready money for every-day expenses, the position was considerably improved.

1810 By 1810 they were able to reject the offers of a commercial company to buy the Hall as 'inexpedient'. The next year there came the reminder that others too were in financial distress, that, in fact, the war was still going on. There were subscriptions to be found by Clothworkers for the 'Relief of the Sufferers in Portugal by the French Invasion' and for the 'Poor Suffering Inhabitants of the Different Governments of Russia through which the French Armies have passed in their late Invasion'. This last – the invasion of Russia – had they but known it, was a signal for the end of those

---

* The remainder, it was noted with approval, amounted to nine pipes of Port, one pipe of Lisbon, eleven dozen Madeira, twelve dozen Sherry, and three dozen Hock.

long years of war. Soon their subscriptions and their testimonials would be towards the celebrations of victory and of the beginning of a long period of peace. The presentation of the freedom of the Company to Lieutenant-General Sir Thomas Graham, 'in Approbation of his eminent and gallant services wherein he had displayed the most Consummate skill and valour on various memorable occasions in the Cause of his Country during the War in the Peninsula'. The 'Relief of Sufferers from the Battle of Waterloo' – a subscription for 'a Triumphal Column in Massive Plate of such Magnitude as to form a supplement to the shield of Wellington now executing . . .', those were subscriptions it was a pleasure to pay.

A pleasure, too, to have painted a portrait of the Clerk, Mr Giles Crompe, Senior, who was nearing his fiftieth year of service with the Company. The portrait – a reward of zeal and fidelity – was executed by a Mr Lane* 'who to give balance to the room where Mr. Crompe's portrait is to be hung is pleased to present the Company with a duplicate likeness of Lord Nelson' the same size as Mr Crompe's portrait. In this he was actuated by a wish to show gratitude for getting the commission from the Company. Not to be outdone in generosity, the Court gave Mr Lane an additional twenty guineas for his 'masterly performance'.

The wars were indeed nearing their end when, in 1814, the Court prepared to give a grand entertainment at the Hall to the Dukes of Kent and Sussex. The Master, Mr Samuel Favell,† and the 1814 Wardens, 'with a Military Band of Music were in the Lobby in the Hall to greet their Royal Highnesses who arrived a little after 3 o'clock and were conducted first into the Long Parlour and then up Stairs into the Court Room where they conversed with great Affability with the Lord Mayor'.

At half past four dinner was announced and they proceeded into A Great the great Hall, the Upper and Under Beadle leading the way with Entertainment

---

* Presumably either William Lane, 1746–1819, or Samuel Lane, 1780–1869. Neither was of the first rank though both exhibited in the Academy. Samuel was 'chiefly known for the accuracy of his likenesses: though wanting in the higher qualities of his art he had some distinguished sitters'.[5]

† See Appendix F.

their staves, 'the Royal Dukes supporting the Lord Mayor on their Arms, right and left. The tables were ornamented with Arches and Frames of Pastework and decorated with artificial Fruits and Flowers. The Dinner consisted of every Thing in Season; and the Wines were such only (Madeira and Port) as the Company use at their Entertainments at this Hall.'

There were many speeches, all subsequently reprinted, and a number of toasts, including one to 'the Emperor of Russia and our brave allies (Nine cheers). . . . In the course of the Entertainment several appropriate songs and glees were sung by the professional Singers and the whole concluded with the greatest Harmony and Satisfaction.'

In the century and a half that had elapsed since the eulogistic greeting in song of General Monk, nothing had been lost in the way of inappropriate flattery. Upon the health of the Prince Regent being drunk, a song called 'The Prince and Old England for Ever' was performed by Mr Taylor.[6]

Let Envy's dark Daemon unceasingly toil
Let the arrows of calumny fly
The South on their mischief looks down with a smile
His virtues their venom defy!

Like Anacreon of old, the Myrtle's soft power
With the Vine's purple branches he blends
No dull stupid maxims that bosom can sour
Who delights in his country and friends.

Let Britons rejoice in that fortunate hour
That gave birth to this favourite child
At which Envy and Tyranny only could lour
While Commerce and Liberty smil'd.

Now let each British bosom with rapturous glow
And effusions of joy rend the skies
For Fate has ordained him to heal all our woe
And the arts of our foes to despise.

This estimate of 'Prinny' was in later years to be challenged.

HALL AND COURTYARD, CIRCA 1820

CHAPTER TWELVE

A TIME OF TESTING

* *

*

THE Company now had a credit balance of more than £2,000 and settled down to the prospect of a prosperous and pleasantly uneventful period of their existence. The Irish estates occupied the greater part of their time and there was, too, a certain amount of difficulty over the administration of their charities. With the tendency of the period for investigation and reform and with the widespread popular view that the City Companies were misusing the money that 'properly belonged to the working classes', Parliament began to look a little narrowly into the whole question of the Corporate bodies of the country.

The matter was suddenly raised in 1819 and a Committee was formed to advise the Clerk in any future enquiries that might be made: it was Lady Anne Packington's Charity that was the first to be investigated. Dame Anne Packington had left, in 1559, her lands in Islington to the Company – lands upon which there were rents amounting to £16 6s 9d – and in 1823 proceedings in equity were taken against the Company. For, said the Vice-Chancellor, in 1825, 'they did not know the boundaries of the said Estate: nor did they keep any distinct account, or apply to the purposes directed more than £16. 6. 9. although the lands had increased in value', and were now worth some £440 a year. It was thought that on a true construction of the will the payment should be increased with the advance of rents and a scheme for the charitable redistribution of the increased amount was approved by the Court of Chancery.

The next to be investigated was Lute's Charity (1585) for lending money to young men and to honest householders. A bill was filed

Marginal notes: Charity Investigation · 1819

against the Company in 1832 by the Attorney General at the instance of two members of the Company, Thomas Spencer Hall and Effingham Wilson. The prevailing opinion in the Company was 'that the sums lent had been lent and lost (although proof thereof could not be established)'; and the Company, 'admitting that no sums had for the last twenty years been lent to freemen of the Company (and no application as it was stated having been made for the same)', a new fund was set up to revive the Charity.

Thomas Spencer Hall was not content to rest upon his laurels, and Effingham Wilson, as will shortly be seen, being otherwise engaged, he laid further information against the Company about Lese's and Middlemore's Charities. The Company thought, probably correctly, that the informations were 'vexatious and oppressive' – in the case of Middlemore's Charity at least, though the money bequeathed had, in the year of the Charity's creation, 1657, for some reason not been applied in the purchase of specified investments, the Charity had been secured in 1658 on another of the Company's own funds and had always been disbursed.

In order to avoid the expense of having to defend further vexatious actions, it was thought expedient to look into all those trusts by which trifling sums were to be lent to deserving young men. In some cases the trifling sums had been lent and lost, but to avoid any further unpleasantness the Company were prepared to set up again such trusts as those of Burnell, Heydon, and Stoddart. And, since the question of charities was now thoroughly stirred up, the Court investigated one or two of the other charities – Lambe's, for instance, and Blundell's.

In the case of Lambe's Charity the court found, somewhat to their dismay, that, although they held the Lambe estates upon condition that a service be held at Lambe's Chapel in the forenoon of Wednesdays, Fridays, and Sundays, such services had not for many years been held. In Blundell's Charity, when examined, there lurked the same dangers as were inherent in the Packington estate: the specified sum of £2 a year had been paid, perfectly correctly, to Bridewell, but the residue from the increased rents had gone into the general fund. That, too, was adjusted.

The same year the first Royal Commission was set up under Sir Francis Palgrave to enquire into the nature of the municipal corporations. Considerably less mischievous in its intent and scope than the commission that followed fifty years later, it is chiefly of interest in the history of the Clothworkers' Company for the evidence it provides of the difficulties encountered at the beginning of the nineteenth century by a Freeman of the Company who wished to be admitted to the Livery. In the great majority of Companies, upon payment of the required sum, admission to the Livery was fairly accessible to every Freeman. The Apothecaries and Stationers were exceptions and in the Clothworkers 'access to the Livery [was] guarded with a certain degree of jealousy'.

This jealousy, according to Mr Effingham Wilson (who has been noted above), had been carried to extremes in his own case. He had become a Freeman of the Company by birth and had taken up his Freedom in 1810. In 1812 he had made application to the Clerk of the Company with a view of becoming a Liveryman, in order that he might be qualified as a voter for the City of London. He was told, so he affirmed, though this was disputed, that he had no chance of success in getting on to the Livery unless he had some friend or acquaintance on the Court, and he was given a list of the members of the Court in order that he might canvass and exert himself amongst them for support.

The results of his canvassing were, to say the least, discouraging. For some years Mr Wilson gave up the attempt until a member of the Court urged him to try once more. Accordingly he again started to canvass and this time received the promised support of sixteen members, a fairly safe margin since it was necessary to receive eleven votes to be elected to the Livery. It was therefore doubly disappointing that at the election he only received five votes in all. After this, even though in his twenty-first year of being a Freeman the Master had himself urged him to come on the Livery and had promised him the support of the Court, he had never tried again, especially as the passing of the Reform Bill had given him the elective franchise without the necessity of coming on to the Livery.[1]

Exclusiveness of Livery

Allowance has to be made for the fact that Mr Wilson was now a bitter man with little love for his Company, but those who were called as witnesses for the Clothworkers spoke without rancour of themselves having had to canvass for anything from three to six years before they succeeded in being elected.

The exclusive nature of the Livery was, generally speaking, to prove for the Clothworkers' Company a most excellent thing. By the time the next Royal Commission sat, the Company had set its house in such order that it was expressly excluded from many of the criticisms levelled at the City Companies. The fact that membership was difficult to obtain made it the more highly prized, and the more highly prized it was the greater was the incentive to serve the Company well. It fostered an admirable feeling of solidarity among those who had finally achieved admission.

*　　*

*

Sutton Valence

The section of the Charity Commissioners investigating, in 1819, the charities for the education of the poor found no fault with Sutton Valence School, and, indeed, the Company were at first well satisfied with the Schoolmaster, Mr James Buckland. But by 1828, when the Company was becoming ever more deeply engaged in heart-searchings about its affairs, this satisfaction had turned to alarm. The numbers had again fallen away and there was considerable absenteeism among such scholars as remained. To make matters worse there had sprung up a rival day school run by a young man who had forty scholars paying ten shillings a quarter. The grammar school providing free education had only eighteen scholars. The Master had been disappointed by the falling away of his hopes of establishing a flourishing boarding school, and this disappointment, 'attended with the cares and difficulties of a numerous family had had an unhappy effect upon his temper so as to lead him to inflict severe and undue punishment in more than one instance thereby creating a prejudice very hurtful to the character of the School . . .'. For this reason, and in spite of the fact that Mr Buckland's morals were irreproachable and he taught writing in an establishment for young ladies in Sutton Valence 'of

1828

great respectability', the Court felt that there was nothing to be done but to remove him from his office: they appointed in his place Mr John Rugg, of High Wycombe – a step that was attended by the most gratifying results. By 1834 the number of foundationers (thirty) was complete and there was a waiting list of a dozen more. In addition there were twenty boarders and for the first time two ushers had to be engaged.

*　　*

*

The years 1819–36 were a time of testing for the Company. Three hundred years of accumulated tradition had inevitably collected with it a certain amount of lumber which, with the spring of the new century, the Company busied themselves in cleaning out and reforming. And in this great reformation the Company stumbled suddenly upon a horrid skeleton in a cupboard where they had least expected it.

The whole sorry business started simply enough, as such things will, when Mr Thomas Alsager, a Member of the Court, 'was besieged with applications by a poor woman who claimed an appointment to a pension of £5 as the relative of Mr. and Mrs. West which she stated to be in the gift of the Clothworkers' Company'. Mr Alsager had, as it happened, never heard of these pensions and asked the Clerk, Mr Giles Crompe, Junior (who in 1826 had succeeded to the position that his father had occupied with such fidelity for more than fifty-five years), for information on the subject. He was told that 'there were no funds applicable to such a purpose, or that if there had been they were all exhausted, or something of that effect'.

Not satisfied by this 'evasion', Mr Alsager moved the Court that the will of Mr and Mrs West be produced by the Clerk. 'The document was produced at the ensuing Court, but at so late a period of the proceedings as to render any investigation of the tenor of it out of the question.' Mr Alsager, now thoroughly aroused, received the permission he sought to investigate the matter personally. 'The document produced turned out to be not a will but a Trust Deed, most strictly binding upon the Company.' To his horror, upon inspecting the trust income, it became apparent that not only was a less sum than was therein directed being paid to the beneficiaries but that no audit had been held of the West Trust books for four years.

An Audit Committee, for that purpose, was at once convened and

at the first meeting...the Clerk absented himself, without any apology, or assigning any reason for so doing, which excited great suspicion, though they hesitated to express it, in the minds of all present. .... It would have been better perhaps to have instituted an enquiry at once into the general affairs of the Company, but it was hoped that the Clerk, as he must have seen the suspicion that was excited, would himself have made an effort to set them right, and the subject gradually dropped.

But others, beside Mr Thomas Alsager, were now suspicious. Two of the Wardens, in March 1836, expressed their dissatisfaction at the manner of taking the audit and

requested the Clerk to attend them and furnish such further explanations as appeared to them to be required. The Clerk on that occasion made a sort of cash account, than which nothing could be more crude and unsatisfactory, in which he admitted a balance as against himself of £1,198, which sum was not at the Bankers, and he declined producing any books or accounts whatever relative to Hobby's Charity, though he exhibited for the current year a balance in his favour under that Trust.

The news was so appalling that many of the Court were frankly incredulous:

Owing to the friendship and good opinion entertained of the Clerk by a majority of the Court, the Wardens were not able to extend the impression which they themselves had received and the time passed on without that further examination into the accounts which these circumstances obviously called for.

But in August 1836 Mr Thomas Alsager became Master and, with the encouragement of those who were increasingly aware of the position, the reformer, whose great services to the Company have perhaps been most undeservedly forgotten, swept into action.

Being desirous of avoiding all abruptness with the Clerk for I still shared in a certain degree the good opinion of him entertained by the Court, I addressed him a letter . . . in which I told him that there was a growing dissatisfaction with the accounts and pressed him to take the lead in originating such alterations as were required, engaging, in that case, to remain in the background and give him the whole credit of them. This suggestion was, by no means fairly and openly met. He evaded the question wholly at first: then promised to introduce it at the October Court, but suffered it to pass by, and in short convinced me by his conduct that I could not hope to make him a volunteer in this business.

Court orders were therefore made for an entirely new system of accounting to be introduced in time for the next audit in March 1837 but, in the meantime, the Clerk had died

and so entirely unimpaired was the confidence reposed in him up to that period that at a Special Court summoned on the occasion . . . every mark of respect was paid to his memory and his funeral was ordered to take place attended by the Master and Wardens and at the expense of the Company.

It is, indeed, not impossible that the Clerk was guilty of no more than being the victim of an antiquated and no longer efficient system of accountancy. It must be pointed out that no defalcations were ever actually proved against him.

The election of a new Clerk was deferred until the affairs of the Company had been straightened out, and, with the zeal that marked a man of the highest character, Thomas Alsager set out to straighten them 'so as to leave no doubts hereafter as to the purity of its administration'. The task was one of fantastic difficulty. There were, it was true, two men of great ability who had ostensibly been the Clerk's assistants 'but', said Alsager, 'they had been entirely excluded from his confidence and knew scarcely so much of the Company's general affairs as I knew myself'.

No attempts had been made to carry out the new system of accounting 'and the only record of the transactions since the Audit of March 1836 was a sort of rough cash book, in a very irregular and imperfect state even for a book of that description'.

'With some labour a balance was struck on the current cash account' and it was found that there was a gross deficiency, not accounted for, of £1,400. 'Never,' said Mr Alsager, 'was there, as I firmly believe, a more perplexed and difficult situation.' For, while the every-day business of the Company was being carried on, the mass of confusion had to be unravelled.

Gradually, working far into the night and with a sacrifice of time and energy 'seriously detrimental' to his private affairs, Alsager, pursuing his examination into the accounts and records of 300 years, began to get a clear picture of the Company's trusts. He was greatly helped by the Upper Beadle, Hughesdon, who had for some time past been entrusted by the Clerk with the collection of various rents which he had entered into a private journal of his own. Many of these rents had not been conveyed, subsequently, into the accounts and these had to be added to the deficiency. There was no official record of the appropriate trusts to which rents were applicable – all this had to be sorted out.

The case of Hobby's Charity was particularly difficult. 'There is no part of our Trusts,' commented Alsager, 'which casts so deep a reproach on the past or conveys so impressive a warning respecting the future management of our affairs as this.' Up to 1821 the accounts of this charity had been kept 'on a very loose and vicious system', and the Court, discovering this, had ordered that 'no part of the rents and profits (as it may be inferred must have previously been the case) should be carried to the Company's own account and also that separate books should be kept for the Charity'.

By the most unaccountable laches and neglect that probably ever occurred in the administration of any public body, the accounts were, from this period, wholly lost sight of. No books were ever produced on the subject; no enquiry was made at the succeeding audits whether a balance existed for or against that trust; and it was as completely excluded from all future audits up to the death of the late Clerk as if it had never existed.

It is not meant by this to say that the trust was left wholly unadministered, but that of the fact whether it was so, or not, the Company had no cognizance. The Clerk used his own discretion in the matter! How

THOMAS MASSA ALSAGER

that discretion was exercised I had opportunity of judging from the perusal of proceedings in Chancery instituted against the Company in 1832 for the administration of this Trust, which fell into my hands among others of the Company's papers . . . the remarkable fact to be dwelt on here is that neither the proceedings themselves nor the decree by which they were closed ever came under the cognizance of the Court.

The Vice-Chancellor's decree that the surplus proceeds, some £1,000, were to be divided *pro rata* among the objects of the charity had been simply ignored by the Clerk,

the same total neglect of the Trust went on, it was left out of the audit while the Clerk still held the control of it, or was, perhaps, the only person in the Hall who knew of its existence. There were other proceedings in Equity, though not attended with such important consequences, with respect to which very little more ceremony was used; but this case of Hobby is so instructive, that if I can only perpetuate the memory of it, that alone would justify all the trouble that has been taken and be a perpetual beacon to our successors against the danger that had passed. I say passed because the subsequent acts of the Court have made the most ample and honourable amends to the Charity.

That the danger, the most horrible danger perhaps which the Company had ever faced, was passed was due to Alsager and Alsager alone. Had some enemy of the Company stumbled upon the terrible secret before the Company had had time to right it and to make the amends they undoubtedly did, there can be little doubt that the Company would have been in grave peril of losing their Charter.

It was to Alsager's credit that their honour was saved, and it was Alsager who set about the reorganization of the Company upon modern lines which would render such dangers impossible of recurrence. It was he who, faced with the chaos of a system which, suitable though it might have been for the simple accounts of the early days of the Company, had grown lamentably antiquated and quite incapable of coping with the complexities of a great corporation, created order and the rule of law. By the institution of standing committees and by a complete remoulding of the system of accountancy – a task in which he was generously helped by those old allies, the Fishmongers, who placed their own newly-reformed accounting system (and Mr W. B. Towse, the son of their Clerk) at his disposal as a guide – Mr Alsager slowly but surely led the Company back to that state of perfection they had once enjoyed.

It is hardly an exaggeration to regard him as the founder of the modern Clothworkers' Company and, wherever prayers are said and benefactors in piety remembered, there should be always found a place of the greatest honour for Thomas Massa Alsager.*

Passed though the floodtide of danger might be, it left behind a trail of mud and jetsam to be cleaned away. In the first place, though the Clerk, whether it be from sins of omission or commission, was primarily to be condemned, it was impossible to acquit members of the Court from a share in the blame for having permitted such things to be. To Alsager it had occurred very early in his considerations that the defects in Constitution were

mainly owing to the responsibility imposed upon gentlemen, filling the office of Master and Wardens in regard to the Government of the Company: and who succeeding to office by rotation and not by election, are not always competent and are generally disinclined, to take so active a part, not to mention that their limited experience previously, leaves them without the proper control over the Clerk for the time being.

Committees, on the contrary, if elected for their talent, leisure and general fitness for such duties, would be liable to no such objection. . . .

Like all reformers, Alsager involved himself in considerable personal unpopularity, for the Committees 'taking cognizance necessarily of matters which devolved usually upon the Master and Wardens the latter felt themselves slighted and complained

---

* In closing his report on the irregularities, Alsager wistfully hoped that his service might 'deserve to be held in perpetual remembrance by all well-wishers to the honour and prosperity of the Clothworkers' Company'. It is probable that this great name would earlier have been rescued from the general oblivion into which it fell if there had not, most understandably and properly, existed well into the middle of the twentieth century the feeling that the whole subject was unfitting to be discussed. But with the passing of time and viewed in the light of the Company's great history of good works and efficient government, it can be allowed to fall into its correct perspective, no longer tending to injure the reputation of a Company above suspicion. So, at last, can honour be paid where honour is so abundantly due.

very freely of such neglect'. But his reforms were permanent, and most properly the Court, before proceeding to elect a new Clerk, studied a report on the whole nature of that Office.

*   *

*

It had been in the past the habit of the Company to pay the Clerk and for him to employ his own assistants. This had led to underpaid assistants who, if they had any knowledge of irregularities, would not dare to point them out. It had also meant that, although the Clerk's salary had been increased in 1826 for him to be able to employ assistants who could carry on in case of his illness or death, those assistants, now that he was dead, knew nothing at all of the Company's more important affairs, though often they had asked for information. 'Such an arrangement was in fact only calculated to take all power from the ruling body and to create a perpetual mastery over them.' In future, therefore, it was the Court who would appoint and pay the subsidiary officers, and the Clerk's vacancy would be advertised to the legal profession. The Clerk's Duties Reorganized

Among the duties of the Audit Committee – one of the three to be set up – was the appointment of a Sub-Committee to report on means of retrenchment, for economy had become urgently essential. Not entirely surprisingly the state of the finances of the Company were found to be far from sound. Expenditure was now the same as, if not more than, income. The Company owed many bills, some of them very big and one of them for as much as £850. The immediate deficiency for the next quarter year was £5,725, or £3,885 if outstanding debts to the Company were paid. Stock was sold to meet this gap and arrangements made to repay the capital at the rate of £1,000 a year. Financial Difficulties

'Very strong and decided measures for the future were held to be unavoidable.' The new Master, Mr Atkins, took a gloomy look at the accounts. The approximate income of the Company was now altogether £14,000. From this total the trusts demanded payments of £6,500; charities due to be paid from the corporate funds involved another £1,730; expenses amounted to £2,800; and entertainment would cost £3,000.

Of these figures (which it will be seen involved a loss on the year of £30 and did not include the capital repayment of £1,000) entertainment was the only item capable of being reduced.

But, fortunately, there were also economies that could be made in the existing expenditure and it redounds greatly to the credit of the Beadle that many of the retrenchments he personally suggested to the Committee involved reductions in his own emoluments. Among other extravagances committed at the Hall was that of an allowance of five bottles of wine weekly to the Beadle and the same quantity to the Under Beadle, beside what remained after Dinners 'in every detail of which the most prodigal waste was committed'. The noble-minded Beadle also discovered 'a large quantity of plate in the Hall which had never been used though it had been a long time in the possession of the Court'.

The Committee also redeemed the character of the Company in respect to dealings with the various tradesmen with whom it had been customary to take such long credit that in the instance of the wine-merchants, Messrs. Raikes and Newbury, it was ascertained that a higher charge was made to this Company than to others, on account of the long credit taken: they made arrangements for the early payment of all claims and saved thereby large sums to the Company in discounts and allowances; they greatly reduced the expense of entertainments and other disbursements by opening them to contracts instead of confining them as heretofore to the same parties who notoriously abused the confidence thus placed in them. . . .

Not everything that was found among the debris left behind in the great Crisis was entirely displeasing: indeed, in preparing for 1838 the Audit of 1838, Alsager had discovered one item of considerable value namely

that a dividend of £500 declared payable by the Irish Society in April 1836, to each of the twelve Companies was withheld from this Company on account of claims to a participation in it by the Butchers' Company and the Upholders' Company who had protested against any payments to us by the Irish Society until those claims had been decided upon. Those Companies, it seems, had been refused on application to our Clerk all information on the subject, or, rather, had been put off by the assurance that he could not give any for all our books of the period referred to had been burnt at the Fire of London in 1666. This was totally false . . . but it was the only answer these Companies could obtain and being, of course, dissatisfied with it they took the course described of attaching our dividend.

Here occurred the first conspicuous and signal service performed for the Company by Mr. Towse. He discovered that the interest of the Butchers' and the Upholders' in the Irish Estate had been purchased by us; the former in 1675 for the sum of £130; and the latter in 1680 for the sum of £40; both these dates, let it be observed, being AFTER the Fire of London. . . .

Had this evidence been produced the Company would have had the dividend nearly a year earlier. As it was, further search produced the legal conveyances from the Butchers and Upholders, and in the face of the irresistible evidence 'the dividend of £500 was obtained at a period when our funds were getting low and the money particularly acceptable . . .'.

Gradually and with pain the Court awoke from the long nightmare. Gradually the realization dawned with the new day of the Company's fulfilment that now everything was going to be all right. Never again would they have to live through such a period of strain. Severe though their financial losses had been, at any rate they had been offered at Mr Alsager's hand, and had gratefully seized, the chance of personal redemption. They had acted like men of honour; and by comparison how small did their monetary losses appear now that, the hard way, they had achieved their own salvation.

It is sad to record that, when, broken down in health by his exertions on behalf of the Company, his own personal crisis was upon him, there was none at hand to help him, and Thomas Massa Alsager, who had solved so many problems, failing to solve his own, died in circumstances of great tragedy.

* *

*

Somewhat to their surprise and certainly to their relief, the Clothworkers found in 1838 that, when all the trusts had been properly set out* and the books brought up to date, their responsibilities were 'less than they had imagined' and possibly not more than £3,000. But great austerity was necessary *under the Order* to replace each year £1,000 of the stock sold.

The italics are their own: the Order had been made and it spelt austerity, but there was a growing feeling that perhaps the Order had been unnecessarily strict. After all, the Irish estates were falling in, which would mean capital coming to the Company, and it was 'desirable not to abridge our usual hospitality except under the pressure of strong and absolute necessity'.

Gradually, in fact, life was getting back to normal, and, although it took time to settle down to the new routines, the new system was working with great efficiency. With this efficiency the financial state of the Company, by dint of the most careful economies, at first improved. In 1839 the Company were £2,500 in arrears, but as £1,500 of that was due to the inefficiencies of the old system of accountancy and as the rate of yearly loss was, generally speaking, decreasing, it was felt that there was some cause for optimism.

1840   In 1840 it was possible to speak of the 'altered circumstances of the Company's affairs by which the advantages both immediate and prospective to be derived from admission to the Livery have greatly improved', and to increase the Livery admission fee by £30. There was still a slight deficit but it was hoped that the following year it might be wiped out.

Further Setbacks   But these high hopes were dashed by a sudden and alarming series of setbacks. First of all came a totally unexpected expense of £1,200 for repairing the Hall. Then the Irish Society, which for 230 years had been paying dividends, ceased altogether to make a profit and indeed showed an accumulated and increasing deficit of £6,500. By 1842 the Company's financial state had reached a new and alarming state of insecurity and 1843 was even worse. Great heart-searchings were made for means of reducing the burden of debt. Would it help appreciably if all Court Dinners were 'Rump

---

* Among his many activities Alsager had produced in 1838 a most useful Register of Trusts, to which reference was still, a hundred and twenty years later, occasionally made.

Steak Dinners without expensive wines or desserts'? What were
the expenses of the various committees? The Court were desper-
ately worried. One member even went so far as to suggest that the
legacy of £20,000, bequeathed to the Company in 1835 by Mr
William Thwaytes for making the Company 'comfortable',
should be used for paying off arrears, but this was turned down.

But the lowest state of the tide had been reached. Things were on
the turn. By 1850 the excess of income over expenditure had
reached nearly £2,000 and the capital deficit was no more than
£3,300. In 1854 the profit on the year had reached £3,000; by
1854 it was £4,000 and there was a credit balance in the accounts of
£7,000. The finances were at last upon a sound footing. The real
times of testing were ended.

CHAPTER THIRTEEN

THE GOLDEN YEARS

*   *

*

I N the meantime, even in the darker days of financial depression the business of the Company had not been without its lighter moments and, indeed, had on occasion attained even a certain old-style magnificence.

1839
Sutton
Valence

In 1839 there was a grand ceremonial re-opening of Sutton Valence School upon a new system, determined upon by the Court and administered under the Schoolmastership of the most auspiciously named Reverend Mr Goodchild. The opening ceremony was attended by 'a considerable number of respectable male and female inhabitants of the parish and neighbourhood, the pupils of the School and the parents and friends of several of the latter who partook of a cold collation provided by the Company'. The Company, for their part, were gratified to receive 'a most hearty and courteous welcome from the respectable classes and from the parents and friends of the pupils, and very respectful conduct from the poorer persons there'. The boys, it was pleasing to record, were 'in a very healthy condition and a cheerful, yet orderly, state'.

But by 1845 there was no great competition to enter the School, and a petition was received from Protestant Dissenters asking that their sons might be admitted. As they hastened to point out, they could 'remember the time when considerable eagerness manifested itself among the inhabitants of the parishes concerned to obtain for their Sons a share of its educational advantages, but a very different feeling has now for some time existed . . .'.

The Court replied stiffly that a most sacred Trust had been created 'from which this Company cannot depart without loss of character and principle and without endangering their position as one of the recognized Public Institutions of the Country'. And, at the prizegiving, to encourage healthy orthodox thought, the prizes handed out to the little boys included such works as Sharon Turner's *Sacred History of the World*, Nesbit's *Landsurveying*, Bakewell's *Philosophical Conversations*, and Dr Paris's *Philosophy in Sport Made Science in Earnest*.

But not all the festivities were parochial. There were considerable junketings in 1843 at the swearing-in of Alderman Musgrove,* Master of the Company, as Sheriff, with processions both by land and water. And in 1844 it was decided that Sir Robert Peel should be invited to dinner and made a Freeman and Liveryman of the Company.

1843

1844
Entertainment of Sir Robert Peel

It was the first time, since the Clothworkers had entertained the Dukes of Sussex and Cambridge, that any such important occasion had taken place, and the Company were as full of breathless preparations for the party as a young bride entertaining for the first time in her own home. Those old rivals, the Merchant Taylors were chosen as the arbiters of taste. 'A list was procured through their kindness of the distinguished persons usually invited by them to meet the Duke of Cambridge and Sir Robert Peel as Freeman of that Company', and the invitations were to be written on 'post paper of the folio size with gilt edges such as that used by the Merchant Taylors when sending Invitations to the Ministers and other distinguished persons'.

There were so many things to be thought of: the awnings, the tent for the band (in uniform, by kind consent of the Colonel of the Coldstream Guards), the arrangements with 'King and Rymer' [*sic*], the selection of suitable glees and songs, the fitting of a screen carrying gas lamps outside the painted window so that it should look its best during the dinner – the whole thing took an immense amount of arranging, and so much attention was paid to the details that the impression is given that, at the back of their minds, the Clothworkers – and who shall blame them after the ordeals they had been through? – were not entirely sure of themselves.

* See Appendix F.

Invitations were sent to the Chancellor of the Exchequer, the Lord High Chancellor, the President of the Council, the Lord Privy Seal, the Home Secretary, the Foreign Secretary, the Colonial Secretary, the First Lord of the Admiralty, the President of the Board of Trade, the Secretary of State for War, the Paymaster General, the Postmaster General, the Lord Chamberlain, most of the Law Lords, and a host of other notables. But of all these, in addition to the Guest of Honour, the only one to accept was the Chancellor of the Exchequer. And when the grim old Duke of Wellington wrote to refuse the invitation in consequence of 'business in the House of Lords', the Company clearly did not believe this excuse and vainly wrote 'to Mr. R. L. Jones to request his interference in the hope of inducing his Grace to change his intention'. None the less, the banquet proved a great success and afterwards Sir Robert Peel was graciously pleased to accept the freedom of the Company.

*   *
*

Opening of the Royal Exchange

The year 1844 witnessed another occasion a little reminiscent of the early days of splendour when the Queen came to the City to open the Royal Exchange. The Company were summoned to the Hall, 'from thence to go to a Station provided on the Queen's Route to pay their respects'. The front of the Hall was 'most Brilliantly illuminated with a Crown, Brunswick Star and the letters V.R. in jets of Gas that outshone all other illuminations'.

To the Company this breath of former City glories came quite naturally, but the Gresham Committee responsible for the general arrangements seem to have made very heavy weather of the proceedings. After considerable initial confusion, when the procession from the Clothworkers' Company arrived at their place in the Poultry,

it appeared that the space allotted to the Company was quite inadequate for them and the Band and Banner men were under the necessity of occupying that part of the road appropriated to the Carriages of the Visitors to the Exchange and therefore interfered with the line of Route that was intended to be kept clear for Her Majesty and attendants:

a most dangerous position to be in when the Horse Guards made their appearance within the Barriers. . . .

Ultimately rescued from this 'perilous situation' by the good offices of the City Solicitor, the band, placed in front of the Mansion House, 'gratified all within hearing' and when it played the National Anthem, 'the Company received the most marked condescension from Her Majesty and Prince Albert'.

It was almost the last of the old-style pageantry for the Company. In 1850, when Alderman Musgrove became Lord Mayor of London, the Clothworkers did, for the last time, proceed in procession both by land and by water. They hired a barge for themselves and a shallop for the musicians; they borrowed javelins from the Goldsmiths. But the old simple pleasures of 'dressing-up' for the occasion had largely been lost, and the idea of an outing on the water held no appeal. *Lord Mayor's Show*

The previous year the Lord Mayor had actually sent them a precept, requesting their attendance in their barge on the occasion of the Queen visiting the City to open the new Coal Exchange. The Company no longer had a barge, and a member's suggestion that they should hire a steamer for the occasion met with little support. The bleak reply was made to the Lord Mayor that, having no barge, they were unable to comply with the precept. Proceeding by river, so natural to their ancestors in the days of appalling roads and narrow streets, was an anachronism they no longer even enjoyed.

Nor did they enjoy some of the Clothworker ceremonies that tended, as they thought, to make them look faintly ridiculous. In the very earliest days of the Company, on the election of the Master and Wardens, the same ancient ceremony had been observed of crowning them with garlands fashioned like a heraldic wreath but made of red velvet with pieces of silver engraved with the Company's arms fastened to them. The ceremony had been as follows: *Ancient Ceremonies Discontinued*

First: The two Wardens at the dinner (at such time as the Master shall be served in) shall rise to go out and then shall come in with the garland, for the Master only, in the Chief Warden's hands, with the minstrels before them and the Beadle; and making their obeisance to the Master shall remain and attend by the Master till the Master hath assayed the garland upon the heads of such of the most worshipful as he shall think meet. And then the Master to receive it again and set it on his own head. And then the Wardens to depart, the garland still remaining on the old Master's head.

And immediately the Wardens to come in again with the Beadle and Minstrels before them, either of them having his garland on his head, and one to bear a cup before the Chief Warden and to go once about the house; and, after obeisance made, the Chief Warden to take the cup and deliver it to the old Master. And then the Master to take off the garland off of his head and set it on the new Master's head.

And then the Master to take the Cup and drink to the new Master. And after that the Wardens (after due reverence) to depart to assay their garlands as they shall think meet; and then to go out and come in again with the Minstrels and Beadle before them with their garlands on their heads and either of them having his cup brought before him and to go twice about the house: and then the chief old Warden to go and set the garland upon the new Chief Warden's head; and to take his Cup and drink to him and so to deliver the same Cup to him. And likewise the Younger Warden to set his garland upon the other new Warden's head.

1850   This proved too much for Victorian pomposity to swallow. In two notes, scribbled and passed across the table, apparently at a Court Meeting in or about the year 1850, an exchange of views took place between two of the Assistants, J. Carter and T. Francis:

'What is your opinion of the practice?' wrote Carter. 'It appears to the present Wardens to be a ridiculous practice'. 'My dear friend,' replied Francis, 'I am a great advocate of Old Customs when they are not of an offensive nature.' Carter passed back another note: 'Some of my colleagues mean to rebel, it being particularly offensive to them. For my own part I care not which way it is: although it may be an old custom, it certainly is only newly revived.' His friend closed the exchange upon a very proper note: 'I shall not join in the rebellion but quietly submit to the majority.'

Unfortunately the majority was against the practice, and so – although the Master's chaplet was still extant in 1858 – passed the

THE HALL, 1857

ancient custom from the Clothworker scene. One result of this iconoclasm, was that thenceforth, in processions through the City, the Master and Wardens, having no traditional hats to match their traditional gowns, were for many years forced to proceed incongruously crowned – if crowned at all –with top hat, homburg, billycock, or bowler. But this was simply an expression of the new *Zeitgeist*. In all the City, in all the country it was the same.

The Clothworkers, as always, were typical of their age. And, as the century approached its half-way mark, the Company were perhaps as great as ever they had been: wealthy and respected, they were preparing to take a definite lead among the Twelve Companies.

* *
*

The times were changing. The golden age of the Victorian era was being ushered in. The years that Harriet Martineau had called the 'Thirty Years' Peace' had given the country all the benefits of long freedom from Continental warfare; this and a new stability at home, following the passage of the Reform Bill and the institution of religious toleration in politics, had led to great prosperity in which the whole country, however inequably, shared. It was to lead to further immense changes in the country's way of life, and these found faithful reflection in the Clothworkers' Company.

Prosperous agriculture and a fantastic output in trade and commerce were 'the rich advantages of the lead [the Country] had gained by reason both of her political stability and of her industrial revolution and inventiveness',[1] and if this golden age produced a mood of complacency and self-satisfaction (and a theory that the reward of virtue is Heaven and 5 per cent), that seems to later generations a little odious, it must be comprehended as being an integral part of the contemporary scene – it must be comprehended and not merely dismissed with the condescending smile more often reserved for the carefree orthographical oddities of the Elizabethans. And it may well be recollected with regret that, while the ideals of virtue largely died out with the Victorians, the ideals of materialism did not.

There was a social conscience at work which, with the growth of liberalism, helped to offset some of the more aggressive forms of materialism. It was social conscience that found its expression in all the new charities, some of them with curious titles, that the Company began to help by their subscriptions: The Asylum for Idiots, Earlswood; The Benevolent Society of Blues; The Establishment for Gentlewomen During Temporary Illnesses; The Friendly Female Society; The Invalid Asylum for Respectable Females; The Gentlewoman's Self-Help Institution; The City of London Truss Society for the Ruptured Poor; The Provident Clerks' Benevolent Fund; The Plumstead Soup and Bread Society; The Royal Sea Bathing Infirmary, Margate; The British Penitent Females' Refuge; The National Society for Promoting the Education of the Poor in the Principles of The Established Church; and The Society for the Suppression of Vice. The list is one that is comprehensive of almost all the Victorian virtues.

1851
Great
Exhibition

This new and golden age was ushered in, symbolically, by the Great Exhibition of 1851, a project of which the Company had been invited to become promoters. After enquiring cautiously whether any financial liability would be incurred, and being assured that it would not, the Company subscribed 100 guineas. The Clothworker Plate was lent to a grand ball at the Guildhall to celebrate the opening of the Exhibition – the fact that the Lord Mayor for this exciting year was a Clothworker, Alderman Musgrove, must greatly have added to the Company's feeling of participation in the dawning of a new era. This feeling must have been heightened, too, by the Master of the Clothworkers' inclusion in the civic party that attended (much to Mr Punch's insular amusement) the fêtes in Paris that celebrated 1900 years of that City's foundation.

Distinguished foreigners, in London for the Exhibition, were entertained at the Hall, and it soon became obvious that the old building that had seen so many brilliant occasions and stirring events was doomed. In 1855 Mr George Meek drew the attention of the Court 'to the ravages of time' on the Hall and the Company's architect, Mr Samuel Angell, was asked to make a report. Like so

Rebuilding
the Hall

many of the buildings that had sprung up after the Great Fire of London, the Hall had been jerry-built. The foundations mouldered and trembled: they were of soft and ill-burned bricks as was the whole superstructure of the building. Bricks had been used in places where stone was called for. Speculating upon the reasons for this laxity the report concluded, probably correctly, that it had been due to the 'difficulty of obtaining a sufficiency of good materials upon so sudden and large a demand'. But, in addition to the brickwork, 'the timbers of chestnut had the dry-rot and were in a fearful state of insecurity'. The old Hall was condemned with some reluctance. Apart from its historical associations 'it had an aspect of comfort as well as of state'.

A contract for the erection of a new Hall was given to John Jay for £33,846 and on 6 September 1856 the Company moved out of their old home. The building was gutted. The delicate Georgian furnishings, the sofa-tables and writing desks, the pier-glasses and girandoles were disposed of, at a period when they were not at all esteemed, for trifling sums. The mellowed brickwork, ill-burned though it might be, and the old timbers were sold.

The Clothworkers, while this distressing operation was going on, rented Barbers' Hall in Monkwell Street, and it was recalled with a pleasing sense of the continuity of tradition that it was to Monkwell Street that they had gone, to Lambe's Chapel, when they had been dispossessed after the Great Fire. There they remained until 6 April 1859, when it was possible to report that a 'splendid structure stands where stood its predecessors, an ornament of this great and wealthy metropolis. The only regret is that owing to the circumscribed nature of the locality its beauty is imperfectly seen.'

The Times gave an excellent description of this building[2]:

The New Hall . . . is one of the finest of which the City can boast. Boldly carved enrichments adorn the facade which is of the Italian style of Architecture of the Renaissance Period. The Arms of the Company surmount a lofty portal with bronze gates in the centre. This leads to an arched corridor and vestibule which form the approach to the entrance Hall over the doorway of which are four relievi executed in Caen Stone by Mr. C. Kelsey, representing the attributes of the Company – Loyalty, Integrity, Industry and Charity. From the entrance-hall – from which it is partially separated by coupled columns – springs the grand staircase. On each side of it, on the ground floor, are the several offices of the Company for the purpose of business. This floor contains, also, the culinary departments – essential portion of a City Hall – on the construction and arrangement of which no ordinary amount of care and skill has evidently been bestowed.

At the foot of the grand staircase are two bronze griffins, admirable both for execution and design, the work of Mr. Kelsey.

On the first landing are to be seen the Royal Arms in alto relievo and in all the propriety of heraldic emblazonment. A lofty pendentive dome surmounts the staircase itself which leads to the piano nobile where, as in Italian palaces, are the State apartments. Here are to be found the reception rooms of the Livery, and a drawing room for the Court of Assistants and their guests. Here also stands the banqueting hall, the chief feature of the building. It is a room of noble proportions and perfect harmony of design. In extreme length it is 80 feet, 40 feet wide and 80 feet in height. Corinthian engaged columns of Aberdeen granite, highly polished and resting on granite pedestals, with a stylobate of richly veined Devonshire marble, divide it into five bays at the sides and three at the ends.

Above the entablature surmounting these columns is an attic from which springs a coved ceiling. Of this ceiling the cove is pierced with semi-circular windows in which are represented the arms of the Twelve City Companies beautifully executed by Mr. Lavers.

Female figures, in alto relievo, emblematical of twelve of the principal commercial Cities of the Empire adorn the spaces between these windows. . . .

There were, *The Times* noticed, five other stained glass windows with the arms of prominent Members of the Company as well as the two statues of James I and Charles I, and, although as yet the gilding and enrichments in colour were incomplete, 'the general effect of this portion of the building is somewhat like that produced by the gallery of the Hotel de Ville in Paris'.

The first meeting in the Hall was held on 6 April 1859. The Company were back, after two and a half years of exile, in their own home, and, as mementoes of the occasion, various homely gifts were made to the Company – a representation of the Company's barge, modelled in 1689, a steel engraving of the Waterloo Banquet, a bronze equestrian statuette of Her Majesty, and an eight-day dial for the Clerk's Office, the oak case turned from a beam of the old Hall.

Plans were excitedly made for the grand re-opening ceremonies which H.R.H. The Prince Consort had agreed to attend.

On 27 March 1860, the 235th anniversary of the death of the last royal member of the Company, the Freedom and Livery of the Company were bestowed upon Prince Albert amidst scenes of rejoicing. 'The Hall, which was tastefully decorated with flags and flowers and illuminated with gas chandeliers, presented an appearance of great brilliancy; the presence of the ladies assembled in the gallery at the south end of the Hall added, in no small degree, to the attractions of the festival'. During the dinner, which was attended by the Marquess of Salisbury, Lord Stanhope, and Mr Disraeli, a band played. There were thirteen speeches made and toasts drunk; and glees, catches, and part-songs – some nine in all – enlivened the proceedings.

In proposing the health of Samuel Angell, the architect, the Prince Consort remarked shrewdly: 'I am not able, indeed, to say what the building cost but this, at all events, is obvious–that the Company do not need to look very narrowly into the amount'. The Company's finances were now, in fact, upon a very sound footing. The money for building the Hall had been borrowed from the Union Assurance Company at 4½ per cent. There was a very respectable excess of income over expenditure and the rent roll was increasing.

Once again, the only cloud in an otherwise cloudless horizon was over Sutton Valence.

* *
*

There had been a lot of trouble over the expulsion of a young bully named Steers whose father considered he had been the victim of 'ferocious and brutal treatment' and had brought lawyers, who

Sutton Valence

threatened dire penalties, to his aid. There had been a lesser amount of trouble from the Archbishop of Canterbury who had complained that pupils were attending dissenting places of worship – and in their school caps too. But the real trouble was that the School again was in a most depressing decline. In 1858 there had only been nineteen boys at the School 'due to the reluctance of parents in Kent to give their sons a Classical Education'. By 1859 the number had dropped to fourteen. At the examinations only nine of them were present: they were all 'very idle' and almost totally ignorant.

In 1860 the Committee, set up to investigate whether it was worth carrying on with the School or whether they should discontinue it altogether, reported that they had read through the records of the School since its foundation in 1576, that it had always been a trouble to the Company either because its rules did not encourage entries or its buildings were inadequate or its Masters incompetent. It would cost £5,000 to set it properly upon its feet. It says much for the Company's determination to carry out their obligations that, after a decision to close the School temporarily at Christmas and consider the matter calmly and reflectively, the money was spent, the School rebuilt and re-organized and generally turned into the excellent institution it at last, after 300 years, became.

* *

*

Municipal
Reform
1858

About this time there came a great new burst of enthusiasm for reform, and the City did not escape the movement. In 1858 the Corporation Bill was before Parliament – a Bill which proposed the overthrow of the Livery Companies' rights to elect the Lord Mayor and Sheriffs in favour of election by the Ratepayers of the various Wards. This attack, backed by Lord Palmerston, on private property – a nineteenth-century measure of confiscation without compensation – was defended by its sponsors on the rather doubtful grounds that Corporations should not be allowed to have the same rights to protection of property as individuals – an article of faith that attracted a growing number of supporters.

The City immediately petitioned both Houses of Parliament

against the Bill, and eventually it failed to reach the Statute Book. But the question of the administration of the Companies' charities came to be raised again. A report was prepared for the Charity Commissions by a Mr Hare, a report of such great importance and use that after the passage of a century it was still being consulted. The Charity Commissioners went carefully into Hare's Report and had no faults to find with the Clothworkers.

The Endowed Schools Act of 1869, which supervised the administration of many of the Livery Companies' charities, and the Charitable Trusts Act of 1871 – although they were hotly opposed with such familiar protests against the wielding of 'unconstitutional powers' and the undesirability of the Commissioners of the Treasury having 'unlimited powers to increase the Salaries of the Charity Commissioners and their Secretary' – both became law. 1860

Whatever may have been the attitude of the other Companies towards these measures, the Clothworkers, although in Committee they spoke against them, showed great readiness to resort to the good offices of the Charity Commissioners. The Charities of Burnell, Hitchin, Hobby, Lute, and Middlemore were all placed in the name of the Official Trustee of Charities, and Lambe's Islington Charity was administered under a Private Act of Parliament of 1872 passed with the co-operation of the Charity Commissioners.

These were the first fruits of the reform movement in the eighteen-sixties. That the Company were so ready to ensure that their house was properly in order was to stand them in the most excellent stead in the attacks which, as will be later seen, were to be made upon the very existence of the Livery Companies.

These were outward reforms. Within the Company other minor changes were taking place to bring the Clothworkers into line with contemporary thought. The various offices and their emoluments were kept in continual review. The duties of the Standing Committees were closely scrutinized. The method of admission to the Livery and Freedom was carefully considered – due to the increase of the fine to £100, admission by purchase had almost died out and entrance by servitude or patrimony was now practically universal. A Committee reported that 'owing to the alteration in the mode of transacting business and to the facility of acquiring the Freedom of the City without the intervention of the Companies, the number of the Apprentices bound is now considerably less than was formerly the case and, with few exceptions, those who are bound do not look forward to the advantages which these ancient Guilds originally offered for their advancement in business and society'.

Further Decay of Apprenticeship System

This falling-off in the number of apprentices had reduced entry to the Company largely to admission by patrimony. Pleasant though this might be in the way of producing a Company existing largely through family ties, it severely restricted the numbers available and limited the choice. Looking to the future, it was suggested that the cost of Freedom by purchase should be reduced to £50. A rule was restated, too, that 'no member already Free of any other Company might become a Member of the Clothworkers' except by Translation', though this rule of course did not apply to the Honorary Freemen of distinction who continued to be elected to the Company, and, after the death of the Prince Consort in 1862, the royal connexions of the Company were maintained by the presentation, with much ceremony, of Freedom and Livery to the Prince of Wales.

Another Honorary Freeman created at this time, interesting not only in his own right but from the indication which the presentation gives of the fact that the Clothworkers' recognized the social conscience that he typified, was Mr George Peabody, 'the munificent friend of the Poor of this Metropolis'.

The entertainment of these and other guests brought the condition of the new Hall into prominence. The decorations were completed at a cost of nearly £5,000 and the Court decided to purchase full-length portraits of the Queen and the late Prince Consort.

1870 The entertainment of Royalty in the persons, first, of the Prince Consort and, later, of the Prince of Wales, after the passage of many years in which Royalty had been absent from the Company, reminded the Clothworkers of the fact that James I had presented them with a brace of buck in perpetuity, a gift long since in abeyance. In 1841 there had been an unsuccessful attempt to get the grant renewed and in 1870 the effort was made again. The Lord Steward felt, however, that to grant the request would open the doors to a whole host of similar requests and there would be insufficient venison in the country for the purpose. If the Company were insisting on this as a matter of right then they must apply to the First Commissioner of Her Majesty's Works, the man in charge of the deer in the Royal Parks.

But although the Company threatened to pursue the matter further, nothing more was done about it and the Clothworkers continued without their venison dinners.

The dinners of the Clothworkers in any case were, though entirely adequate, no longer the gargantuan feasts they had been. The quantity of wine drunk by the members, with the exception of Lisbon and Port, had fallen off most markedly, but unfortunately this had not been reflected in any increase of good behaviour on the part of the Livery, behaviour which made the Court comment that 'the recent tendencies to disorderly conduct manifested at the Livery Dinners might lead them to discontinue invitations in certain quarters on a recurrence of complaint'.*

It was such similar frailties of human nature that were later to be used as a contributory charge against the City Companies when the great attacks of 1883 were made against them.

*　　*

*

The Clothworkers' Company was by the beginning of the eighteen-seventies flourishing in an unexampled manner. Never had they been so rich, never had their affairs been in such perfect order. As the great tidal wave of Victorian prosperity rolled on, bearing on its crest the cargoes from the empire, the fruits of trade that made London ever increasingly the greatest port of the world, the wealth of the Company increased with it. For, naturally, as

Prosperity

---

* Subsequent experience would indicate that disorders usually occurred among the younger members of the Livery after the eighth or ninth of the speeches by distinguished guests.

231

London became more and more the centre of a thriving commerce, so the demand for land and accommodation increased and so did the Company's properties appreciate in value.

Irish Lands
Sold
1871

In addition to this appreciation there had been a further source of capital for reinvestment – at a time when re-investment was most profitable – from the sale, in 1871, of the Irish Lands to Sir H. H. Bruce. Upon news of the sale reaching Ireland, the tenants there wrote asking to be allowed to buy their own holdings: they were prepared to pay £165,000 to do so. Unfortunately, the sale to Sir H. H. Bruce had already been agreed at £120,000, a figure that caused the Butchers' Company to hold up the sale on an objection as co-partners. The Butchers' memories must have been short, their records incomplete. It was barely thirty-three years since it had been pointed out to them that they had long since ceased to have any share in their partnership, that they had sold their rights in the estates in 1675. Their objection collapsed utterly when this was pointed out to them and the sale went through.

It was at this moment that the Clothworkers' Company, instead of sitting back as they were perfectly entitled to do and contemplating the pleasing spectacle of their material prosperity and the conscientious way in which their trusts were being administered, showed their shrewdness and their essential quality by an action of incalculable importance.

CHAPTER FOURTEEN

EXPERIMENT IN EDUCATION

* *

*

ARLY in 1872 the attention of the court was drawn 'to the desirability of affording some encouragement to the Movement for Technical Education in connection with the Cloth Trade at the principal centres of that industry or otherwise'.

The movement had first been noted as early as 1867 when it had been remarked that 'without education we cannot expect to have skilled workmen of the highest class. . . . The adoption of similar schools [to those in operation on the Continent] in Britain will, before long, become a necessity and the sooner they are established the better.'[1] Foreign competition had 'directed the attention of manufacturers to the instruction given in Continental schools whereby so high a standard of design and execution of textile fabrics [had] been reached as to threaten the supremacy of English goods'.[2] But before anything could be done on similar lines in this country the British mistrust of innovation had to be overcome.

There was no disguising the fact 'that these Continental schools have not been regarded with favour in this country. Manufacturers have expressed contempt for instruction given away from the mill. However,' continued the Report, 'manufacturers have unwillingly in many cases come to the conclusion that if they are to hold their own in the markets of the world, it will not do to cling any longer to the absurd notion that an Englishman is worth many foreigners and that, in the future, as in the past, foreign competition can be lightly treated. . . .'[3]

Nor was the artisan's attitude much more enlightened than that of the employer. Although there were many just complaints of the lack of artistic skill in English work that placed it at a disadvantage in competition with the foreigner, 'the workmen's Trade Unions not only do not promote but actually disallow improvement in manipulative skill – by forbidding the accomplished workman to compete with the incompetent except at a disadvantage'.[4]

But now the movement for technical education was fairly launched. It was intended, ultimately, 'to provide a greater supply of foremen and directors of labour skilled in the practical and technical application of recent scientific discoveries, a want which is . . . very much felt by manufacturers of every description'. In other words, the wonders of the mechanical age which was upon the Victorians had outstripped the workers' ability to employ them.

As far as the Company were concerned, the thing started in a very small and very hesitant and uncertain way, but the important point is not only that it started at all but that it started in 1872 before the popular outcry against the City Companies began to be raised and that, therefore, as far as the Clothworkers were concerned, the action seems a spontaneous one, prompted by a genuine desire to do something useful toward the trade which, in name, they represented. And since it was the cloth trade, the technical interests of which they wished to further, they had to look outside the City in which their interests had always lain. With the scarcity and dearness of coal in London, the cloth trade had long since migrated towards the Midlands and the North; for this reason the first direction in which the Company gazed was towards Yorkshire in general and Leeds in particular. But when the financial requirements of technical education in Yorkshire were first stated – they were from £2,000 to £5,000 per annum for ten years – the Company felt that this was more than they could afford to pay for something that was still very much a new-fangled idea.

They were, however, prepared to get things moving by commissioning a history of the woollen trade as a means of stimulating practical interest in the subject. A Mr James Holroyd, 'the best Authority on the Woollen Trade,' was 'willing to undertake such a History con amore provided his expenses, say £900 to £1,000, were guaranteed by the Company'.

It is possible that these expenses seemed a little high to the Company. At any rate, for the present, the history was left in abeyance but immediate encouragement was given by the presentation of medals at the Vienna Exhibition. The Committee further thought, early in 1873, that it would be right to give encouragement 'to deserving workmen and apprentices in the centres of the Cloth Industry' and, with this in mind, they invited the Mayors and Chairmen of Chambers of Commerce in Leeds, Huddersfield, Halifax, and Stroud to confer with them.

It was at this moment – eighteen months after the Company had conceived the idea – that the City awoke to the fact that something big was stirring in the land: a circular was sent by the City Chamberlain, asking the Livery Companies what were their intentions towards technical education. The Clothworkers replied that 'the Company are taking independent steps for the promotion of Technical Education in the Cloth Trade which will, in due course, be notified to the Public'.

The first of these steps was, in fact, the gift of 100 guineas to the Society of Arts to help in the establishment of a prize fund 'for the encouragement of Artizans distinguishing themselves'. Then, after the earlier scheme for presenting medals to the Austrian Exhibition had fallen through, by reason of a lack of agreement on both sides, the Committee recommended that £500 a year should be given in money grants 'to deserving and industrious artizan Clothworkers at the seats of the Cloth Industry'. 1873

All the time the Company were really groping in the dark to find the best way in which they might aid the industry. They were pioneers and had no one to guide them as they fumbled towards the final triumphant conclusion.

* *
*

As early as 1869 a meeting had been held in Leeds to promote the foundation of a Yorkshire College of Science but it was not until 1872 that a really serious attempt was made to collect sufficient funds for the project. By 1874 such slow progress had been made that of the £60,000 at first required only one third had been sub- The Yorkshire College scribed. It was then that a former Mayor of Leeds, Mr Obadiah Nussey, drew the attention of the Clothworkers' Company to the excellence and suitability of the project. At the conference of Yorkshire Mayors and Chairmen of Chambers of Commerce summoned to the Hall the idea of the College fired the imaginations of the Committee with great enthusiasm.

With an inspired munificence a capital sum of £10,000 was given for the provision of a building to house a Department of Textile Industries, and the former proposal to grant £500 per annum for industrious artisans was switched to the establishment of a professorship there.[5]

In this way, and at a time when the work was something new and revolutionary, the Company had, in the new field, set an example of leadership which they never lost. From henceforth education was the moving force in the Company. The minutes contain, for the remainder of the century, hardly any record – apart from estate administration – other than that of munificence in education. The Company, in their first enthusiasm, went far out of their way to look for objects deserving of educational support. The Bristol College of Science, for example, to which in 1876 the sum of £525 a year for a probationary three years was granted, came to the Company's notice as the result of an advertisement in the newspaper read by the Clerk, the inspired Sir Owen Roberts.

It was a great spontaneous movement which included in its scope not only technical education for the artisan but the higher education of women and the schools at Sutton Valence and Peel in the Isle of Man.

*   *
*

Philip
Christian's
School

The School at Peel, to which Philip Christian in 1653 had left £20 a year, had never caused the Company the trouble that had come from Sutton Valence. In 1644 there had certainly been a slightly awkward situation by reason of the fact 'that the Estate left by Mr Christian for the maintenance of this and other charges being in houses was by the dreadful fire in London consumed to Ashes, so that the rents were by the Judges then sitting at Clifford's Inn reduced to one moiety'. But this moiety, at the request of the Bishop of Sodor and Man, was paid and eventually restored to its full amount. Apart from this, the existence of Peel School went almost unnoticed. A subscription towards translating the Bible into Manx was one of the few reminders that the Clothworkers had any footing on the island.

In the burst of educational enthusiasm the Company turned towards Peel with new offers of help. The yearly payment of £20 had already, in 1840, been increased to £48 and, again in 1850, to £66 10s. Now, in 1873, the Company offered £1,000 towards the building of a new school for boys plus £260 a year – 'a princely payment' as the school rightly regarded it – on condition that the inhabitants of Peel should raise the rest of the money needed for the site and the new building.

This offer, a generous and quite spontaneous one, was received with considerable local acclamation, but for several years acclamation was all – the necessary money was simply not forthcoming, and it was not until the inhabitants of Peel realized that without the Company's aid their rates would be increased from 3d to 3s that the citizens rallied round and produced the sum that was necessary.

The higher education of women, another revolutionary scheme, received its first impetus from the request to the Company to do something in the way of Exhibitions for the lady students of Cambridge, and the first Clothworker Scholarship to Girton College was the result. Girton College

As for Sutton Valence, there were fine schemes for its re-organization put in hand. It was not that the School was now being any trouble. It had settled down to a quiet mediocrity with forty-eight boys – a number which, in the old days, the Company would have regarded with complacency. Now, however, plans were set in train for raising it to 'a school of the first rank of 300 or more as in the case of Uppingham'. But, said the cautionary voice of the Reverend E. A. Abbott, who was making the report as Examiner, it must be added, 'though . . . with great regret, that in the present state of social feeling in England no first grade public school would Sutton Valence have much chance unless it were of a somewhat exclusive character. I am very proud of the comprehensive nature of my own school [Plasnewydd] where pupils of every station in life mix freely together, but I fear public feeling is not at present prepared for a first grade boarding school of this kind.'

In 1876 the School was enlarged, and from thence forward the Company had no further trouble from Sutton Valence: they noted with approval that the Headmaster was of an enlightened turn of mind in his belief – at that time by no means universal – that 'access at proper times, etc., to water is good for health, for cleanliness, knowledge of swimming and, even, for morals'.

It is not surprising, with all this expense on education, that in 1873, for the first time in many years, the Company found itself with a deficit on the year's account. There had been a number of capital accounts opened and loans for building made – Lambe's Chapel was to be demolished and a new Church erected in some more populous spot where it would serve some more useful purpose. The crypt of the Chapel was to be removed to the Churchyard of Allhallows Stayning and the bodies from the crypt re-interred. The finances of the Company were sound enough but there was an immediate shortage of ready money which called for a certain amount of retrenchment. It was therefore particularly unjust, as far as the Clothworkers were concerned, that at this moment, at this high tide of their benevolence, a series of virulent attacks upon the City Companies began to be made.

*   *
*

The City Companies Attacked

There seems no doubt that these attacks were most carefully organized and timed. If the City Companies were totally unappreciative of the necessity for advertisement and propaganda, a necessity that the majority were still ignoring three-quarters of a century later, their opponents suffered from no such failings.

1876

In 1876 the Member for Gateshead, Mr Walter James, after the ground had been broken by a number of inspired attacks in the popular press, demanded in Parliament an investigation into the affairs of the City Companies.

There is evidence that these attacks had been building up for some time from the fact that as early as 1874 there had been suggested the formation of a Committee of the Twelve Companies for the protection of mutual interests. There were some who refused to be moved by the signs of the times: the Goldsmiths, for instance, refused to join any such association and the Grocers refused the use of their Hall for any meeting of the Committee.

But, with the new attacks of 1876, everyone realized that something must be done and an Executive Defence Committee of the Associated Livery Companies was formed. The Company subscribed £100 towards the fighting fund and the older Committee of the Twelve Companies was merged in the new organization. But it appears that little or nothing was done in the way of counter-propaganda: the Companies set their houses in good order and sat back to await the attack.

There was some retrenchment on the Company's expenditure for entertainments but whether this was due to the somewhat reduced circumstances that have been noted or to a desire not to attract further criticism, or to both, is not entirely clear.

Certainly, when in 1874 the Company had presented their Freedom and Livery to Sir Garnet Wolseley for the success of his Ashantee Campaign, no dinner was held for the occasion and in lieu £550 was given towards the dependants of those in the services killed on the Gold Coast.

But the Clothworkers, in any case, had little to fear from any such investigation. Thanks to the pioneer work of Mr Alsager that had awoken them to such a sense of responsibility towards their affairs, they were being extolled as the Company that had set the example to all the others.

'To the Clothworkers' Company . . . is due the initiation of a movement that bids fair to become of national importance'[6] was a typical comment, and, in referring to the attacks being made upon the City Companies, a newspaper, after advising the Companies to adapt themselves to modern demands, added: 'In some cases it would be of great advantage if the Guilds, following the example of the Clothworkers' Company, could assist in maintaining existing colleges, schools or societies for instruction in the mechanical and applied sciences or in art.'[7]

There was one snag in the way of this. There were, in London, very few such institutions. Leeds, where the Textile Department of the Yorkshire College of Science was now, after a shaky start – there was some trouble with the first Professor – firmly established, was inseparably connected with the cloth trade, but what were the other Companies to do? Were the other Companies, it was demanded, to go outside the City? Should the Cordwainers look to Northampton, the Weavers to Norwich? Because, if they did so, then the City Companies would cease to be primarily interested in the City to which their responsibility was owed and could not be said to fulfil the terms of their organization which was for the purpose of promoting and improving the trade of London.

To the Clothworkers again fell the task of leadership. After consultation with the Drapers' Company, who had been the next to show interest in the scheme, and at the suggestion of Sir Sydney Waterlow, it was thought

desirable that the Clothworkers' Company should initiate a movement for establishing in London a City Guilds Technical Institute or University with affiliated branches for the local centres of the various Industries in the Suburbs and Provinces generally, where the latest applications of science to the trades and manufactures generally may receive practical illustration and impetus by way of supplying a want arising from the partial disuse of the system of Apprenticeship still offered by almost all the Livery Companies . . . which was, in fact, the rudimentary Technical Education of former days. . . .

The Clothworkers joined with the Drapers in a Committee to confer with the Mercers and to get both their support and the support of other Companies. From this leadership was formed an educational system of incalculable importance and to which further reference will be made later.

In the meantime something was being done to appease public opinion which, so it was said, 'demanded that the Livery Companies should provide Technical Education not leastly because those in the Companies were now laymen and outsiders who had inherited a vast estate and had done nothing to further the interests of those for whom the Estate was founded'.[8] As the Bishop of Chester had sonorously quoted in 1869, 'He that will not apply new remedies must expect new evils for Time is the greatest Innovator, and they that reverence too much old times are but a scorn to the new'. It was agreed that those reformers 'who desire to level all alike have in the neglect of Technical Education a great grievance'.[9]

But although these grievances were being rapidly righted, the reformers continued their organized campaign of propaganda, and – with a sense of publicity that the Companies might well have emulated – they fomented what was an uninformed public opinion into a state of indignation by a calculated series of innuendoes, half-truths, and downright lies.

The insistence of the Member for Gateshead that there should be an enquiry into the affairs of the City Companies led, in 1876, to a demand for a return to be made of the number of those in each Company entitled to vote at the City elections, but, apart from this and apart from a further return to the charge by Mr Walter James in 1877, no more was heard in Parliament about the matter until 1877 in 1880 a change of party from a Conservative to a Liberal Government under Mr Gladstone led inevitably to the appointment of a 1880 Royal Commission.

The views of the Prime Minister on the subject were already known, for in a speech at Greenwich in 1875 he had said that it was particularly desirable that efforts should be made to give instruction in science to enable the British artist and workman to hold his place in the markets of the world. It must depend, he said, primarily upon the mind and will of the individual artisan:

All that others can do is to offer assistance and who should offer that assistance? I confess that I should like to see a great deal of this work done by the London Companies. I have not been consulted by the London Companies, but if so I would have besought and entreated them to consider whether it was not in their power to make themselves, that which they certainly are not, illustrious in the country by endeavouring resolutely and boldly to fulfil the purposes for which they were founded,

From this derogatory reference it was clear on whose side in any Royal Commission Mr Gladstone was likely to be.

Public interest in this Commission had been greatly stimulated by the chief enemies of the Companies who had diligently been filling the popular press with articles about the wicked behaviour of the City. There was Mr Phillips, a magistrate, writing articles under the name of 'Censor'. There was Mr Gilbert, a frequent contributor to the *Contemporary Review*, the *Fortnightly*, and the *Nineteenth Century*. He had also written a booklet called *The City* in which he quoted as authority and example a writer sinisterly hiding behind the pseudonym of 'Nemesis'.

'Nemesis' of the *Weekly Dispatch* was, so it transpired, none other than Mr James Beale who also wrote in the *Echo* under the name of 'Father Jean', a writer who showed that he owed considerable inspiration to Mr Firth, Member for Chelsea and author of a virulent attack on the Livery Companies in his work *Municipal London*. All these writers enjoyed one common factor: they wrote with extreme inaccuracy and in a spirit of complete antagonism. They used many of the more calculated tricks of demagogic propaganda by describing ordinary functions in a derogatory way. No one at a City banquet could be described as 'eating'. Instead an imaginative picture was painted of the 'guttling' that went on; nobody ever drank – they 'guzzled'.

Perhaps the most irresponsible of the conspirators was James Beale. In addition to his literary activities he was a member of the London Municipal Reform League and chairman of the Metropolitan Municipal Association. He was also a prominent member of the Liberation Society, which was working to prevent the devolution of money to the Church – a Church already, in his opinion, sufficiently rich. He was the presiding genius of such Workingmen's Clubs as the Eleusis, the Cobden, and the Hammersmith; and, in addition, he went round all the similar clubs in the metropolis lecturing on the subject of the iniquities of the City Companies. As it is safe to assume that the majority of his listeners had, before his visits, never heard of a Livery Company and had certainly never heard any other side of the picture than that presented by Beale, it is hardly surprising that, as he himself affirmed, 'in every case they universally assent to the ideas expressed'.

Now, it should be one of the essentials of a Royal Commission that the members of the Commission should seem to be absolutely impartial. Yet the Commission of 1880 not only consisted of nine members (out of twelve) of the predominant political party, but – and this was the most serious criticism of it – of three men known to be sworn enemies of the Companies they were judging. Among those were Mr James, Member of Parliament for Gateshead, and Mr Firth, Member for Chelsea and most prominent of the City's accusers.

Typical accusations that had been made against the Companies were as follows:

The show of charity covers a maladministration of trusts and a reckless disregard of charitable intentions such as find no parallel. The fact is that in many cases these votes of money to charitable purposes are neither more nor less than conscience money.

The conduct of the Companies has been such in their Trusts as, if they had been private individuals, would have subjected them to have been treated as criminals.

The vast sums they hold and which were designed for charitable purposes are being wantonly wasted in weekly feasts and orgies of unbounded wastefulness.

Large salaries and monies in shape of attendance fees on Courts and Committees are rewards paid to members of the Courts and that, in further addition to these moneys on the occasions of such feasts are slipped under the plates of dining members.

Relatives of Members of the Courts are educated in the Companies' Schools and there accommodated with Exhibitions in the Universities free of expense.

Members of the Companies are granted leases of Company properties at most advantageous terms and are thus enabled to make enormous profits from subletting.

City dinners are not a very elevating sight and nothing could be more disgusting than the condition of the Companies' Halls after these weekly orgies.

Decayed Company pensioners receive anything up to £300 a year and such Companies as the Goldsmiths' [whose income was alleged to be over £150,000 a year*] spend £30,000 a year on dining.

The £20,000 left by Mr. William Thwaytes to the Clothworkers' Company was a lunatic bequest and should be overthrown.

With so great a list of wrongs it is curious that the adversaries of the Livery Companies found so few to substantiate their criticisms.

With possibly the single exception of the former administration of trusts – and that was old, dead history for which reparation had been amply made and which could never again occur (the Charity Commissioners gave evidence of the faultless way the charities were now administered) – the collective conscience of the City Companies was entirely clear. One by one the charges fell to the ground and from the evidence there emerged a very different picture from the one that their accusers had tried to draw.

As the tale of the extraordinary lengths to which the Companies' good deeds extended was unfolded – a tale which it would have been wiser to have made public earlier and more consistently – it became apparent that the Companies were, in reality, very different organizations from those described by their detractors.

By the time the hearing was over only two of the hostile and prejudiced political majority were still prepared to vote for the complete dissolution of the Companies. In spite of this, and perhaps from its constitution inevitably, the report of the majority of the Commission was hostile to the Companies. The principal feature of the majority report was the appointment of Commissioners who were to compel the Companies to allocate their incomes to the support of 'objects of public utility'. They were to effect an entire change in the management of the City Companies' properties and 'to relieve the Courts and Liveries from the labours known to attach to properties and charities the accumulation of ages, now grown into a magnitude only to be dealt with under a well-devised system of centralisation and management in conformity with the spirit of the age and commensurate with the vastness of the possessions requiring to be dealt with'.

* Their total income, both corporate and trust, was at that time approximately one-third of this amount.

Subsequent twentieth-century experiments in 'well-devised systems of centralisation' (in other spheres of activity) were to be attended by results not universally effective. That the recipients of the Companies' charities were not subjected to such control was perhaps fortunate for them.

There were many Clothworkers who found it a matter for regret that a member of their Court, Sir Sydney Waterlow, should have voted for State control.

It was after the long battle was ended that there came a curious confirmation of the prejudiced nature of the struggle against the Companies. The Secretary of the Royal Commission, who should certainly have been without partisan feeling in the matter, writing without consent in the names of Lord Derby, the Chairman of the Commission, and his colleagues, circularized the newspapers, drawing their attention to the Report and asking them to comment favourably upon it, for, said he, it was a matter with which the Government intended to deal in the next session of Parliament and 'Consequently nothing is more necessary than to educate the opinions of the Liberal electors of the provinces who have little acquaintance with London matters'.

This attempt to influence provincial opinion upon the civic affairs of London, which can scarcely be held to have affected the provinces for the worse by anything that the City Companies might do, was typical of the biased attitude of the attackers.

As it happened, the report of the Royal Commission met with the fate of many other Royal Commissions. Not only did the matter sink slowly out of sight but a change of Government in 1885 – the session in which it had been hoped to introduce legislation – reduced the immediate danger of further attacks.

From the whole incident there emerged nothing but good; not only were the Companies kept on their mettle, but also, for the first time, their case was publicly stated. That their defence received less prominence than the attacks upon them is probable, but it was now on the record for all to read.*

---

* Of particular interest was the vindication published in 1885 by L. B. Sebastian, a member of the Skinners' Company.

If the City as a whole, and the Livery Companies in particular, could have learned from it that, while modesty is a most noble attribute, it can also be a dangerous one; if they had learned the lesson that it pays to advertise, the affair of the Royal Commission of 1883 would have been more useful still.*

All the time these attacks were being carried out the good work of the Clothworkers' Company was being continued without a pause. Huddersfield and Glasgow were brought within the scope of technical education. The City and Guilds of London Institute was given £10,000 and the promise of £3,000 a year. The Yorkshire College received an initial grant of £13,500 and an income of £1,200 a year. The Bradford Technical Weaving School got similar gifts of £3,000 and £150 a year. In every direction prizes were awarded and encouragement given to industry. Sixteen gold medals to the Woollen Exhibition at the Crystal Palace, prizes for industrial design at the Yorkshire Union of Mechanics Institutes, scholarships at Bradford – the munificence appeared endless.

The Yorkshire College was erected to the designs of Mr A. Waterhouse 'in the Gothic style of the fourteenth century freely treated'. The fact that it was spared from being covered with terracotta dressings was due to the provincialism of Leeds where they were 'not sufficiently known to calm the fears which some have of innovation'.

As a result of all this activity on the Company's part and, no doubt, of the attendant notice that the Clothworkers attracted in the local press, there came a curious echo of activities long since abandoned. The Company were asked in 1885 to intervene in a trade dispute. The Cloth Pressers' Association of Leeds brought to the Company's notice that

1885

A Trade
Dispute

> It has become during the past few years a custom with the majority of manufacturers in this neighbourhood to make all their low cloths (Unions, Tweeds and other kindred fabrics) in various lengths up to 100 yards and in not a few instances upwards of 100 yards, whereas the

---

* It was not until 1951 that the City and Guilds Institute thought it worth while having a Committee for Public Relations and at first only in the most embryonic form.

same kinds of cloth were formerly made 40 to 50 yards long. Our objection to the present enormous lengths is the difficulty we have in lifting and moving them about as required. ... When prepared or otherwise filled with paper ready for the press some of the pieces weigh (including paper) upwards of four hundredweight each; these unreasonable weights have in many cases to be lifted and moved from place to place by two men and the strain necessarily caused by these enormous weights has proved very injurious to many of our fellow workmen.

Our object in writing to you, Gentlemen, is to endeavour to obtain your sympathy and to ask for your influence with the manufacturers of the District and to prevail upon them, if possible, to discontinue the practice of making ends or pieces longer than 50 yards. Our efforts to accomplish this object have hitherto failed and, as we do not wish to take any step that would bring us into direct collision with our employers if it can be avoided by the intervention of a third party, and having already applied for assistance from the Leeds Chamber of Commerce who say they cannot help us in consequence of not having a Clothworkers' Committee in the Chamber.

We appeal most respectfully to you, Gentlemen, to assist us, feeling assured that you will readily see the injustice under which we labour. . . .

It is fascinating to speculate on what might have been the effect on trade relations if the Clothworkers had stepped forward and, with the same bold leadership as they had shown in education, had taken up again a controlling interest in the manufacturing side of industry. Perhaps the whole thing was really quite impossible; perhaps, after so many years, it would have been out of the question to reassume the status they had held, the status they had let slip away from them in the gentle processes of evolution. But there must remain a feeling of the faintest regret – for the chance would never again occur – that, probably inevitably, the Cloth Pressers' Association were told

that, although there may be some grounds for dissatisfaction with the growing practice of manufacturing cloth of increasingly greater length with a view to diminishing the cost of production in the face of competition at home and abroad, entailing as it does a greater amount of exertion and labour on the part of the Cloth Pressers and Carriers, yet the question on analysis involves so many difficulties and infringes on so many delicate interests and susceptibilities that this Committee, while desirous of utilizing the position of the Company for any good purpose in connection with the trade, albeit altogether outside and removed from the suburban circuit of three miles to which the jurisdiction formerly contemplated by the Charter was confined. Resolved that the matter being essentially a question between the Employers and their workmen the Committee does not consider the Company can usefully intervene.

For the future, then, the Company's interest in the cloth trade was clearly delineated as being confined to education and benevolence alone. That this benevolence was not limited to the English industry may be gathered from the fact that in 1881 they were quite prepared to give a special prize at the Crystal Palace Woollen Exhibition for Irish cloth ('a sound cloth of lasting colour . . . much appreciated by all who wear it'), although in earlier years the competition feared from Ireland had caused the abolition of the woollen cloth trade in that country.

All over the North of England technical colleges and mechanics institutes were springing up and soliciting the aid of the Clothworkers. Eventually the spate of applications for grants in aid became so overwhelming that it became necessary to rule that the time had come to refuse all such grants except through the City and Guilds Institute to which the subscription in 1885 was raised to £4,000 a year.

It must not be thought, however, that this enthusiasm for technical education was universal. There were those who considered that the whole thing was too much of an experiment to justify the expenditure of so much money, that the market would become overstocked with skilled artisans who would fail to find employment. Nor would they allow themselves to be persuaded that if an artisan were unemployed he would have more chance of getting work than one who was unskilled. But these critics were in a minority. The 'experiment' continued.

CHAPTER FIFTEEN

THE EXPERIMENT SUCCEEDS

*   *
  *

IT is from this juncture that the Textile Department of the Yorkshire College provides the focal point of the Company's history.

The original Textile Department, built at the Clothworkers' expense, contained

on the ground floor a lecture room and room for experimental weaving on small hand looms; on the second floor a museum, students' common room, drawing office and the instructors' private rooms. A large weaving shed is detached from this portion of the buildings in order that the noise of the machinery when in motion may not disturb the students in the lecture room. It contains eight power looms, all differently constructed, representing the classes of looms made by the best workers for the fancy woollens and worsted trades; seventeen hand looms, eight of which are mounted with jacquard and nine with witch or dobbie machines; also a twisting frame for producing a large variety of twist yarns.

There was also a Museum.*

* Museum exhibits of specimen wools, yarns and dyed textiles were becoming an inseparable part of Technical education. The Clothworkers' Company possessed a unique collection of samples of raw wool – it was found to have the moth but was saved in time – mostly from the colonies, which they were prepared to lend for such exhibitions as the Colonial and Indian Exhibition of 1886 – an exhibition which brought to England many official visitors. In addition to being feasted at Clothworkers' Hall, the visitors were entertained by the Company with such varied pleasures as a field day at Dartford for the trial of Nordenfeldt's Machine and Quick Firing Guns, a visit to the Continental Submarine (Channel) Tunnel Works, and a visit to the Asylum for Idiots at Earlswood. The Company later conferred the Honorary Freedom and Livery on representatives from Victoria and New South Wales.

The Textile Department was not established without difficulties and, indeed, opposition. Inevitably the buildings cost more than had been budgeted. More accommodation was required and still more money was called for. The Company promised in 1883 a further £10,000 and a future increase from £1,250 to £1,500 per annum for maintenance. This additional estimate, in its turn, proved to be too low and a long correspondence ensued on the subject. Eventually, somehow, the money was forthcoming[1] and the good work proceeded to an accompaniment of some adverse criticisms from – among all unlikely sources – the *New York Dry Goods Reporter*, which considered that the project was wasteful and did not teach students how to make a living.*

The truth of this latter assumption – readily disposed of in the loyal columns of the *Textile Recorder* – remained to be tested: if examination results provided any criterion, the efforts of the Textile Department were an immediate success – 'a standard of Excellence of the very highest order' was reported by the Examiners. No doubt encouraged by this result, the Company in 1885, when again the call came for more money for Leeds, agreed to provide a further £3,250.

1885

Although the Yorkshire College and the City and Guilds Institute – the latter at the time being in financially low water and having but little success in examinations – provided the chief outlet for munificence, the other educational and charitable activities continued unabated. The blind pensions in 1885 exceeded £5,000 per annum. The Technical College of Glasgow received £150 per annum for its Weaving School, Bradford Technical College had been given £3,500 towards its building fund – though unfortunately £1,300 was subsequently embezzled – and from Bradford too came a distant echo of the old search procedure when the Company gave £250 towards the establishment of 'a Conditioning House . . . where Tops, Noils, Wools and Yarns may be tested and certified for weight, workmanship etc.'.

* This was a form of criticism constantly levelled at technical education. The hard-headed north country mill owners were scarcely convinced three-quarters of a century later.

This Conditioning House provided in effect a revival, outside London, of old Blackwell Hall, and Article 12 to the provisional order for its establishment read: 'A Certificate issued by the Corporation [of Bradford] under their Seal, either alone or together with the Seal of the Worshipful Company of Clothworkers of London shall be deemed and taken as conclusive as to the accuracy of the contents thereof without further or other proof...'.

The general principle by which the Company was guided in distributing grants was the great Victorian virtue of self-help. When a town had raised on its own behalf from its inhabitants some considerable sum towards the creation of its own establishment for technical education, then, and not before, the Clothworkers' Company would make a grant, usually based on a percentage of the amount raised by local subscription. A general trade depression about this period was apt to make the local response to appeals a little tardy, but generally the money was somehow raised – the Jubilee of 1887 provided stimulus to such towns as Dewsbury – and a Clothworker grant received. *Per contra*, as soon as a technical institute was municipalized, the Company withdrew their support since they saw no good purpose in subsidizing in effect the ratepayers of the towns where the local council had taken over the responsibilities of technical education.

All the while, in the background behind the fanfares from the local press that heralded each new stepping-stone towards universal technical education, the other educational and charitable activities of the Company were continuing, as they had always done. In addition to the existing pensions for the blind the Company were soon to administer another trust arising from £70,000 left to them by William Wing for blind charities.*

* A close watch was kept to ensure that these charities were dispensed solely upon the deserving blind, and it was seldom that mistakes went undiscovered. In 1883 the owner of a house worth £80 a year and used as a brothel got a blind pension before being found out. 'That her expenditure is slight would appear from the fact that she has been in the habit of calling weekly at a nobleman's house to receive bits of bread and other waste scraps.'

Sutton Valence was in a better state than it had ever been and the recommendations that had been made by the Charity Commissioners in 1875 that it be turned into a boarding school for girls were rejected. This showed no anti-feminine attitude on the part of the Company. The higher education of women was bearing good fruit; it was a Miss Dawes, a Clothworkers' scholar of Girton who became the first 'Lady Master of Arts' at London University – for the first time in the country according to press reports.

School prize-givings provided many pleasant occasions for the Company. At one such ceremony at Peel, in the Isle of Man, 'Misses Lily Joyce, Gert Nelson, Susan Crane and Lena Foyle . . . recited – the last named receiving long and continued applause which only ceased on Miss Foyle's reappearance when she repeated the last portion of a most pathetic poem descriptive of a ship-wreck . . .'.[2]

Senior members of the Company were kept busy laying foundation stones and opening new buildings such as the Ossett Mechanics Institute.

It must have seemed the darkest kind of ingratitude – though it was, in fact, due to a total neglect of the arts of propaganda – to the Company that at such a time of munificence and charity and sheer hard work in far-sighted welldoing the Company found itself once again attacked by the ignorantly envious.

*　　*
*

1885　The first of these attacks came in the Corporate Property Security Bill, introduced by Sir Charles Dilke in 1885, a measure which 'purported to be merely to protect the property of such Corporations as our own' and to prevent Corporations being brought to an end and their property divided among the members.

Antagonistic Legislation　The Clothworkers' approach to this Bill was cautious. Although they had always held themselves to be entitled – though never intending such a course – to wind up the Company and divide their property as they might think fit, they thought that so long as the Bill meant no more than was purported it was not worth while to fight it. As, however, the City Guilds Association had decided to petition against the Bill, the Company, in order to have a *locus standi* in case of amendments, agreed to being joined to a modified form of petition.

A second attack comprised in the London Livery Companies Bill, another piece of legislation introduced by Dilke, was hotly opposed.

But the third onslaught, the Bill to impose a Succession Tax on Property held in Mortmain was thought by the City Livery Companies to be not unreasonable and no opposition was made to it. Under the terms of the Act the Clothworkers found themselves liable for the raising of some £1,800 a year – an imposition that called, in spite of the flourishing state of the Company's finances, for a corresponding degree of retrenchment. The retrenchment could hardly come from any other source than internal expenditure on entertainments and the like* and, since it was the internal expenditure that had been most critically investigated by the Royal Commission, it was on internal expenditure that the cuts fell. There seems, in any case, to have been at the time a prevalent feeling that nothing, however innocuous, must be done that could in any way be misinterpreted as politically provocative.

It was decided, for example, in 1895 that boxes of *bon-bons* should not be distributed to all and sundry at Thwaytes Dinners because it might so happen that a Member of Parliament might be presented with such a gift and deliberately exaggerate its value to the world at large. The *bon-bons* were in future to be distributed, seasonally, to Clothworkers at Christmas time.

The custom of fees being paid to the Master and Wardens on the occasion of their attending Church at the distribution of certain charities was abandoned except where the fees were payable under the wills of ancient benefactors. Many of the ecclesiastical charities themselves came under the purview of the City Parochial Charities Act which in 1883 was passed to remedy an obvious defect. As *The Times* put it some years later:[3]

* It is not clear whether this retrenchment was responsible for the appearance in 1889 of whale steak upon the menu of a Clothworker banquet – a dish greeted with the unfavourable and ribald comments of some eminent guests.

Originally possessed of modest funds distributable among large numbers of poor, the conversion of the City from an inhabited town to a mere place of business at once vastly increased their property and left scarcely anyone to be benefited by it. It was rumoured that an income of £100,000 a year resulted in nothing more than the maintenance of Church Services to which no one went.

The Charity Commissioners investigated and found that there was an ecclesiastical income amounting to between £30,000 and £40,000 and general property yielding over £50,000 per annum. A general tidying-up took place and a capital sum of £150,000 was devoted to buying open spaces and another of £163,000 for building polytechnics and free libraries.

Further
Attacks
1892

But the most unjust criticism of all came from members of the London County Council and the London School Board. In 1892 it was reported in the City Press that the Clothworkers

were constantly being told . . . that they spent their money solely upon guzzling, and that therefore they ought to be deprived of it, the more especially as it belonged to Londoners at large. . . . Either [the critics] were entirely ignorant upon the subject about which they were speaking . . . or they belonged to the peculiar and not altogether enviable class of politicians who looked upon persistent misrepresentations as a legitimate and very necessary weapon of warfare. . . .

. . . The gross income of the Company at the present time was about £56,000 a year. Out of that amount no less a sum than £16,000 was trust money which had necessarily to be devoted to certain specific purposes. That money was not only expended upon the objects for which it was left but the whole cost of administration was defrayed out of the private or corporate funds of the Company and was not in any way a charge upon the Charities. Further, wherever and whenever it was considered necessary or advisable, those charities were supplemented by the Company to the extent of several thousands of pounds a year. The Charity funds were roughly a little less than one-third. The question might very reasonably be asked: What do you do with the remaining two-thirds? Well, out of that money, which amounted to something like £40,000 a year, less than one-third was expended upon the personal wants of the Company. The remaining two-thirds was wholly applied to public and useful purposes – to education, to charity, to the support of aged and necessitous persons. It was necessary . . . to understand that out of the one-third that was devoted to the personal needs of the Company, the rates and taxes, including the Corporate Succession Tax of 5% and the establishment expenses, were defrayed, together with the charges of the estates and the costs of the entertainments that were given from time to time.

Regarding the entertainments which some people declared were the sole *raison d'être* of the Company, the total cost was only about 6% of the corporate income and that no less than one-third of that was supplied by a fund specifically left for the purpose by a member some 40 years ago.

Was it reasonable to suppose that the London School Board, with its jerry buildings, its doubtful contracts and its superfluous pianos would make better use of the money. . . ?

The following year the London County Council approached the City Companies with a specific proposal. Although, said the Council, technical education was being carried on excellently in various parts of the metropolis, nonetheless, it fell below the standard of the country as a whole, with the result that, though London contained a larger artisan population than anywhere else, its skilled artisan class was being largely recruited from the provinces with the result that many Londoners, from lack of training, swelled the ranks of unskilled labour. Would the City Companies be interested in the setting up of a Technical Education Board? 1893

L.C.C. Proposals

To this, as the *St James's Gazette* wrote,[4]

A very proper reply [was] made by the Clothworkers' Company to the invitation . . . to contribute towards the Council's tardy scheme for subsidizing Technical Education in London. . . . Considering that the London County Council is the last of the County Councils to make provision for Technical Education and even now only proposes to devote a third of the money available to the purpose, the demand was particularly arrogant. But still more so when the facts are known. For years the Clothworkers' Company has been helping technical and secondary education. Apart from its interest in the 'clothworkers' of Leeds and Bradford, it subscribes £4,100 (a tenth of its income) to the City and Guilds Institute and makes large donations to the Central Technical Institution in Exhibition Road and to the Islington Polytechnic.

Out of an income of £40,000, £17,000 is spent annually on secondary education alone [– a state of affairs which, as the Clothworkers claimed, showed that they had] anticipated years ago and long before the country generally was awake to the cardinal importance of Technical Education the claim now somewhat imperiously made upon their corporate funds.

They further pointed out that they administered £16,000 of charitable trusts' income free of charge, and that, if they were to do any more for technical education, these charities would have to suffer.*

It was an answer that should have been enough for most people but there were still those who refused to believe that the City Companies were not possessed of a vast hoard of illicitly gained wealth that they spent with vulgar lavishness. That in the years 1878–92 the Company (second only in generosity to the Goldsmiths) had given £61,700 towards technical education in London was a point that their attackers chose to ignore. That these same attackers were hard to satisfy is shown by the case of Mary Datchelor's School.

1894
The School
of Mary
Datchelor

In 1871 a scheme had been made out by the Charity Commissioners appointing trustees to administer the funds of an eighteenth-century bequest known as the Datchelor Charity. The major part of this scheme consisted of the establishment of a middle-class day school for girls. In 1877 the School had been opened in Camberwell. It grew rapidly and soon the income from its endowments was found to be too small. Sources of extra income were for long sought in vain. Now, in 1894, the Trustees approached the London County Council and asked them to become responsible for the maintenance of the School. The London County Council refused. And when, later in the year, the Clothworkers offered to take over the management of Mary Datchelor's School and give to its support an extra £400 per

* None the less, pursuing their own chosen course of technical education, the Company managed to find another £3,000 towards the building of new art rooms at Leeds, another £150 per annum for the teaching of drawing and design there, and £1,000 towards the People's Palace.

annum, their opponents on that very Council that had refused support denounced the Company for seeking to gain control for a mere £400 of monies which, they averred, should no longer be devoted to the middle classes but to the deserving poor. They added, with a single-trackedness of mind that was worthy of a better application, that the enormous incomes of the City Companies should be immediately applied to technical education.

The London County Council moreover, as well as pressing for an amalgamation of the County and City of London, urged that the accounts of the Livery Companies should be deposited with some public department and subject to public inspection – a suggestion that had been made ten years earlier and rejected by Parliament.

So tiresome did this constant sniping become that the London Municipal Society was formed for 'opposing attacks made by the London County Council upon the Trust and Corporate Property of the Livery Companies'. The Clothworkers subscribed £100 to the Society towards organizing 'a constitutional and legitimate league of defence against the wanton, systematic and unjustifiable misrepresentation of the Detractors and Enemies of the Corporation and Guilds of London'. With these constant, ungrateful attacks from their own countrymen and with the international scene gravely disturbed, it is not to be wondered that the Court spoke of the times as being 'of unexampled anxiety and suspense in the History of the Country'.

In 1889 the Lord Mayor had appealed for £100,000 to form a Patriotic Volunteer Fund fully to equip in the metropolitan area a volunteer force 'so as to enable them to take and keep the Field in the possible event of Invasion'. The Company gave £2,500 in five yearly instalments of £500.

But there were limits beyond which generosity could not be carried. When Sir H. Hervey Bruce, who had bought the Irish estates on mortgage, got into difficulties and asked the Company to excuse him the payment of £30,000 'which is not a matter of great moment to a wealthy Company while to me and my family it is a matter of great moment', the Court could not agree with him but forced the conclusion of a new, unsentimental, and businesslike bargain.

* *
*

1895
Limits to
Extent of
Technical
Education

There were limits, too, to the amounts that could be spent on technical education where that education was either ineffectual or with too remote a connexion to the Clothworkers' Company. The Northern Polytechnic Institute had received altogether £17,500 from the Company when in 1895 it was decided to have nothing more to do with the Institute – an attitude caused by the 'want of vigour which has unfortunately characterized the prosecution of this enterprize from the very commencement'. And when from Glasgow in 1897 came an appeal for more money, the chilling answer was given:

I suppose it is quite an unprecedented case that a London Guild, whose funds were intended for the benefit of Londoners and the local Trade associated therewith, should have given any support to a Weaving College in Scotland, and, so far from increasing the subsidy of £50 now given towards the Weaving and Dyeing College of Glasgow, it may become a question whether that amount may not have to be reduced or withdrawn. The total amount contributed by this Company since 1878 has been £1,900.

Moreover, when the Prince of Wales sought money for a hospital fund to celebrate the Diamond Jubilee, the Clothworkers, in agreement with the other Great Companies, flatly declined to take any appreciable part in raising the £12,000 a year required to place the hospitals out of debt.

As the Clothworkers pointed out, they were already giving 7 per cent of their corporate income to hospitals and dispensaries and were doubtful if this could be increased. And the giving of £20,000 to the Yorkshire College at Leeds had left no spare capital which could be devoted to the Prince's fund.

But this tightening up of the financial controls did not imply any increase in personal luxury for the members of the Company. Indeed, amidst all this expenditure on the welfare of others the expenditure lavished upon themselves was, with an eye on their

THE NINETEENTH-CENTURY HALL

enemies, radically reduced. In 1881 the new-fangled telephone had been installed in the Hall, but it was not until 1895, after protracted discussions, that electric light was also introduced. The Hall windows had been brightened with the arms of such Honorary Freemen as the Duke of Leeds, the Marquess of Dufferin and Ava, Viscount Wolseley, Lord Iveagh, Lord Masham, and Lord Kelvin. Copies of the portraits, belonging to the Duke of Leeds, of Sir Edward Osborne and Sir William Hewet had been commissioned. But beyond this the tale had been mostly one of internal austerity. Expenditure on the Ball had been cut, the Clothworkers had refused in 1892 to send an exhibit illustrating their particular craft to the Lord Mayor's Show, replying that 'this Company's utility is shown by their action in furtherance of Trade Education in various Clothworking districts of the country ... more especially Yorkshire – but it would be difficult if not inappropriate to present any Exhibit illustrating the craft of our Company'.

There was a pleasing exception to this self-denial when in 1889 a long outstanding obligation was fulfilled and £250 was allotted for the purchase of plate to commemorate the donors and benefactors whose gifts had been melted down in 1643 – an act which had been most earnestly commended to posterity nearly 250 years earlier. Now a silver salver, designed by Mr Edward Falkener, was bought and engraved with the names of the benefactors.

It was not until the Diamond Jubilee of 1897 that the Clothworkers felt that they could indulge in any outward display of expenditure upon themselves. At a cost of well over £800 they occupied 500 seats on the stands erected in St Paul's Churchyard. Over the Hall gateway the letters 'V R' were placed and illuminated with gas. For the first time in seventeen years the drawing rooms, at a cost of £1,500, were redecorated and recarpeted. There was none who could justly deny that they had earned this beautifying of a Hall from which so much money had been poured towards the upkeep and well-being of others.

1897
Diamond
Jubilee

As the nineteenth century drew to its end the fruits of their enlightened sowing were beginning to be garnered.

CHAPTER SIXTEEN

END OF AN ERA

*   *
*

Success of Yorkshire College 1894

THERE was no doubt about it, the Yorkshire College at Leeds was being a triumphant success. As the *Yorkshire Daily Post* had written in 1894:[1]

When one compares the character of the trade of Leeds and the district of two decades ago with what it is at the present day and considers that many of the more important mills in the locality are supervised by Yorkshire College men it becomes evident that the instruction imparted in that institution has in no small degree benefited the weaving industries of the city and neighbourhood.

There has been a complete change in the classes and styles of fabrics made in the district since the textile departments of the College commenced work. Some years ago Leeds was noted for its productions of plain textures: now fancy fabrics both of woollen and worsted materials in very extensive varieties are made in the neighbourhood.

Not only Leeds but other centres of weaving in the country have benefited, for from year to year a fair number of Scotsmen, for example, have received instruction at the College which they have utilized in their work north of the Tweed.

The amount of business daily transacted had now become so great that an Assistant Clerk and professional auditors had to be appointed: the blind charities that were yearly administered, to take but one example, amounted to £7,000, and in the last year of the old century the Company had accepted new responsibilities for education in the Isle of Man where 720 boys were receiving a free schooling. With such an amount of business to be transacted it was natural that there should be a somewhat closer scrutiny made of those who were responsible for transacting it.

Each year the Court were reminded, when it came to choosing from the Liverymen those who were 'auncientest, meetest and ablest' to be elected as Wardens, 'that there are other qualifications beside technical solvency required for succession to an office of such high dignity, trust and responsibility'.

The Court took notice, too, of a paragraph that had occurred in the return to the Royal Commission: 'The Livery or Clothing of the Company was intended to designate the more substantial and leading order of the Freemen and women, for it should be observed that Freewomen are under the Charters eligible for the Livery.'*

There had been an order of the Court of Aldermen in 1697 declaratory of the consensus of the Livery Companies on the point that a person qualified as a Liveryman of any of the Twelve Companies should have an estate of £1,000 and of the lesser Companies £500 – the spirit of the rule being still acted upon although there was no absolute property qualification. For their admission Liverymen now had to pay, in addition to their £20 fine, the sum of £85 as a composition fee for the Stewards' expenses in providing a banquet – a sum which had grown with the cost of living from the £25 of earlier times.

As a result, as the twentieth century dawned – and with it, symbolical of the old Company's forward-looking modernity, the Mastership of Lord Kelvin – the Company had never been more secure, both financially and morally. It must have seemed, as the Company read Dr Phene's† *Victoria Queen of Albion – an Idyll of the World's Advance in her Life and Reign*, that there was no end to the brilliance of the country's high noon.

---

* It is not entirely certain that the Royal Commission were accurate in this assumption. Although in the Charters it was stated that the Master and Wardens 'may be able every year or every two years or otherwise at their pleasure to make and have one Livery or Livery Clothing of One Suit among the Citizens of the said City, the then Bretheren and Sisters of the same Commonalty most sufficient thereunto', there is a school of thought that maintains that this does not refer to the Livery as it is understood today: at one time all freemen and freewomen were provided with Livery or Clothing by the wealthier Companies but later they restricted the wearing of a Livery to the elders of each Guild.

† Member of the Court.

There were, however, a few small clouds in the glittering sky. The political enemies of the Company still gave cause for alarm, and once again Sutton Valence was in very low water, with a great shortage of boys. The Headmaster, blaming the distance of the school from the railway and the typhoid epidemic for having caused such a falling away, resigned. And these clouds were the forerunners of approaching storm. The long years of peace and prosperity were nearly over.

South African War 1900

First there was the South African War; insignificant series of skirmishes though it might appear compared with the horrors that were waiting in the succeeding years of the century, it constituted an unwelcome drain on the corporate funds. Masters of the Twelve Great Companies and a number of influential and wealthy bankers and merchants were called to the Mansion House to consider the suggestion – allegedly from the War Office – that the City should 'provide, equip and despatch a special Corps of at least 1,000 Volunteers for special services in South Africa, to be selected from the various Metropolitan Volunteer Regiments, all of whom to be first-rate marksmen and half to be mounted'. £100,000 was required: the Corporation of London gave £25,000 on the spot. City company merchants and shipowners flung into the fund money and shipping for the force.

After some discussion the Clothworkers promised £2,000, which was raised out of income by abolishing the entertainments for the years 1900 and 1901 – a contribution which earned them the South African War Medal.

The war pursued its inevitable course. Losses among the Company, were, fortunately, few. Lieut-General Sir G. S. White, the defender of Ladysmith, was given the Freedom of the Company, and so was Captain Beachcroft Towse, the double V.C. But before final victory could be celebrated, the old Queen, who had led the country through years of unparalleled prosperity that it would be hard ever again to realize, was dead. And with her death, quite suddenly, everything seemed to change – and to change for the worse.

*　　*

*

For the first time the drive towards technical education seemed to falter and lose its momentum. At Bingley the textile classes were but poorly attended and local subscriptions amounted to no more than £11 16s 6d. In future, said the Company, their annual subscription of £50 would be dependent upon the aggregate of local subscriptions amounting to £250 – any sum less than that would mean that the Company's contribution would drop to 20 per cent of the lesser sum subscribed. But worse, far worse, was the fact that at Leeds there was reported the falling-away in quantity, if not in quality, of students at the Yorkshire College – particularly in the Dyeing Department – a development that caused much heart-searching in the Company.

The industrialists charged with investigating the state of affairs reported that the falling-off in numbers was due largely to competition from such nearby technical institutes as Bradford, Halifax, and Huddersfield. It was not to be regarded as a fault of the teaching at Leeds: the popularity of certain courses went in cycles. Just after the discovery of coal tar colours everybody had wanted to learn chemistry. Now electricity was the fashionable study and – an additional factor in decline – the new colours had made dyeing a matter of working to a recipe: the Germans had recipe books and how to apply them. It was thought that teaching must in future concentrate more on developing intelligence than on imparting mere technical skill – training for leadership in industry must be the new target.

A difficulty in the way of this was the attitude of the cloth industry itself. It was the old story of the conflict between science and practice: the hard-headed mill-owners were either apathetic or even hostile to college technical training. Even those manufacturers who had reluctantly given their children a higher education were complaining of the length of the vacations – the sons who were preparing for the long dour struggle of competitive industrialism were, they said, not having to work hard enough.

The curriculum of the Clothworkers' Department at Leeds was reorganized, students were told that practical study was expected of them during the vacations, and the authorities were told that, if they were to expect any support for their idea of forming an independent Yorkshire University, they must make their working-year longer.*

In 1903 the Court of the Clothworkers' Company was informed that Leeds had decided to ask for a Charter as an independent Yorkshire University. The Company's first reaction was both hasty and unexpected. The Clerk wrote that the Clothworkers had no more money to spare – they had already given Leeds all that they could afford. They thought, as they had said before, that the terms were too short, the training insufficiently strenuous, and that, considering all things, it was a mistake ever to have had anything more than a Technical College at Leeds.

To this sudden outburst, Leeds replied with a great calm that they thought there must be some misapprehension; they were not asking for money; they were simply keeping the Company informed of the College's actions.

Mollified by the softness of the reply, the Clothworkers announced that they would be prepared for the Clothworker Departments to become part of the new University and would give £4,000 per annum to them, as long as they were allowed to continue on the same footing as the Departments of Agriculture, Engineering, and Leather – otherwise they would withdraw the departments altogether and form a technical college quite apart from the new university. The Company pointed out that this yearly grant they offered showed an increase of £300. They had already spent more than £70,000 on Leeds and the £4,000 a year represented a capitalized sum of upwards of £200,000.

The Council of Leeds gratefully accepted the offer and in 1904 a Royal Charter was given to the new foundation of Leeds University. In deference to objections from Sheffield and Bradford the claim to be known as Yorkshire University had been abandoned.

Looking back on the event twenty-one years later, it was considered 'not too much to say that the guaranteed support of the

* The Yorkshire College at Leeds was originally a college of the subsequently disbanded Victoria University, which consisted of Liverpool, Owens, and the Yorkshire College.

Company was one of the determining factors in the success of the Yorkshire College's petition for an independent University Charter at the beginning of this Century'.

*   *
*

But if the Clothworkers offspring in the North was from henceforth to flourish, the Company were much worried by the sickly condition of their London brain-child. For some time past the City and Guilds of London Institute had been in financial difficulties, as one by one various Livery Companies fell off from their support. When in 1904 there arose a first-class financial crisis, the Clothworkers reacted strongly and indignantly. Steps must be taken to avoid 'such a catastrophe as the weakening or dissolution of this great organisation'. They wrote to the Institute, pointing out that the present income was barely sufficient 'to maintain the efficiency of its various branches in face of the improvements called for by foreign competition'. To offset, in part, the default of other subscribers, the Clothworkers were prepared to vote £3,500 for the current year – 'the largest annual grant they have made to it since the Institute discontinued its subsidies to local Technological Classes in Yorkshire and other places connected with the Textile Industries, thereby necessitating additional direct subsidies from the Company ... '.

1904 Crisis in Affairs of City and Guilds of London Institute

The following year they would increase this sum to £4,000, 'if as the result of the present crisis it is shown that the other Companies will do their share in maintaining this Institution for which they have a joint responsibility. Should, unfortunately, no satisfactory arrangement be made the Clothworkers will be forced to reconsider their own position in respect to the Institute.'

The only response, almost immediately forthcoming, was that the City Corporation reduced its subscription to the Institute.* And, although early in 1905 a meeting was held and the repre-

1905

* There was a minority suggestion among some diehard members of the Corporation that technical education was a waste of time, energy, and money, and that it had only been taken up by some of the City Companies 'to save their bacon' – an innuendo which, however true it may have been of some Companies, was clearly not applicable to the Clothworkers.

sentatives of the Livery Companies attended, holding out hopes of increased subscriptions, by November it was found necessary to report a 'meagre response' in spite of the fact that there had been 'munificent support' from the Goldsmiths and a generous contribution by the Fishmongers.

The Court were asked to 'remember that the Clothworkers' Company subscribe £4,000 per annum to the Leeds University for the provision of Technical Education specially suited to their own – Textile – Trade, and they see no reason why they should fill up the gaps caused by the laches of other Companies as regards the City and Guilds Institute'. However, the Company considered 'that the abandonment of a national and valuable work which has conferred such lustre on the Livery Companies would be disastrous on public grounds and would undoubtedly cause a revival of serious attacks on the constitution of the Companies'.

Somehow the City and Guilds Institute contrived temporarily to overcome the financial difficulties which continued for many years to be a feature of the organization – and indeed the more successful it became the more it needed extra funds from the City. But the survival and evident success of the Institute did not in any way prevent the further attacks – that had been foreseen – upon the Constitution of the Companies. In 1909, for example, a strong attack by the 'Progressive Party' of the London County Council was made against the City Companies, reminding the public of the Royal Commission and its recommendation for 'the allocation of a portion of the corporate income of the Companies respectively to objects of acknowledged public utility'. Among these objects were services which were borne by the rates – 'education, baths, parks, workmen's dwellings, etc.' – but the obvious unreasonableness of the attack caused it to fail, as other later attacks were also to fail.

With all the expenses that beset the Clothworkers' Company in their well-doing, it is not surprising that those responsible for the finances began to talk of 'overburdened resources'. There had to be taken into consideration a capital overdraft of £35,000, 'still remaining to be liquidated out of the Company's income in the

Further Attacks on City Companies

1909

Company's Finances Strained

matter of the Land, Building and Equipment of the Clothworkers' Wing of the Leeds University, Christian's School Building, etc. etc.'. It became necessary to off-load some of the responsibilities that they had borne so long.

As early as 1904 it had been reported that the Clothworkers, being dissatisfied with conditions of the School at Sutton Valence and finding their expenses in connexion with it considerable, 'were seriously considering closing the school altogether and handing it over to the Kent Educational Authorities to be utilized as a Board School under the recent Education Act'. This the Company strenuously denied – 'under the present excellent Headmaster it is doing good educational work, although the numbers are disappointing'. It was just possible, the Clothworkers admitted, that some kind of arrangement might have to be made with the Kent Educational Authorities but never with the idea of turning it into a Board School, and 'if as the result of improved access and locomotion Sutton Valence should become a resort for Retired Officers and those who would appreciate a cheap and almost free education of a higher type . . .', the Company would be particularly loath to weaken a connexion of 300 years' standing.

However, by 1908, a year when the Company were spending more than £1,000 per annum on Sutton Valence – a school which the Headmaster referred to as 'Rugby at half-price' – there were still no more than sixty boys there, and the Clothworkers began publicly to wish that it could 'be drawn within the orbit of the Kentish Secondary Schools'.

There was, however, another suggestion that was taken up: that an amalgamation be arranged with the United Westminster Schools who were looking for a place for a boarding school in the country. Much correspondence ensued to ensure the full protection of the various interests involved. Land for new buildings was promised. The connexion with the name of William Lambe was to be kept. The Clothworkers agreed to help the United Westminster Schools over the cost of the new buildings – they would pay £5,500 over a period of ten years; £1,000 of it being paid in the first year. A generous gift of land was made by Sir Edgar

Horne. Places were to be reserved in the school by the Governors for Lambe Scholars.*

1910   In 1910 the Clothworkers at last handed over the responsibility to the United Westminster Schools, although they were forced by the Board of Education to retain some share of the estate management of the place. As a parting gift they presented to the new school buildings a 'suitably inscribed' clock with Westminster chimes. But, at the last prize-giving and visitation of the old regime – a regime that had lasted 335 years – only one Clothworker could be found to represent the Company. It made a sad contrast to those great occasions of the nineteenth century when visitations were made in splendour by all the members of the Court and their ladies, when the members of the Company, after a drive in carriages through the grounds of Filmer Castle, were received 'with every token of esteem and respect by the poorer sort among the inhabitants' and regally entertained by the scholars.

With relief from the weight of Sutton Valence in sight and with considerable retrenchment in many directions, it was agreed in 1910 to give £5,000 to Leeds University to complete the Clothworkers' buildings there. By 1912, when the new buildings were opened, the Company had spent, since 1876, £160,000 on Leeds University.

*   *
*

The new reign, that of George V, began uneventfully enough. The Company were in a commanding position among the leaders of the technical education movement. This position was owed, it was generally agreed, in a great measure to Sir Owen Roberts – a Clerk of quite exceptional merit and ability, who had retired in 1907 after forty-one years of service.

In spite of this position, however, the Clothworkers had taken no corporate part in the Coronation ceremonies. Quite ended now

---

* There was a proposal too from Sutton Valence that the William Lambe Almshouses there should be done away with and non-resident pensions put in their place – a proposal to which added point was given from the fact that they had been largely destroyed in a fire.

were the customs observed from the reign of Charles II to that of George IV when the Masters and Prime Wardens of the Twelve Great Companies were chosen to assist the Lord Mayor of London 'as Deputy Chief Butler of England to the Most Noble the Duke of Norfolk, Chief Butler, in presenting a cup of wine to the sovereign on the occasion of the Coronation banquet and thereby to testify the loyalty of themselves and the Companies over which they preside to the Throne of these Kingdoms'.

This year, once more, the Coronation banquet had not been held and there was no way in which the Companies could be represented at the ceremonies. Even their attendance at the rejoicings was greatly whittled down. At the Coronation of Edward VII* the Clothworkers had been allotted 500 seats in St Paul's Churchyard: now in 1911 there were only 1,000 allotted for all the City $\quad$ 1911 Companies together – a state of affairs that led the Clothworkers to decide against applying for any for themselves. Now they settled down in the new reign to the dull but necessary task of completely reorganizing their trusts and charities – a task that was suddenly interrupted by the outbreak of the first of the great world wars.

In an age when the development of the flying machine and the $\quad$ 1914 rocket was insufficiently advanced to bring about any great realization of the concept of total war, the physical dangers to the Company's lives and property were inconsiderable. The first $\quad$ World divisions went to France, Clothworkers amongst them, and those $\quad$ War I who remained at home did what they could in circumstances in which the inconveniences were more mental than physical. All the Company's entertainments were suspended for the duration of the war, and War Relief Funds – some of them with very queer-sounding titles, such as The Imperial Maritime League (Villages

---

* In connexion with this Coronation ceremony, it is of interest to note that some of the diamonds in the Crown supplied for the Coronation of Queen Alexandra were afterwards embodied in the new Master's Badge of the Clothworkers. This Badge, presented by Mr F. Morgan in 1905, was copied from a design earlier suggested by J. B. Carrington and prepared 'from the point of view of how to get the most definitive and simple effect of the character of a sixteenth-century jewel while preserving and adding to the symbolic and heraldic details thereof and enriching the same withal by the best stones and workmanship available'.

and Rural Districts) Enlightenment and Recruiting Campaign; The Emergency Committee for the Assistance of Germans, Austrians, and Hungarians in Distress; The Sportsman's Battalion; and The Royal Army Temperance Association: Appeal for Recruiting Bands – vied for the Clothworkers' charity.*

1915 In Leeds the Clothworkers' Departments took on a new importance. The loss of German dyestuffs added a greater significance to the tinctorial chemistry and dyeing that was being carried out there; and when in 1915 King George V visited Leeds and saw for himself what the Clothworkers were doing in the way of high explosives and aniline dyes, he thanked the Master for the Company's munificence.

But Leeds and the constant call for subscriptions to war charities apart, the Great War – as it was called till another greater had dwarfed it in the public mind – is reflected in the Company's records as little as those early wars in the first days of the Company's life. The great war leaders of the Empire were honoured by the Clothworkers: W. M. Hughes of Australia, W. F. Massey of New Zealand, Jan Smuts of South Africa, Sir William Robertson, the C.I.G.S. – all were made free of the Company.

Wounded colonial soldiers and those who had formed the first seven divisions were entertained at the Hall, but, such occasions apart, the War scarcely intruded into the minutes and certainly offered but few physical dangers to the Company. It is true that in **1917** 1917 the Ironmongers were accommodated at the Clothworkers' Hall after damage had been done to their Hall by an air raid, but devastation such as was to strike the Company not a quarter of a century later was unthinkable.

Owing to the uncertainty of the times – it seemed that it would be long before entertaining could be resumed – much of the Company's champagne was, in 1917, sold. £750 was given towards equipping the research laboratories at Leeds – in spite of all the effort there it was alleged that the dyestuffs industry was still in a deplorable state.

* £2,000 was given to the Prince of Wales's National Relief Fund and £500 to Belgian Relief.

And then, quite suddenly, the War which had seemed unending 1918 was over and the Company could sit back and take stock of their position.

During the war years more than £22,000 a year had been given from the Corporate Funds to charities – a term which included £2,500 a year to the City and Guilds Institute and £4,000 a year to Leeds where valuable research was being carried on. As the University had noted:

With a fuller recognition of the need for technological and scientific research the textile and dyeing industries will realise more clearly than in the past the enormous debt which they owe to this London Company for its far-seeing and munificent action in establishing, equipping and maintaining the Clothworkers' Departments of the University.

In addition to these gifts, £20,000 a year had been paid out of the Charitable Trusts Fund, and the Company were more than ever identified with the welfare of the blind; out of their own trusts £8,500 was yearly paid to blind charities, and, in addition, the Blind Man's Friend Charity with an annual income of £3,800 was administered entirely free by the Hall Staff. £14,500 had been given to war charities – the list seemed endless.

With so many financial preoccupations there had come grave Post-War worries, worst of which the occasion when the Clothworkers Difficulties

were carrying the £71,000 Bank Loan raised to help the Government, when the outlook was not very promising and securities kept falling in value, and when the Bank was inclined to press us to realise our securities and cut our loss; a loss represented at one time on paper at over £10,000 but fortunately reduced by waiting to £1,100 and, if the Court could have waited a little longer, even this would have been turned into a profit. . . .

In addition, the Company were worried by the great rise in taxes, rates, and prices. Income and property tax payable by the Clothworkers had risen from £2,573 in 1913 to £12,600 in 1919. It was thought unlikely that entertaining on the old pre-war scale would ever be reintroduced.* There were reasons too, quite other

---

* Fortunately, loss of life had been on a smaller scale than loss of treasure – no more than thirteen members of the Livery were killed in action.

than financial, why it was impolitic to think in terms of too great personal expenditure. Inevitably after the war was over there was political unrest which not only led to further attacks upon the City Companies but also put certain physical difficulties in the way of resuming the entertainments.

In 1919, before St Thomas Eve, the Court decided that 'having regard to the possibility of further industrial unrest and consequently of difficulties in travelling, particularly for elderly persons, and in view of the uncertainty as regards both food and coal supplies . . . it would be safer, under such circumstances, not 1920 to attempt to hold the usual entertainment this year'. It was not until the following year that – in the face of some opposition within the Company – entertainments again got under way to the extent of two Livery Dinners a year.

1921 Some members of the London County Council too began again to agitate for an enquiry into the funds of the City Livery Companies and, in 1921, arranged a meeting to enquire into the educational activities of the Companies. They could hardly have arranged any enquiry that was less likely to reward them with opportunities for attack. The Twelve Great Companies gave the Council an imposing list of the educational activities in which they were engaged – the Clothworkers' contributions to Leeds University, the City and Guilds Institute, and the Mary Datchelor School being by no means the least – and by 1924 the Council were at last able to decide that enough was in fact being done by the City Companies in the way of education.

The Clothworkers principal educational charity had, as it happened, been a source of some recent anxiety to them. At the Leeds end of World War I, Leeds University had been financially speaking in extremely low water. 'In spite of the huge profits made by the textile firms in the neighbourhood, the University appeal for funds had been but poorly responded to compared with Newcastle, Liverpool, Manchester and Bristol and the situation at 1922 Leeds is at present one of great anxiety.' The Clothworkers had rallied round with an immediate gift of an additional £1,000 for the year 1922 and somehow the University had survived the difficult post-war period. Now in 1925 the University gave vent to an appreciation of the work the Company had done there, work that was 'the outstanding feature of the financial history of the University'. They noted that the Clothworkers had given 'capital donations amounting to £80,000 . . . and annual grants for maintenance, aggregating by the end of the year 1923–24 the sum of £140,000'. And, as has been noted elsewhere, it was 'not too much to say' that the guaranteed support of Leeds by the Company had been one of the determining factors in the granting of a Charter to the new University. 'The Clothworkers' Departments are well-   1925 housed,' the report continued, 'but their efficient maintenance requires an expenditure greater than their income and consequently entails a disquieting drain on funds which are wanted for University development.'

The Company's response to this new appeal was startling in its generosity. They proposed to increase their grant to £7,000 a year for seven years, provide £1,300 for the purchase of special equipment, and a capital sum of £17,000 for building additions. The University was quite overcome by this new munificence. 'The Company has not merely created the leading Textile School in the world. It has also been largely responsible for creating a University which is the most virile institution that I have ever had experience of,' wrote A. M. Wheeler. And it was pleasing to note, too, that gradually the dour practical opponents of technical education were being won over from their attitude of disapproval. Two farmers reported that 'the whole outlook with reference to woolgrowing' had been changed by Leeds Textile Departments, and one of Yorkshire's best-known industrialists was said to have spent two hours at the University stand at the Yorkshire Show and had afterwards actually admitted that he had found it very interesting.

*   *

*

Meanwhile, the domestic affairs of the Clothworkers were reverting almost to the old pre-war normal routine. Loyal gifts were made on the occasion of such royal weddings as those of Princess

Mary and the Duke of York. In 1924 Prince George of Kent became a Freeman and was presented with the Honorary Livery of the Company. Several substantial sums were voted towards such varied appeals as those of the preservation of the Old Vic and of St Paul's. There was talk, too, of rebuilding the Company's own Hall in conjunction with some commercial undertakings whose rents would pay the costs involved in the scheme. The Cloth-workers' Hall and offices were to be, so it was suggested, on the third and fourth floors of a building of which the lower floors should be let as offices. There was – as many thought, rightly* – considerable opposition to this plan. A large income was not, it was implied, everything, certainly not everything if there were to be lodgers in the house; and it was eventually rejected. Rejected, too, was the suggestion that at the British Empire Exhibition at Wembley 'the Master and some Members of the Company should take part on horseback in the forthcoming Pageant repre-senting the Livery Companies in the time of Queen Elizabeth'. The organizers were told that 'this suggestion was quite impossible.'

Four years later, on 18 January 1928 was celebrated the 400th anniversary of the Company.

---

* Being, however, wise after the event, the reverse is perhaps true – a new, modern building might well have withstood (as did many such buildings nearby) the air attack of May 1941.

CHAPTER SEVENTEEN

THE GREAT UPHEAVAL

* *
*

As the Clothworkers entered the fifth century of their existence, it was permissible to look back briefly over the long road they had trodden.

Of the old forms and practices of the original Company outwardly little was left. Control of the trade, the merchant body, the artisans, yeomanry, and apprentices all had disappeared except for vestigial remains. The decay of the Company's physical control over workmanship and working conditions had begun to be felt even during the days of Elizabeth, and, although the Company had formally appointed searchers until 1754, it had been little more than a formality for at least a hundred years earlier. Arbitration had also long since fallen away since they had no powers to enforce that arbitration. All that was left, indeed, of the old day-to-day Guild observances was the assistance of their sick, infirm, aged, and decayed Clothworkers and the provision of the traditional occasions for good-fellowship amongst their members.

Apprenticeship had long since become a matter of form. The Yeomanry remained, if they remained at all, only faintly to be seen in the body of Freemen outside the Livery, some of them bearing Elizabethan names and, no doubt, descended from the old craftsmen of the Company. But if these remains of the former days seemed to the uninformed largely nominal, they were in fact still very much alive and still intensely vital. Apprenticeship, for example, had been replaced by technical education – which of course furthered the Company's old ideals, constantly improving by research at Leeds the standards of workmanship.

Moreover the Livery and the Court, the Master and the Wardens had – apart from ceasing to control the working cloth trade – altered but little throughout the centuries. They had been well nourished by the early prudence and frugality of their fellow Clothworkers.

From the property they had bought or been left in the young days of the Company had grown the great estates which provided the source of their munificence. Some of the original properties still survived the centuries. The Hall in Mincing Lane, Nos. 46, 47, and 48 in Fenchurch Street, the Billiter Square and Billiter Street properties, had been handed down from the days before the amalgamation of the Fullers and Shearmen. 118 Fenchurch Street and Nos. 4–6 in Hogarth Court had been left to the newly-founded Clothworkers by the Countess of Kent in 1540. The site of the White Swan in Tudor Street had been bought in 1577. The original site of Wood Street Square had been left to the Company by William Lambe. And 77 Wood Street had been bought by the Shearmen as early as 1520. There were others too,* including the Moorgate and Copthall Estates – some original properties, some of later purchase or bequest – which, with the vast increase of property values in the City, had supported the Clothworkers through the many financial crises of their history.

1928   Now, as they celebrated their 400th anniversary – a celebration which included the presentation of a copy of the Chetwynd Cup to every member of the Court and Livery at a total cost of £1,400 – it was fortunate for their peace of mind that,they could not foresee the holocaust that only thirteen years later was to consume the buildings on many of those sites and the rents that sprang from them. But in 1928 the world seemed a tolerably safe place to live in and the question of the percentage of foreign students at Leeds – 22 per cent in the Textile Departments – was a matter of concern for trade rather than for ideological reasons. Was it a good idea to spend money, the Company had to ask themselves, on teaching foreign students who would eventually go home and set out to obtain our trade – a trade which was somewhat distressed?

* See Appendix C.

But in 1929 there was still room for liberal views to be heard and 1929 to prevail, and it was decided that, since for the most part foreign universities admitted without discrimination the students of countries other than their own, Leeds would also do so.

*   *

*

The years immediately preceding World War II were almost entirely uneventful in the Clothworkers' annals: it was a time in which the efficient administration of their estates was a business which had reached such proportions that it became necessary in 1934 to appoint, as ten out of the eleven other Great Companies had already appointed, a professional auditor to protect the Cloth-workers' own auditors.

They were years whose records every now and again aroused echoes of their past – a desire (quickly resisted) to renew to some more active extent their old connexion with Sutton Valence, an invitation (refused after much divergence of opinion) to go with the Lord Mayor to open a new bridge at Londonderry.

But, looking to the future as they were, they resolutely re-   Clothing frained from opening old and long-concluded negotiations. They   Charities also brought up to date some of the old surviving customs. The Clothing Charities were simplified by the granting of a £5 gift voucher from a well-known but inexpensive store. And the Clothing Cakes, distributed on the occasion of Webb's Charity but no longer generally appreciated, were superseded in 1937 by chocolates.

There was an echo of the days when the Company still controlled   1937 working conditions and entry into the cloth trade in the reminder, sent out in 1937, that no Clothworker might be a member of any other City Livery Company. Ten Clothworkers had unwittingly disobeyed the Ordinance in this respect but *nunc pro tunc* were given permission to do so.

There was, moreover, in spite of the need for economy that had curtailed entertainments in 1932, no stinting in the Company's charities. Leeds University was now receiving £6,000 a year, London University was granted £2,000 a year for ten years. And, in celebration of the Royal Silver Jubilee, the Mary Datchelor School – a school which had more than justified the Company's fondest hopes – was granted £2,000 towards the building of a new combined Hall and swimming pool.

No one can grudge them the comparatively small sums that they spent on their own entertainment and on the gifts made to each member on such occasions as the Silver Jubilee and the Coronation of King George VI. In any case, the entertainments and gifts, the dinners and the receptions, were the last that the Company were to enjoy for many years to come, the last that many Clothworkers were to enjoy in a Hall of their own.

1938   In 1938 there came to the City the first serious threat of War. Part of Clothworkers' Hall, it was arranged with the City Corporation, should become a first-aid post. In the Upper Still Room, gas masks were to be stored. Prayers for peace were offered up and, 'while the Prime Minister was actually on his way to Germany on 15th September for the first of those three historic meetings with the German Chancellor, Herr Hitler, Clothworkers' Hall was closed for ten minutes and [in the Court Room] was held an informal intercession Service attended by everyone in the building, workmen included, the Westminster Abbey form being used'.

For a few brief months the sun broke again through a gap in the clouds. The normal business of the Company continued more or less as it had always done. The annual grant to Leeds University was increased by £500. The Company's plate, which had been lent to the Congress of *La Ligue Internationale des Adversaires de la Prohibition* at Vintners' Hall, was lent, in part, to the New York World Fair. Only the Livery reception failed to come up to expectations during the brief lull. No more than nineteen members of the Court and forty of the Livery accepted the invitation, and to fill the Hall the Company's lessees and tenants were invited to make a total attendance of 350.

1939   Then the sunlight faded again, and for the second time in a quarter of a century Great Britain and Germany were at war.

*   *

*

278

For the first few months it seemed almost possible that, in spite of World War II all the preparations, the City might go free from danger, but for safe custody the plate that had been lent to the United States remained there. Moreover, an alternative strong-room was provided at Hays Wharf for the Pepys Cup and some of the Best Plate. Duplicates of the Company's records were made on microfilm and stored at Morden.

Just for those first few months the Company remained poised in the vacuum of the unreality of a war that seemed to be no war – the Freemen were regaled as usual on St Thomas's Eve and chocolates were distributed to the Livery at Christmas – and then, in June 1940, the normal world disappeared in the fantastic debacle that flung the Allied armies from the Continent.

As the troops came streaming back to England it was thought 1940 that the Livery Halls would be used for billeting and the Clothworkers announced that they could accommodate 150 or even 200 soldiers in an emergency. And though this was one of the emergencies that did not take place, there were soon others – such as the Fishmongers and the Girdlers occupying the Hall as air-raid after air-raid upon the City made increasing numbers homeless.

On 1 October 1940 the Hall narrowly escaped destruction when a bomb fell into the churchyard, bringing to light a plague pit but failing to explode. The building was rapidly 'evacuated', and 'to allay local anxiety and apprehension ... the Company's Union Jacks in Mincing Lane and Fenchurch Street' were displayed. The Bomb Disposal Unit was also informed, and since it proved impossible to render the bomb harmless by defusing, it was exploded *in situ* after filling the pit it had made with 10,000 sandbags. Such care was taken in this operation by Captain Davies (who subsequently was to save St Paul's) that the Hall suffered no damage other than the destruction of the kitchen annexe and the wall at the back of the Court Parlour.

From henceforth the City was for many months to be almost continually attacked. The first Court meeting of 1941 opened with a 'short prayer in recognition of the Hall having been preserved from destruction in the Fire Raid in the City on the night of

Sunday, 29th December, which destroyed Guildhall and so many Livery Halls and historical buildings'. That the Hall had escaped on this occasion was due largely to the initiative of the Beadle and the Porter when fire bombs fell on the roof of a nearby building that was without fire-watchers or occupants – and for their action on this occasion they were made free of the Company.

But, though the Hall had for the moment escaped, all the Company's property in Wood Street Square had been that night destroyed, and with it had been destroyed the source of income for St James's Church, for the Exhibitions at St John's College, Oxford, and for some of the Clothing Charities.

On 8 March 1941 another unexploded bomb under the back wall of the Court Parlour led to another partial 'evacuation' of the Hall. This time the bomb – which brought to light some Roman pottery of the first century at a depth of 30 ft – was successfully defused and the business of the Company continued. It was business conducted under extreme difficulties. With the willing consent of the Court the Clerk was serving part-time as Commander of a Home Guard company; the Assistant Clerk, too, was similarly engaged on confidential work with the police force; the Beadle was involved in City air-raid duties; in fact every man on the Company's staff was engaged in some form of National Service, either wholly or in part. In spite of this a 'Government week' of forty-six hours was faithfully worked in the Clothworkers' Office and the affairs of the Company, although kept to an absolute minimum, continued. Court and Committee meetings were held as usual. Many of the blind pensions were transferred to the Metropolitan Society for the Blind, who acted as agents for the Company, and special emergency arrangements to carry on the work of the Court Committees in the absence of a necessary quorum were agreed. In Clothworkers' Hall the Fishmongers and Girdlers carried on their own disrupted businesses. In the Company's shelter a City firm, important to the War effort, was given sleeping accommodation. A fire-watching force was established.

But when, during the night of 10 May 1941, another spectacular raid, lasting for five hours, devastated the City, no fire-watching force could hope to stem destruction on a scale unknown since the Great Fire which had destroyed that earlier Hall.

1941
The Hall
Destroyed

The bomb damage of seven months earlier was still being repaired when the first incendiary bombs fell among the builders' timber piled in the churchyard adjoining the Library. These were quenched, and immediately the fire-fighters had to rush into the Hall to deal with three isolated incendiaries which pierced the roof of the Livery Hall and another which fell through a ventilator into the Clerk's room.

There then came a plea for help from the nearby London Tavern, but while it was being answered another shower of incendiaries – quite impossible for the few helpers to cope with – fell upon the Tavern which quickly became an inferno, 'particularly as it contained much woodwork'.

By 2 a.m. the Hall was ringed about with fire but still stood intact among the flames when suddenly the telephone rang eerily among the chaos as the Clerk managed to make contact from the suburbs with the beleaguered fire-fighters whose

difficulties ... were much increased by the blast from various high explosive bombs which fell at intervals, completely stunning our men, but, though knocked over on several occasions, no-one, fortunately, was blown off our roofs or badly injured by falling walls. One result of these bombs was, of course, to destroy every remaining window and door in the neighbourhood and to blow through them flaming debris of all descriptions, the fires from which were continually fed by fresh deluges of incendiary bombs. The various official fire brigades were employed elsewhere and it was not until early morning that we were able to secure their help.

By this time, however, the South East corner of the Livery Hall was catching fire from the adjoining Dunster House which, in its turn, had become involved in the Mark Lane inferno started by the London Tavern.

About 7 o'clock on Sunday morning it was clear that the Hall was doomed as the volume of flame from Dunster House was overwhelming and as the Fire Brigade ... had not sufficient pressure to reach the top of the Livery Hall.

Within an incredibly short time our whole building was on fire from top to bottom and our gallant band of workers could do no more than endeavour to protect the back of No. 48 Fenchurch Street which had already been on fire several times but was eventually saved.

By the time the Clerk arrived at the Hall it was nothing 'but a smoking ruin whilst fires were still raging in Fenchurch Street and Mincing Lane'.

Owing to lack of water pressure the fire services were helpless and, in spite of all attempts to save it, the Beadle's house caught fire in the afternoon and the Clerk was knocked downstairs and nearly killed by the fall of a heavy iron bath. After this there was nothing to do but salvage such goods as could be moved before the ceilings fell.

Fortunately, No. 48 Fenchurch Street, a recently built Cloth-workers building adjoining the Hall (in which the Company's business was later carried on) had been saved, entirely due to the efforts of the Company's staff after the official fire services had declared it doomed and had abandoned it to its fate.

By 5 o'clock in the afternoon, after eighteen hours of the battle, most of the fires were out and there was nothing left for the Clerk to do, since all telephones were out of action, except to make his way sadly to the Master's house in the suburbs with the dreadful news.

* *
*

When the Master, Thomas Girtin, arrived next day in Mincing Lane there was some difficulty in reaching the ruins of the Hall, for the police had erected barriers. However, a chance meeting with the Clerk, whose 'rough and dusty attire and rubber top boots showed the part he had been playing', provided him with a pass and he was able to see for himself the extent of the damage. So great had been the heat that there was scarcely any ash or dust left and the shimmering chandeliers, which had once enchanted the dining Company with their iridescent lustres, had been reduced to solid blocks of glass. All the furniture, the model of the barge, the statues of Charles I and James I that had survived the Great Fire of London and had not been removed to places of safety – all were gone. The Library, the fine wines, the office equipment, the working files, and much property in store for almspeople and City tenants had disappeared as though they had never existed. Only the strong room and the safes had stood up to the fire, though so great was the heat that it was five whole days before the staff dared to open the strong room. The Plate, both at the Hall and at Hay's Wharf, had escaped and, together with the Charters, some 100 boxes of title deeds and the old minute books, dating from 1520, had survived. So also, the Master was delighted to notice, had survived a small clock and the coat of arms over the doorway leading into the vestibule, together with the wall plaques of Industry, Integrity, Charity, and Loyalty, each with its appropriate inscription. It seemed, in that dark moment, to be an omen for the Company's future and, as the Master said: 'Grievous though our loss may be, surely it is but the outer casing and shell of the Company that has gone – the whole core and heart and spirit of the Company remains of course as sound as ever.'

* *
*

Already the stricken Clothworkers were looking to the future. Nor were they without friends in their time of trouble. Overwhelmed by offers of help and hospitality, the Company finally chose to take up their business residence in the offices of Christ's Hospital 'for the duration of the War, or until such earlier date as the Clothworkers may desire', as their hosts in Great Tower Street graciously phrased their invitation. The Library was re-founded with gifts from other Companies and with certain purchases. Gradually the threads of life were again picked up. From the chaos created by the loss of the working files, order was gradually restored.

There were certain unforeseen difficulties that attended the restoration. The office safes, for example, were so warped by the heat of the fires which had destroyed the Hall that it was found necessary to ask their manufacturers to open them. So many safes, however, throughout the City were in like condition that several months' delay was forecast until the Clothworkers' turn upon the waiting list should arrive. Fortunately the Clerk, happening to encounter some hungry members of the safe company going among the ruins of the City and having about his person, by chance, no less than three packed luncheons, was enabled to strike up a friendship which ended with the Clothworkers' safes attaining a high priority.

The same problems existed, too, as had existed after the destruction of the Hall by the Great Fire of 1666. Then a pale of timber had been erected to hinder thieves. Now a brick wall was speedily built around the strong room, and only the presence of resident staff prevented its immediate destruction by would-be looters. In spite of indignant letters from the Master to the Lord Mayor and the Commissioner of Police, the attacks continued until such time as the contents could be removed. Meanwhile the rain falling on the melancholy scene percolated into the vaults and damaged many of the portraits that had escaped the flames.*

None the less, slowly and painfully, the business of the Company was resumed and returned to as near normality as was possible in a City continually under enemy attack and under conditions in which vast sections of the Company's properties – particularly in Islington – were utterly destroyed.

From a corporate income which in 1942 had fallen to about two-thirds and in 1943 to less than half the figure at which it had stood before the war, the Clothworkers contrived to play the part they had always played, although it proved sometimes necessary to modify their benefactions. From the corporate income, Lambe's Trust, amongst others, was now paid. In the absence of facilities for research, the annual research grant of £3,000 to the City and Guilds College was reduced to a token payment of £500 a year and the additional research grant of £1,000 altogether abandoned. The rationing of textiles led to the Clothing Charities being paid out, for the remainder of the war, in cash instead of kind.

---

* In one respect, however, the history of 1666 did not repeat itself. The system of two 'large dogges' then employed was not again adopted; nor would any food have been available to sustain them.

With Court and Committee meetings being held at Vintners' Hall, the inevitable demands of defence were met. Warship weeks and Wings for Victory weeks followed one upon another until gradually, almost imperceptibly, it became clear that a period might be put to the years of destruction and the endless depletion of the Company's revenues.

The girls of Mary Datchelor School, who had been removed first to Ashford in Kent and then to Llanelly, after an earlier decision in 1944 to return to London had, with the beginning of the attacks by flying bombs, been reversed, at last came back into their own.

By 1945 all the plate had been returned from the United States of America and the Clothworkers, with many protestations of their gratitude, had quitted the hospitality of Christ's Hospital for offices of their own on the fifth floor of No. 48 Fenchurch Street, already mentioned. They had, it was true, no office furniture save for one desk and one table that had been salvaged from the Hall, but two members of the Court promised to remedy this in part, and what was still lacking was to be purchased. As things turned out, the office furniture was lent by their erstwhile hosts to whom in gratitude the Clothworkers had given, in parting, both £500 for a life nomination of twenty years and a silver inkstand for their Treasurer's room.

Though Committee meetings were now held in the new offices, the Court still met at Vintners' Hall, and in the peace year of 1946 they there decided that a thanksgiving scheme should be evolved 'as a token of the Company's feelings in regard to the termination of the War and the relatively small loss of life amongst the Members of the Freedom and Livery'. The scheme proved to be a noble one. To St Paul's Cathedral was given £1,000 as a contribution to the Twelve Companies' new windows there. A sum of £20,000 was granted to Leeds University for extensions to the Clothworkers' Departments of Textiles and Dyeing: with this spectacular gift went the offer of three post-graduate scholarships of £500 per annum apiece, to be allotted to students from an American university. It was an offer made with the avowed object of fostering good-will and understanding between the two nations and it was hoped that similar facilities might, in due course, be offered in exchange to British students by the American university concerned.

Mr John Humphery* suggested that this scheme should be further extended to cover a similar system of exchange, with the same objective, between Guy's Hospital, of which he was Chairman, and some American hospital or medical foundation. And although, as it turned out, it was subsequently found difficult, if not impossible, to arrange the scholarships offered to Leeds University, the Hospital part of the scheme proved highly successful. Two eminent practitioners from Guy's Hospital annually exchanged duties for three months with two of similar standing at the Johns Hopkins Medical School at Baltimore. To cover their expenses they were each paid by the Company £500.†

The large donations to Leeds University were made, moreover, without prejudice to the Clothworkers' regular grants which now amounted to no less a sum than £10,500 a year. And when, two years later, it was estimated that the extension to the Textile Departments would cost £10,000 more than had been thought, the Company cheerfully and readily footed the bill.

* Master, 1937.

† The first beneficiary from the United States, Dr Alfred Blalock, in 1947 introduced to this country a technique for cardiac operations which achieved the spectacular results known to the popular press as the Blue Baby operation. From his Clothworker-sponsored visit resulted a clinic for the treatment of congenital heart cases where a surgeon carried on the treatment initiated by Dr Blalock.

CHAPTER EIGHTEEN

A TIME FOR GREATNESS

*   *
*

GRADUALLY normality – or what to a new generation passed for normality – began to return. By February 1946 it was possible to hold a dinner at Grocers' Hall, in May that year there was a dance at the Connaught Rooms, and in July the Court and their ladies enjoyed a trip by river to Hampton Court.

Yet unwelcome restrictions still remained, and although in 1947 another river trip was made, this time to Greenwich, for the first time for many years the Saint Thomas' Eve luncheon to the Freedom (which had been held every year throughout the War) had to be abandoned owing to the severity of the food rationing that still persisted.

But two years later it was possible to think of laying down a cellar once again and the Company made a small purchase of vintage port. Moreover there came other faint reminders of the more picturesque past when, on the 150th anniversary of the establishment of the Thames River Police, the twelve Great Companies were represented in a water pageant by a dozen skiffs – the Clothworkers' was manned by the London Transport (Trolley Buses) Rowing Club – each bearing the appropriate arms.

The Company's arms also appeared on a set of rugs – specially woven by the University of Leeds – which the Clothworkers presented to King George VI and Queen Elizabeth on their silver wedding day, and soon the Company's banner was again to hang in the restored Guildhall.

In their relationships with the other City Companies co-operation had taken the place of the age-old rivalries: there was a joint luncheon – afterwards to become a yearly event – with the Court of the Dyers' Company, of which it was recorded: 'So far as is known this is the first occasion since the order of precedence of the two Companies was settled in 1515 that they have met together.' Moreover the re-building of the Hall in Mincing Lane was facilitated by the purchase of adjoining property from the Haberdashers' Company, and in the redevelopment of the Lime Street–Billiter Square area lands were exchanged with the Fishmongers' Company.

A further expression of the goodwill existing between the various Companies was shewn by the readiness with which the Vintners', Grocers', Fishmongers', Ironmongers', and Drapers' Companies lent their Halls for business meetings and entertainments of the Clothworkers.

These of course were domestic matters; much more important was the ability of the Company to resume – and even extend – their benefactions which by the circumstances of war had necessarily been curtailed. Particularly was this so in the field of education where the outcome of the struggle between the Great Powers now depended, more than ever before, upon a lavish supply of technicians. The centenary appeal of the Imperial College of Science and Technology received a generous response, and, in addition to their annual grants to the University of Leeds, the Company first met the cost of a new wool research laboratory and later made a substantial grant towards the £6,000,000 extension scheme which was primarily intended to assist in meeting the ever increasing demand for scientists and technologists but which also took into due account other aspects of university life.

In 1951, largely due to a handsome donation from the Company, the Ministry of Education granted the Mary Datchelor School at Camberwell the status, under the Education Acts of 1944 to 1948, of a 'voluntary aided' grammar school. The Clothworkers' association with this school, which bears a deservedly high reputation in the world of education, had begun in 1894, seventeen years after its foundation, and for some years the

Company had been solely responsible for its management. And even when this position no longer existed, the Clothworkers still had a majority on a Board of Governors which included representatives of the London County Council and one member appointed by the Company on the nomination of the University of London. In January 1957 the eightieth anniversary* of the founding of the school was marked by (among other things) the publication of *The Story of the Mary Datchelor School* and by a visit on Prize Day of H.R.H. Princess Alexandra of Kent who presented the prizes and gave a short address.

Clifton College, too, profited from the Clothworkers' interest in education, for during the latter days of the War the Company established for a number of years boarding bursaries to enable some boys from primary schools to receive the benefits of a public school education.

Not all the Company's benefactions, however, were confined to education: as part of their Peace Year Thanksgiving Scheme they made a considerable gift to the St Paul's Cathedral Restoration Fund. Under the same scheme they financed an exchange, which became an annual event, between physicians and surgeons from Guy's Hospital in London and the Johns Hopkins Medical School in Baltimore, U.S.A. And though the main object of the Company in establishing this exchange was to foster friendly relations between the two countries it inevitably brought about results in the medical field that were to prove highly valuable.

* *
*

In one sense nothing could again be really normal until the Company once more had a Hall. Hospitality they had received from many sources but the longing for a home of their own was

*It was noteworthy that during the first seventy-three years the school had only two head-mistresses, the great educationalists and great administrators Miss Caroline Edith Rigg (1877–1917) and Dame Dorothy Brock (1918–50). And their successor, Miss R. N. Pearse, early shewed that the traditions of the school were in safe keeping.

one that they shared with many of the country's younger population.

In 1945 the Company had decided that the Mincing Lane frontage of the old Hall site should be used for commercial offices to be erected under a building lease and that the new Hall should be an entirely separate building upon the remainder of the site. Plans were prepared by Mr Henry Tanner; after his death the Company appointed Mr H. Austen Hall as the architect for the scheme. It was of course technically impossible that the building should go forward with the same speed that had characterized the construction of the earliest Halls. Negotiations with the War Damage Commission about the type of payment to be made for the destroyed Hall proved both difficult and protracted. There was no doubt in the minds of the Company's advisers that the building qualified for a 'cost of works' payment but the Commission at first thought otherwise and several years dragged by before their final decision was made in the Company's favour.

In the meantime great and inflationary increases in the cost of building dictated a change of plan and it was decided* to have two floors of letting offices imposed above the Hall. Moreover there were negotiations to be carried on for the widening of Dunster Court and for constructing an exit road into Mark Lane: this project brought the City of London Police into the discussions and, somehow or other, the anti-ribbon-development authorities. In addition, the plans of a neighbouring property company for the development of a site adjoining the Hall were found to be at variance with those of the Company.

But, at long last, the various problems were all, in one way or another, overcome; an amicable arrangement was arrived at with the adjoining owners, the City Police and the anti-ribbon-development authorities were satisfied, and the question of war-damage compensation was settled. In 1950 'planning permission' for the Hall was granted and the Company applied for a building

*A member of the rebuilding committee recorded that a fortuitous ray of winter sunshine which penetrated the Company's temporary offices in 48 Fenchurch Street during a conference with the architect helped to clinch this decision.

THE TWENTIETH-CENTURY HALL, 1958

licence. There was still to be a long delay but finally the licence was granted – as it happened, only a few months before the war-time regulation which called for it was entirely swept away – and competitive tenders were sought.

By this time building costs had become so high that no longer could it be said that, in the words of Prince Albert a century earlier, the Clothworkers did 'not need to look very narrowly into the amount' that the new Hall would cost. Now, although they might be generous in their charitable and educational grants, every expenditure upon their own account must be carefully scrutinized; owing to the destruction during the war of many of their properties and to the results of post-war inflation many embellishments which might have enriched the new Hall were ruthlessly cut out. It was at this stage that the Master, Mr O. Astley Bloxam, suggested drastic alterations to the plans; when these were adopted they not only effected very considerable economies but, at the same time, greatly increased the potential income from the letting floors.

Gradually the building began to take shape and a special sub-committee worked hard on choosing furniture and furnishings which should be worthy of the Company's home. Inevitably there were such set-backs as delays in the delivery of steel but at last the building was sufficiently advanced for the foundation stone to be laid, on 17 July 1956, by H.R.H. the Duchess of Kent, accompanied by her daughter H.R.H. Princess Alexandra of Kent. Beneath the stone were placed a set of coins and a copy of the current Livery Book.

In her speech the Duchess referred to 'the remarkable continuity of institutions of which we in this country are so rightly proud'. For on that summer day the site had, in fact, been in the possession of the Clothworkers (and the Shearmen before them) for exactly five hundred years.

* *
*

It is clear that the War had effected no great changes in the essential Clothworker way of life. They had seen so many wars in the centuries of their existence; so many times of trouble had come and had been surmounted and gone away again. It was a thought that could give a calm acceptance of events as they occurred. The times, it is true, were extraordinary but the Company met them by extraordinary measures. For example, both Field Marshal Sir William Slim of Fourteenth-Army and South-East-Asia fame and Air Chief Marshal Sir Roderic Hill of Fighter Command and Bomber Command were invited to join the Court of the Company immediately after taking the Honorary Freedom and Livery*–an action which it was acknowledged 'will be without precedent, but it is considered that the times themselves are also without precedent . . . '. It was thought that their 'advice and counsel may well be to the advantage of the Company in the years immediately ahead'.

The years that lay immediately ahead, and indeed as far ahead as could be foreseen by any one, were certainly years that would call for skill and cool judgement. The new Elizabethan age in which these events were taking place, in which the Company were shaping and consolidating a future which there were reasons to suppose would be no less brilliant than their past, provided for those who sought them ample comparisons with the reign of that first great Elizabeth under whose rule the early, formative, years of the Company had been spent. There were striking similarities certainly between the moral atmosphere of the two periods, similarities from which it was tempting and possible to draw facile conclusions. But in one great and all-important respect the two ages stood clearly side by side, facing together a fantastic and ever-expanding horizon. In the sixteenth century the little ships had probed the unknown ends of the earth. Now, in the twentieth century, the first tentative feelers were extending into the outer darkness of space, probing with rocket and with satellite the confines of the very universe. Then the frontiers of that first Elizabethan world had been frontiers of earth and of water, frontiers of mountain or raging seas. Now they were the seething

*The war-time Prime Minister of Australia, Mr R. G. Menzies, had been elected to the Honorary Livery in 1941.

frontiers of matter, the awful frontiers of creation itself. And at that moment, when the moral advancement of man had yet to equal his scientific achievement, it seemed appropriate to the Company to recall the words of the official report on the destruction of the Hall given by their Master a dozen years before the young Queen came to her throne:

In their wisdom our forefathers some centuries ago chose a motto for the Company and through all the desolation and destruction in Mincing Lane this motto still stands unchallenged over our erstwhile entrance. In our larger national – nay international – affairs no less than in our smaller and nearer Company life may we never lose sight of those words known to every Clothworker:

MY TRUST IS IN GOD
ALONE

EARLY ORDINANCES

*   *

    *

THE first Ordinances of the Company dated 17 January 1532 give an insight into the lives of the earliest Clothworkers. Too long to be included in this work, some of those not mentioned elsewhere in the text are summarized in this Appendix.

They were to keep thirteen wax tapers burning before the statue of the Virgin Mary in the Monastery of Christ Church – the old place of worship of the Brotherhood.

On Election Sunday (the Sunday following the Feast of the Assumption) at nine o'clock in the morning all members of the Livery and all the householders were to follow the Master and Wardens two by two, 'honestly and sadly', to Christ Church for Mass 'and the same Mass shall hear to the end'. Every one was to put a Penny in the Collection.

Every two or three years new livery was to be given. All members of the Livery were to pay for a sample 3s 4d 'if it be cloth in grain. And if it be cloth out of grain 2s'. Then they could buy what cloth they wanted so long as it was of the correct colour. The money was put towards the cost of a dinner on the occasion.

Anyone elected to the Livery who 'of his obstinacy and frowardness refuseth and will not take it upon him . . . and will not be reformable but continues still in self will and obstinacy' was to pay 100 shillings every time he refused.

All members of the Livery were to keep two suits of livery, best and second best, 'for the worship of the City and the honesty of the Mystery of Clothworkers'.

Four Quarter Days were to be kept at the Hall for 'reformation of the defaults of the Craft and to hear the complaints of the same'. Every householder had to pay 6d quarterage. There were fines for absenteeism on Quarter Days.

Any Clothworker leaving the Company and joining another without express permission in writing was to be fined £20.

Any Clothworker, 'of good fame and name' and with all his dues fully paid up, who fell into poverty was to be 'refreshed weekly towards his needy sustentation' and, if dying in poverty, to be 'honestly buried' in the presence of the Master, Wardens, and such of the Livery as might be ordered to attend.

No member of the Company was to disposses another Member or raise his rent 'for malice'.

No journeyman or newly qualified apprentice was allowed to set up as a householder until the Court had certified him to be worth £10. On being admitted to the Mystery he was to pay 10s. 'Rowers at the perch' were to pay for their 'admission and for a key for the stair where they wash their clothes and for the maintaining both the timber and defending the charge of the water 20s sterling.'

No master-clothworker was to pay his apprentice any wages until he had presented him at the Hall for a test of his skill. If his skill was sufficient he was then 'to work by Journeys and to take his groat a day according to the old custom'. If he failed his test then the Court would 'assign him to work with some other man by year or else assign him what he shall take by the week' until he was proficient.

Householders were forbidden to 'lend out any of their apprentices for to bear any burden or to carry any wares or merchandises from place to place or to bear any buck to and from Thames or to fetch water for other men inasmuch as there be porters and waterbearers and other poor people labourers great number in the City of London that with such business would gladly deserve somewhat towards their poor livings ...'.

'All manner of serving men of the said Mystery ... shall be of good rule and demeanour against the Master Wardens and Fellowship.' Unlawful assemblies and games such as Cloisshe Kayles were strictly forbidden.

Employers of servants hired by the month, quarter, half year, or year on a board lodging wage were to see that they attended divine service, that they were kept in a state of 'reasonable awe and dread' and indulged in no 'riot or misrule'. Not even on Sundays or Holy Days were the servants to absent themselves without leave.

A servant working by the day and living out on the other hand was bound on holy days to do no more than 'to come in the morning and after the old manner and custom to hang out his masters wet cloths and at the evening . . . to come and help take them in and to lay them to the shear board against the morning of the day following'.

He was to come to work on every working day 'both winter and summer at 4 of the clock in the morning. And to leave his work in the summer at 7 of the clock at night without any sleeping hour and then to go to supper. And in winter to leave work at 8 of the clock at night and then to go to supper.'

The Master and Wardens could stop his wages for bad timekeeping according to the rate of $\frac{1}{4}$d per hour.

Before apprentices were taken by Clothworkers they had to be produced before the Court to make sure that the apprentice was 'free-born and coming of a good stock and kindred and also that he be clean of limbs and body and not disfigured'.

No Clothworker was to be so 'misadvised' as to rebuke the Master or Wardens, openly or otherwise; nor was he to offer any other member of the Company 'any word of rebuke or reproach or any other nickname'.

If any Member of the Company failed to pay his quarterage or other dues or did not pay the fines imposed upon him under these Ordinances then the Court could distrain upon his property.

CHARTERS

* *
*

THE following are brief details of the principal Charters relevant to the history of the Company.

1. 20 EDWARD IV 1480. Incorporated a Guild of *Fullers* of the City of London and the suburbs consisting of three Wardens and a Commonalty of Freeman. Gave the power to deal in property and the right of perpetual succession, to sue and be sued. The three Wardens were to elect, yearly, three Wardens to govern the Company by Ordinances.

2. 23 HENRY VII 1508. Incorporated a Guild of *Shearmen* of the City of London on similar lines to the above, with a Master and two Wardens to govern by Ordinances.

3. 19 HENRY VIII 1528. Cited the above two Charters and incorporated both the Fullers and Shearmen jointly as *Clothworkers* of the City of London with similar rights, privileges, and duties to those set out in the two earlier Charters. Government of the Company was to be by a Master and four Wardens, elected yearly by the 'Commonalty that is to say the Freemen of the Mystery of Clothworkers'. The Company were authorized to make 'one Livery or Livery of Clothing of one suit' among the 'Brethren and Sisters of the Company most sufficient thereto and the same clothing honestly to use as often as and whensoever it shall please them and may hold and keep their Feast or Entertainment of meat and drink in a convenient place on the Feast of the Assumption . . . '. The Charter also established the rights of search throughout the City and the suburbs, in company with the Mayor or his deputy.

4. 4 AND 5 PHILIP AND MARY 1558. Confirmed the Charter of Henry VIII.

5. 2 ELIZABETH I 1560. Confirmed the previous Charters.

6. 9 CHARLES I 1633. Confirmed the previous Charters and simplified the titles. It also made special mention that all engaging in the trade were to pay 6d per quarter to the Clothworkers' Company. In 1684 a Writ of *Quo Warranto* was issued against the Company as a result of which the Company surrendered their existing Charters.

7. 37 CHARLES II 1685. Re-established the Corporate Company. It nominated the Master and four Wardens and fixed the minimum number of the Court at thirty-four. The Court were appointed by name as was the Clerk. All including the Livery were to take the Oaths of Allegiance and Supremacy before being admitted to office and to be communicating members of the Church of England having received the Sacrament within the previous six months. The Charter reserved the right to the Crown to remove and appoint officials of the Company at will. It then re-established the trade rights that had been contained in the earlier Charters.

8. 3 JAMES II 1687. Charter to the *Companies of the City of London*. Cited the confusion attendant upon the removal and replacement and in some cases of reinstatement of Liverymen by the Crown and restored the rights of the Companies to elect their own officials.

9. 3 JAMES II 1688. A Grant to the *Clothworkers' Company* confirmed the general grant given in the preceding Charter.

10. 4 JAMES II 1688. Charter of Restitution to the *Companies of the City of London* restoring them to their former rights and privileges.

11. 11 GEORGE VI 1947. Clarified the difficult position which arose from the annulment in 1690 of Nos 7 and 9 (above). This had left the Company, by reason of the laws relating to mortmain, in some ambiguity about the acquisition of property.

SOME COMPANY PROPERTIES

* *
*

118 FENCHURCH STREET, AND 4, 5, 6 HOGARTH COURT
Left to the Company by the Lady Margaret Countess of Kent in 1540. The title deeds, which go back to 1314, are the earliest in the Company's possession.

'THE WHITE SWAN', 28 AND 30 TUDOR STREET
Leased to the Countess of Kent and the Clothworkers' Company jointly in 1537. The freehold was bought by the Company in 1577 and additional land was added to the property in 1654. The Countess of Kent's almshouses stood on this site until 1770 when they were removed to Islington. Part of the site was sold in 1922.

THE COUNTESS OF KENT'S (WOMEN'S) ALMSHOUSES, ISLINGTON
The site was bought by the Company, corporately, at some date between 1583 and 1796.

1–7 (INCLUSIVE) BILLITER SQUARE
9, 10, 11 BILLITER SQUARE
11, 12, 13 BILLITER STREET
Left to the Fullers' Company in 1520 by Roger Gardiner. It passed to the Clothworkers when the Fullers and Shearmen were united into one Company in 1528.

THE JOHN HEATH (MEN'S) ALMSHOUSES, ISLINGTON
The site of these almshouses was bought by the Company at some date between 1583 and 1796 and the almshouses created under the will of John Heath who died in 1641. They were built on a site in Islington other than the one they now occupy, were moved to Monkwell Street in the City in 1825, and in 1872 back again to Islington to the present site.

11 AND 12 FENCHURCH STREET, AND 1 PHILPOT LANE

The Fenchurch Street part of this property was left to the Company in 1585 by John Lute. The Philpot Lane site was purchased in 1874.

6, 8, 10 MOORGATE

Part of the site was left to the Company by William Lambe in 1580. It provides one of the earliest extant examples of a Licence in Mortmain from the Crown (1587). The original document is in medieval Latin and is perfectly preserved. The rest of the site was bought in 1839.

1–11 (INCLUSIVE) WOOD STREET SQUARE

Left to the Company by William Lambe in 1580. The old Hermitage or Chapel of St James-in-the-Wall (Lambe's Chapel) stood on the site for several centuries until pulled down in 1872. The crypt was re-erected on a site at the rear of Clothworkers' Hall. In 1872 the Company bought part of the old London Wall and the site and soil of the Square to round off the property.

77 WOOD STREET

Bought by the Shearmen's Company in 1520, the title passed, in due course, to the Clothworkers on the union of the Fullers and Shearmen in 1528.

134 FENCHURCH STREET

Left to the Company under the will of John Bayworth in 1622.

CLOTHWORKERS' HALL, MINCING LANE

The main portion of the site was bought by members of the Shearmen's Company in 1456 (the earliest title deeds in the possession of the Company, for this property, are dated 1391). Other parts of the site were acquired under the will of Roger Gardiner (1520) and by purchase in 1843 and 1874.

43 FENCHURCH STREET, AND 43 MINCING LANE

Bought in 1844 out of a fund belonging to the Trusts of three benefactors: Oliver Claymond (1540), William Lambe (1568), and Frances West (1723).

45 FENCHURCH STREET

Bought by the Company in 1869.

46, 47, 48 FENCHURCH STREET
Left to the Fullers' Company in 1520 under the will of Roger Gardiner and vested in the Clothworkers' Company on their incorporation in 1528.

49 AND 50 FENCHURCH STREET
Bought by the Company in 1843 with funds raised largely from sale of lands left to the Company by Oliver Claymond.

1 STAR ALLEY
Bought by the Company in 1874.

7 MARK LANE
Acquired by the Company in exchange for 174 Upper Thames Street which had been left to them in 1574 by William Frankland.

9 AND 10 MARK LANE
Bought by the Company in 1871 and 1872.

PART OF THE SITE OF THE FORMER CHURCH OF ALLHALLOWS STAINING (INCLUDING THE CHURCH TOWER)
Bought in 1871.

11, 12, 13 COPTHALL COURT, AND 31 THROGMORTON STREET
Left to the Company under the will of Thomas Ormston in 1556, subject to certain life interests. Possession was finally obtained in 1592.

17–21 (INCLUSIVE) FARRINGTON STREET
1, 3, 7–11 (INCLUSIVE) MODERN COURT
Left to the Company under the will of Robert Pyle (or Peele) in 1538. The property as originally devised to the Company was larger than at present, some of it having been sold. At one time the Fleet Ditch bounded this property which was close to the Fleet Prison.

62 AND 63 MARK LANE, AND 25 ABCHURCH LANE
Left to the Company by Oliver Claymond in 1540, the property passed to the Clothworkers on the death of his widow in 1550.

8 LOVE LANE, ALDERMANBURY
Bought by the Company in 1841 as a reinvestment of part of the funds raised by a sale of the properties in Nicholas Lane, Fox Ordinary Court, and Abchurch Lane, left to them by Oliver Claymond.

SOME BENEFACTORS

*   *
*

	Date of Will	Bequest	Purpose or Beneficiary
Samuel Aaron	1730	£300	Christmas gifts for the poor
Mrs Acton	1837	£1000	Free gift. Income distributed to poor
William Armer	1575	£50	To be lent free of interest to honest householders
James Barkin	1675	£100	To be lent to 5 young Freeman free of interest
John Bayworth	1622	134 Fenchurch Street	Christ's Hospital Church-wardens of Farnham, Parish of St Gabriel, Fenchurch St. Master, Wardens, and Clerk
Peter Blundell	1599	£150	To buy lands, the rent to be devoted to the poor of Bridewell and other purposes
William Blunt	1596	£100	To be lent to 10 poor men
Richard Boylston	1596	£100	Poor of Lambe's Almshouses on attending Chapel
John Bricklis	1440	Premises and rents	Church of Allhallows the Great
Barbara Burnell	1630	£300	To buy lands: rents to be devoted to poor of Stanmore, a poor Scholar at Oxford, etc.
John Burnell	1603	£100	To be lent to 2 young Freemen at 5%, the interest devoted to the poor
Thomas Burnell	1655	£200	Clothing, bread, and Suffolk cheese for the poor at Stanmore, etc.
Francis Burton	1684	£1 p.a.	2 artisan Clothworkers

	Date of Will	Bequest	Purpose or Beneficiary
Phillip Christian	1653	2 houses	For two poor boys in the Isle of Man or to a Free School in Peel, also to the poor of the Company
Oliver Claymond	1540	Lands and tenements	Allhallows Staining, the Vicar of Hitchin
George Cornell	1850	£2000	Annuities for the blind
Thomas Dixon	1574	£250	Lands for the benefit of Christ's Hospital and Cloth-workers
George Neale Driver	1853	Lands	Relief of poverty
William Edwards	1700	£100	Christmas gifts for poor artisan Clothworkers or their widows
Thomasine Evans	1596	5 tenements	Clothes for poor widows or wives over 50. Also coals
Richard Farrington	1613	£60	To buy lands for the benefit of the poor of the Company
James Finch	1508	Premises in Hay Wharf Lane	Profits to maintain a Reader of Divinity at Whittington College
William Frankland	1574	2 tenements	Coals for the poor of Allhallows the Great, also for the poor of Skipton
Edward Gregory	1845	Rents from land in Wiltshire	Aged blind pensioners of the Company
John Halse	1573	£100	To be lent, free of interest, to 4 young men of the Company
Ralph Hamer	?	£100	To be lent, free of interest, to 4 young men of the Company
John Heath	1640	£1500	For building and maintaining almshouses
	1635	£1000	Clothing for the poor, an annual sermon, etc.
Elizabeth Heather	1801	Interest and dividends on residual estate	Six poor widows
William Heron	1580	Lands	On trust for various purposes, educational and otherwise
William Hewer	1715	£100	The poor

SOME BENEFACTORS

	Date of Will	Bequest	Purpose or Beneficiary
William Hewet	1599	£300	Hospitals and an Exhibition at Cambridge
John Heydon	1573	£100	To be lent at 3⅓% to two young men. Interest to Mercers' Company
Robert Hilson	1585	£26 13s 4d	The poor of Great Stanmore
Lady (or Mrs) Hinde	1569	£20	To be lent to 4 young men
Robert Hitchins	1680	£1500	To purchase an estate for the benefit of clothing the poor on St Stephen's Day
John Hobby	1674	£3000	To buy lands to be held jointly by Christ's Hospital and Clothworkers' Company for apprenticing Blue Coat Boys, clothing the aged poor, and releasing debtors from gaol
Margaret Holligrave	1595	Property in East Smithfield	The poor and prisoners' aid
Thomas Hussey	1622	£120	The poor on St Thomas's Eve
Augustin Hynde	1556	£100	To be lent to 4 young men
Alexander Iverie	1588	£100	Poor of the Company
Margaret Countess of Kent	1538	Property and leases and £350	Almshouses for women
William Lambe	1574	Property	Clothing the poor, 4 sermons a year, etc.
		Property	Almshouses at Sutton Valence
	1576	£30 p.a.	Sutton Valence School
Samuel Lese	1639	Lands, etc.	Profits to be lent to honest young men of the Company
Elizabeth Love	1805	£200	The blind
John Lute	1585	5 houses	Profits partly to be lent to 5 young Freemen and 10 honest householders, partly to provide clothing, etc.
Dame Elizabeth Lyon	1556	£40	To be lent to poor young men, free except for 10s for a drinking
John Machell	1558	£100	To be lent to 4 young men of the Company

APPENDIX D

	Date of Will	Bequest	Purpose or Beneficiary
Samuel Middlemore before	1647	£800	To buy land to provide clothing, coals, sermons, etc.
John Middlemore	1647	£100	To buy land to produce £5 p.a. for 20 poor Clothworkers
Thomas Newnam	1800	£10,000	30 blind persons
Thomas Ormston	1556	£3 p.a.	Bread for poor hospitals
John Osmotherley	1642	£2 10s p.a.	Christmas gifts for 5 poor Clothworkers
Dame Anne Packington	1559	Lands	Rents to be distributed among the poor of St Dunstan's-in-the-West and St Botolph, Aldersgate
	1570	£100	Bread for the poor of St Botolph, Aldersgate
Sir William Peake	1672	£100	Michaelmas gifts to 10 poor Clothworkers
William Pennoyer	1670	£10 p.a.	10 blindest, oldest, and poorest Clothworkers
Edward Pilsworth	1603	Messuages	Profits to Churchwardens of Shillington and an Exhibition at Oxford
Sir John Robinson	1679	£300	Augmentation of sum paid to Countess of Kent's alms-women
John Rogers	1551	4 houses	Rents to the poor of the Company
Sir Thomas Rowe	1568	£100	To be lent to 10 poor honest householders
Peter Shales (or Skales)	1584	£100	To be lent to 7 Clothworkers
John Southall	1590	£40	To be lent to 4 poor men
Richard Staper	1610	£110	£1 to each of 5 poor Clothworkers on St Thomas's Eve
James Stoddart	1607	£100	To be lent to young Clothworkers. Interest to provide charcoal for poor, etc.
Sir William Stone	?	£50	To be lent to 2 young Freemen
William Thwaytes	1831	£20,000	The blind
		£20,000	For making members of the Company 'comfortable'
Sir Thomas Trevor	1622	£100	£1 p.a. to 6 poor women

	Date of Will	Bequest	Purpose or Beneficiary
James Trussell	1635	£400	To buy a house: the profits to be paid to the poor, to Christ's Hospital, etc.
John Watson	1555	Houses	Part profits to St Mary, Aldermary, remainder to poorest Freemen the week before Christmas
John Webb	1697	£1600	Clothing for the poor; cakes, wine, etc., for the Livery
Sir Godfrey Webster	1720	£700	1 gn. to each of 20 poor working Clothworkers or their widows on 4 November
John and Frances West	1713	£30 p.a.	To be given on St Thomas's Day to 30 aged poor of the Company
		Other rents	For 26 ditto
	1718	Premises and rents	The blind of Reading and Newbury
	1718	Premises and rents	The blind of Twickenham, Isleworth, and Richmond
	1719	Premises and Poultry	Blind persons generally
Frances West	1723	Premises and Poultry	Honest blind poor of London
	1723	Premises in the City	Apprenticing 2 poor boy orphans, residue among poor and blind
	1724	£2650	To buy lands for the benefit of the poor blind of Reading, Newbury, Twickenham, and the City
Frances West	1724	£650	To buy lands for the benefit of 3 poor blind of Henley
John West	1688	£1000	To purchase lands for maintaining 6 Reading boys in the Blue Coat School there
Roger Wilcox	before 1603	£120	To be lent to 3 honest young Freemen

307

A CLOTHWORKER MISCELLANY

*   *

*

IN this Appendix have been gathered a number of small items, worthy of being recorded, though mostly of a lighter nature, which could not conveniently be included in the narrative.

Cash Customers Only: 1559
> 'All the bretheren of the Company which from henceforth shall come to buy tassels out of this house shall have none delivered them without paying ready money when they receive their Tassels.'*

Hard Currency Control: 1560
> 'All the Company that occupied buying and selling by wholesale or retail were warned to appear and had admonition on the Queen's Majesty's behalf that every of them severally should bring in certificate in writing what sums of money they have paid to any stranger since the 20th day of September last and to certify what day they paid it and in what kind of money their payment was. And so weekly to bring in like certificate every Saturday. . . . '

Improperly Dressed
> On 4 September 1565 a member of the Company was fined for coming to take his oath in a cloak.

Slander: 1573
> An apprentice was fined for reporting 'that his Master had and was laid of the French Pox'.

Behaviour in Church: 1580
> 'Whereas the meeting of our Journeymen in Powles [St Paul's Cathedral] on Sunday morning so near the choir as they use to do is both troublesome to the divine service and disquieting of such well

---

* Such difficulties arose over the supply of teasels that within twenty years the Company seem to have given up dealing in them.

disposed as repair to the same,' it was ordered that they should be warned 'to take some other place there which was thought to be good in the North Aisle, in the body of the Church or some other place else where it shall be thought meet and convenient'.

Laundry Charge: 1588
'To scouring of a cloth that was spoiled at the last feast with venison pasties the sum of 10d.'

Manners Makyth Man: 1591
During a dispute certain mercers in Cheapside were ordered with their workmen and apprentices 'for the good usage and demeanour towards such of the workmen of the fustain shearers and others as deal therein that they may pass the streets and go about their business orderly and quietly, without hissing at or any other misdemeanour or abuse in any respect'.

The Beadle: 1594
The Beadle on 15 January 1594 was committed to ward for fighting.

The Barge: 1594
The Queen's Bargemaster 'came and moved the Court for their pleasure for the Barge because there is no Barge of the Queen's that will carry above 24 persons of the Livery and Trumpeters. Therefore they must have a Gravesend Barge. Which they agreed unto . . . '.

What's in a Name?: 1603
Fined at the same Court meeting, for faulty workmanship, were George Swindell and Ben True.

Putting on a Good Show: 1604
The 'standing' was ordered to be enlarged from 150 feet to 200 feet 'that the Livery may stand with the more grace and ease at the King's coming through this City and that (if need shall require) some of the auncientist of the Yeomanry may stand therein with the Livery for the better show'.

Butler's Perquisites: 1604
The Butler was complained of because his wife carried away food in her basket 'contrary to good order'. In future his wife was not to come with him to the Hall at any time and he 'to have only the Chippins of bread'.

No Night-Gowns: 1611

'None of the Master, Wardens, Assistants or Livery of this Company shall at any time come to this Hall upon any Court Day, Quarter Day, festival or any other day or times of public service in their night gowns or in falling bands but in their livery gowns and ruff bands in comely manner as becometh the citizens of this honourable city.'

A Yearly Account

In 1612 the beer bill was found to have grown to an alarming account, not having been paid for about five years. Henceforth the account was to be paid yearly.

Clothworkers' Stairs

The stairs at the water-side, next to the Steel Yard formed a common meeting place for all Journeymen and Apprentices. It needed four members of the Company to keep order there. Keys to the stairs were issued to householders. Light is thrown on the use of the stairs by a petition made to the Lord Mayor, in 1612, against 'encroachment upon the passage or highway at the end of All-hallows Lane near the Clothworkers Stairs which is intended by Mr. William Campion for the supporting of that part of his house next the said stairs which is in danger of falling down 14 [? inches] further into the said Lane, which should it be affected would be very prejudicial to the poor bretheren of this Company using the fuller's art especially by reason that two of them carrying a wet woollen cloth on a staff between them at their coming forth from the said stairs shall hardly be able to turn them up the lane with their said burden on their shoulders without danger of hurt by overstraining themselves being so heavily laden.'

The Hall Garden

The following flowers or plants are mentioned in the accounts as being in the Hall Garden from time to time. The dates given are those when the plants are first mentioned: vine and eglantine (1530), rosemary and spyke (1537), hyssop, daisies and other herbs (1550), gillyflowers and lavender (1563), creepers for the Upper Parlour (1565), double primroses, mastick, angelica (1584), jarmanders (1601), camomile, pennyroyal (1607). In 1568 there was a Knot garden and in 1607, at Election dinners, two arbours were constructed out of wood and wire covered with birch branches and flowers. In 1610 the apple tree had to be chained to the wall of the Hall. The implication is that there was but one apple tree.

Lord's Day Observance: 1613

' . . . the Sabbath Day commanded by Almighty God to be kept holy and inviolate is not kept as it ought to be but contrarywise is exceedingly profaned to the great offence and displeasure of Almighty God and to the grief of all good men. And that especially the said Sabbath is profaned by men of mechanical arts amongst whom the artisan Clothworkers of this City as well of this as of the Merchant Taylors' Company are not the least offenders. . . . '

Stimulus to Recruiting: 1613

The Soldiers who had been trained for a special duty were paid 1s per day and given 2s feather allowance 'and 10/- over and above was given to them to drink at their departure which they willingly and thankfully did accept. Whereupon it was thought fit and so ordered by this Court that the willingness and conformity of the said 29 persons . . . should be set down and recorded for the better encouragement to others in such and like services hereafter. And when occasion of the like service shall happen those that now served might the rather be spared and excused and be in reasonable part eased in taxations and assessments hereafter to be imposed upon this Company and have the preferment to any benefit in this Company which any free Brother in this Company may be preferred to.'

Please to Remember

The 'most execrable divilish and dampnable complott of the gunpowder treazon'.

Domestic Note: 1616

'The long Turkey carpet upon the upper Table in the Chamber over the Parlour shall be forthwith scoured and laid up.'

311

Shorter Hours, Same Pay: 1618

The Journeymen petition that whereas the unemployed have gone to the Hall on Sunday mornings to be hired, thereby profaning the Sabbath, the meeting should now be held at 5 p.m. on Saturday afternoon 'without any abatement of their wages for leaving their work two hours before their accustomed time'. Many of the Assistants agreed to this proposal but the Master and some others did not and the matter was deferred.

The Latest Style: 1623

'Twenty of th'armours in the Armory shall be put forth into the form and fashion of Armors that are now in use and serviceable.'

Staff Problems: 1626

Robert Sampkin, the Hall Porter, was dismissed 'for his great intemperancy in suffering himself to be very often distempered and overcome with drink'. He was then reinstated but, 'continuing still in that vile and hateful sin . . . he could by no means be reclaimed' and was finally dismissed. The Butler, too, was removed 'for matter of incontinent life laid to his charge whereof he could not clear himself. And for vehement suspicion of other misdemeanours and falsities . . . ' the Beadle of the Yeomanry was then warned to profit by the example of these two others, since he, too, 'hath been noted for distemperature in drinking at sundry times'. He was warned to 'abstain from all excess of drinking and from taking Tobacco. And to take more care and use more diligence in doing the Company's business . . . '.

The Fuller Figure: 1628

'Anthony Sturtevant one of the Livery being a man of a gross and unwieldy body is of late by reason thereof become unapt and in-disposed to travel or stir abroad otherwise of mere necessity and that also unwillingly. . . ' He was dispensed from service or attendance upon the Company upon payment of 20 marks.

Gate-crashers: 1636

Monition was given to three members of the Company 'that from henceforth they presume not to accompany or go with the Wardens, Assistants and Livery of this Company or any of them to the Mayor and Sheriffs of this City to dinner as heretofore they have accustomed to do to the disgrace and discredit of this Company'.

Grievances: 1641

The afternoon of the first Monday in every month was to be set aside for hearing grievances.

The Editor Regrets: 1661

'It is ordered that the Poet's books presented to the Company of the shew and triumphs in the City of London the day before his Majesty's Coronation shall not be accepted but returned to him again.'

You, you, and you . . . : 1661

The Company are ordered 'forthwith to pay into the Exchequer Chamber for the use of the King's Majesty the sum of £200 as a free, voluntary present of this Company according to an Act of Parliament in that behalf lately made'.

Hooligans: 1683

The Court were 'pleased to allow Mr. Lamott at his request two men to watch the young trees lately planted for a night or two to preserve them from being pulled up by Rude Persons against May Day'.

Almswomen: 1692

'Great charge falls upon the Company by electing and chosing very ancient and sickly women into their Almshouses in White-friars. . . .' It was therefore decided that 'upon the next vacancy they would make their choice of one or two good Motherly Women about 50 years of age . . .', to look after the infirm. The first of these was one Dorothy Damask.

Dinner is Served: 1697

To avoid the disorderly scramble for seats at Livery dinners in future 'every Liveryman shall retire himself into the Garden before dinner . . . and shall come forth from there in Order as the Clerk shall call them and place themselves at the Table according to their seniority'.

Putting Pressure on the Verger: 1700

Twenty shillings to be paid to the Verger of St Paul's 'as a Gratuity and no more unless he provide a more convenient place for the Company to sit in'.

No Victimization: 1701

A complaint was made by the Journeymen 'against several Master Clothworkers also free of this Company that they did not row and shear cloths as they ought to do and employed Foreigners upon which complaint the Court were pleased to appoint A Committee to examine the differences between them and also ordered that if any Master Clothworkers should trouble the Journeymen and not employ them by reason of this their complaint the Court would defend them provided they behave themselves Civilly towards their said Masters . . . '.

Musick: 1705

'John Cobb a Member of this Company and a Practitioner in Musick humbly desired that he might supply this Company with Musick upon their Occasions when required.' His request was granted provided that it was 'good Musick and as reasonable as others'.

Trained Bands: 1708

In future 'no officers of the Trained Bands of this City whose beat this Company's Hall is in shall have the use of the Hall yard or garden to meet in or draw up his or their Company except he or they have first leave from the Master and Wardens then being and if leave be so granted then the Company shall be discharged from sending out any person to bear Arms therein . . . '.

Cockneys: 1708

'Aldgate Cockneys to have the use of the Hall.'

Mockmedlys: 1714

'The Cloth that is given by this Company in all their Gifts being Mockmedlys some Gentlemen are of opinion that Kentish Cloth may be better and more serviceable for the poor than the other. . . . '

Apprentices: 1774

This Indenture Witnesseth that . . . doth put himself Apprentice to . . . Citizen and CLOTHWORKER of LONDON to learn his Art, and with him (after the manner of an Apprentice) to serve from the day of the Date hereof, until the full End and Term of . . . years from thence next following, to be fully compleat and ended. During which Term, the said Apprentice his said Master faithfully shall serve, his Secrets keep, his lawful Commands everywhere gladly do. He shall do no Damage to his said Master, nor see to be done of others, but that he to his Power shall let or forthwith give warning to his said Master of the same. He shall not waste the Goods of his said Master nor lend them unlawfully to any. He shall not commit Fornication, nor contract Matrimony within the said Term. He shall not play at Cards, Dice, Tables or any other un-lawful Games, whereby his Master may have any Loss. With his own Goods or others during the said Term, without License of his said Master, he shall neither buy nor sell. He shall not haunt Taverns or Play-houses, nor absent himself from his said Master's Service Day or Night unlawfully. But in all things as a faithful Apprentice, he shall behave himself towards his said Master and all his, during the said Term. And the said Master . . . his said Apprentice, in the same Art which he useth, by the best Means that he can, shall Teach and Instruct, or cause to be taught and instructed; finding unto his said Apprentice Meat, Drink, Apparel, Lodging and all other Necessaries, according to the Custom of the City of London. . . .

The Tea Habit: 1847

This year 20 guineas was given to the Company to purchase tea for poor females.

Old England Still: 1884

A request was received for the loan of some item illustrative of the trade to an enterprise entitled 'Ye Olde Swansea and Dystrycte Bazarre ande Exhibition of Industrie'.

PETTY CASH

Correction: 1543

'Item; Paid to ij men for giving attendance certain times in their frocks for correction of apprentices ij^s. viij^d.'

Workman's Compensation: 1555

'Item; Paid towards the healing of a poor man's head which fell off the frame of the vine in the garden ij^s.'

The Confidence Trick: 1558

'Item; paid to the collector for two years quit rent going out of our Hall for that it was before paid to a crafty knave by a false quit-tance. . . .'

Overtime: 1578

'Item; paid to ij labourers for working after the hour vi^d.'

Press Gang: 1599

'Item; paid to release James Snow from Mr. Bull's Press 1s.'

Christmas Boxes: 1613

To Mr Campion's Drayman, to the Baker and to the Bellman 'for their offering at Christmas xiiij^d'.

Sanitary Services: 1618

'Paid to the nightmen for emptying a Vault at the house at the Hall Gate wherein Thomas Holt dwelleth and carrying away of vij tons of soil at iij^s iv^d the Ton xxiij^s iv^d.

Paid to a poor man for cleaning the bricks vi^d.

Paid for candles for the nightmen spent in part of two nights viij^d.

Paid for bread and cheese and beer for them viij^d.

Paid to the Pitman that stood in the Vault iv^d.

Paid to a poor man for overseeing the filling of the Tons both nights xij^d.

Brewers' Order: 1620

2 barrels of beer at 6s, 9 barrels at 8s, 1 barrel at 10s, and a 'great stone jug pot to draw beer in at 1/2d.'

Get your Hair Cut

'Paid for cutting the hair of certain young men that came to the Hall to be made free having uncomely foretops vi^d.'

SOME CLOTHWORKER PERSONALITIES

*   *

*

(i) GENERAL

THOMAS MASSA ALSAGER. Master 1836. Manager of *The Times* and founder of its City page.

SIR FRANCIS CHAPLIN. Master 1668, Sheriff 1688, Lord Mayor 1678. Samuel Pepys 'dined with little Chaplin who is like to be Sheriff the next year and a pretty humoured little man he is'.

EDMUND DUNCH, 1657–1719. Whig politician, he joined heartily in revolution of 1688. Master of Queen Anne's household. Member of Kit Kat Club.

JOHN ELDRED. Master 1604–5. An enterprising Levant Merchant. His voyage in the year 1583 to Tripolis and his travels thence to Babylon are described in Hakluyt's collection of *Voyages*.

PETER MACINTYRE EVANS. Clerk to the Company for twenty-six years (1907–33). He consolidated the great work begun by his predecessor, Sir Owen Roberts, and unaided bore the whole burden of the administration of the Company's affairs during the First World War. He was a recognized authority on blind welfare work to which, second only to the Company, he dedicated his life.

SAMUEL FAVELL. Master 1813. Eminent Reformer. It was through his casting vote that London Bridge was rebuilt.

SIR SAMUEL FLUDYER. Lord Mayor 1761. His Lord Mayor's show was the last for which a play was specially commissioned from the 'City Poet'. He began his career in very narrow circumstances but 'by extraordinary industry, activity, enterprise, and good fortune acquired inordinate wealth' (Romilly).

SIR DENNIS GAWDEN. Master 1667. Victualler to the Navy. 'Incomparable Benefactor' to the Company after the Great Fire of 1666 (*q.v.*).

SIR RICHARD GURNEY. Knighted by Charles I when the latter returned from Scotland. Master 1633, Alderman 1634, Lord Mayor 1641–2. 'A man of wisdom and courage who cannot be too often or honorably mentioned' (Clarendon). He was distinguished by his great courage, loyalty, and sufferings during the Civil Wars. He was disgraced and committed to the Tower for causing the King's Commission of Array to be read in the City after Parliament had requested the City for supplies of men and money.

RICHARD HAKLUYT. See pages 53–6.

WILLIAM HEWER. Master 1687. Presented new Barge to the Company. Clerk to Samuel Pepys 1660, Commissioner of the Navy 1686, Treasurer of the Garrison of Tangier, M.P. for Yarmouth, Isle of Wight, 1685. Evelyn comments that he had made a very considerable estate out of his career with the Navy but had been put out of office at the Revolution. 'Mr. Hewer lives very handsomely and friendly to everybody.'

SIR WILLIAM HEWET. Master 1543. First Clothworker Lord Mayor 1559. Wealthy merchant with estate of £6000 per annum. Lived on London Bridge. His only daughter was rescued by apprentice Edward Osborne (*q.v.*) when she fell from the Bridge. Later, when this daughter was wooed by many eminent suitors – in particular the Earl of Shrewsbury (Hon. Freeman 1562) – he betrothed her with a great dowry to Osborne, saying: 'Osborne saved her and Osborne shall enjoy her'.

SIR JOHN IRETON. Master 1652, Lord Mayor 1658–9. Young brother of General Ireton, the Regicide; son-in-law of Oliver Cromwell; M.P. for London 1653; one of the Commissioners for Trade 1655; knighted by Cromwell 1657; Commander of London Militia; Deputy President of Artillery Company. At Restoration he was removed from office of Alderman, his knighthood taken away, and with several others reported by the Lord Chancellor to Parliament for having traitorous designs on the Government. He attended in the cavalcade when Charles II made his public entrance into London 'which was exceedingly wondered at, however it did not screen him from being excepted out of the act of Indemnity' (Mark Noble's *Life of Oliver Cromwell*).

JOHN LACY. Master 1583. Friend of Queen Elizabeth I. His great house at Putney (1595) had a drawing room ornamented with the Clothworker Arms. Elizabeth stayed there more frequently than with any other of her subjects. (See *Dictionary of National Biography*.)

WILLIAM LAMBE. Master 1569. Free of the Company 9 July 1568, he was given the highest precedence 'in view of his Will'. His profession was of choral music. It has been suggested that his vocal talents may have pleased the musical Henry VIII to make him benefactions out of the loot from the Monasteries; or he may have become rich by marriage.

'William Lambe, so sometimes was my name
Whiles alive dyd runne my mortall race
Serving a Prince of most immortall fame
Henry the eight, who of his Princely grace
In his Chapell allowed me a place.
By whose favour from Gentleman to Esquire
I was preferr'd with worship for my hire.
With wives three I joyned wedlock band
Which (all alive) true lovers were to me
Joane, Alice and Joane; for so they came to hand
What needeth prayse regarding their degree?
In wifely truth none stedfast more could be,
Who though in earth death's force did one dissever
Heaven yet, I trust, shall join us all together.
O Lambe of God, which sinne didst take away;
And as a Lambe was offered up for sinne
Where I (poor Lambe) went from thy flock astray
Yet thou, good Lord, vouchsafe thy Lambe to winne
Home to thy folde and hold thy Lambe therein
Then at the day, when Lambes and Goates shall sever,
Of thy choice Lambes, Lambe may be one for ever.
I pray you all, that receive Bread and Pence
To say the Lord's Prayer before ye go hence.'

ROBERT MURRAY, b. 1633. Inventor of the Penny Post. 'The Penny Post was set up on our Lady Day (being Friday) A° Dni 1680 a most ingenious and useful project invented by Mr. Robert Murray first and then Mr. Dockwra joined with him. . . . Mr. Murray was formerly Clerk to the general Commissioners of the grand Excise of England and was the first that invented and introduced into the City of London the Club of Commerce consisting of one of each trade whereof there were very many elected and are still continued in this City. And he also contrived and set up the office or Bank of Credit at Devonshire House in Bishopsgate Street Without where men depositing their goods and merchandize were furnished with bills of current credit at two thirds or three fourths the value of the said Goods.' (Malone: *Vindication of Shakespeare* and *Nouvelles*. Aubrey MSS in Ashmoleum Museum.)

SIR JOHN MUSGROVE. Master 1843, Lord Mayor 1850–1. With the aid of Batty's Circus and Menagerie reintroduced pageants into Lord Mayor's Show in which they had been abandoned since 1702. He was greatly ridiculed by *Punch*, a typical joke being 'Parturiunt Montes, nascitur ridiculus Mus(grove)'. According to the *Sunday Times* 'a more inexpensive – we were nearly writing niggardly – mayoralty has never been witnessed within the good old City of King Lud'.

SIR EDWARD OSBORNE. Lord Mayor 1583–4. The gallant apprentice who saved the life of the rich merchant's daughter (see SIR WILLIAM HEWET) and married her. Ancestor of the Dukes of Leeds, he was enobled for his financial support of James I as Viscount Dunblaine.

LADY ANNE PACKINGTON (see Some Benefactors, p. 300), fl. 1560. Widow of Sir John Packington, Recorder of Worcester (a man allowed to keep his hat on in the presence of the Sovereign). She provides an early example of female emancipation, having at one time been a returning officer.

SAMUEL PEPYS. Master 1677. Sufficient has been said elsewhere of this great Clothworker.

SIR OWEN ROBERTS. Clerk to the Company for forty-one years (1867–1907) – 'a Clerk of quite exceptional merit and ability. . . . During his tenure of office the Clothworkers' Company has set an example to every other Company in the City of London, an example which has been widely followed to the advantage of the whole nation and of this the credit in no small due belongs to Sir Owen Roberts.'

SIR JOHN ROBINSON. Master 1656, Lord Mayor 1662–3. 'A prating buffleheaded fellow' (see p. 137). Lieutenant of the Tower of London 1660, President of the Artillery Company 1665. He prevented the Artillery Ground (originally a large Close called Tassel Close where the Teazles grew) from being turned into a burial ground. Entertained Charles II at Clothworkers' Hall 1662.

SIR THOMAS ROWE. A Merchant Taylor Benefactor in 1568 to the Clothworkers (see Some Benefactors, p. 300). He took some English mastiffs to India as a present to the great Mogul. They were of marvellous courage. One leaped overboard to attack a school of porpoises and only two survived to reach India, where one immediately attacked an elephant. The Mogul was very pleased.

JOHN TOWILL RUTT. Master 1816. Eminent Dissenter and Liberal. Took chair at memorable meeting of 'Friends of the People' Society in 1792 in support of French Revolution. Founder of *The Monthly Repository*. Edited Burton's Diary. Disinterested zeal led to acceptance of Jenner's methods of vaccination. 'His public speaking was vigorous, his conversation animated and his verses showed facility and playful humour.'

SIR THOMAS SKINNER. Master 1584. Arrested 1589 by Order of Queen in Council for withdrawing from London without contributing to the forced loan in spite of his fellow-Aldermen's attempts to make him comply.

SIR JOHN SPENCER. Lord Mayor 1594–5, a time of great scarcity in which he caused the City Companies to lay in supplies of corn in their granaries in the Bridge House. He suppressed with severity several tumultuous meetings of apprentices and others in the City. Five youths were afterwards executed on Tower Hill. 'A pirate of Dunkirk laid a plot with twelve of his mates to carry away Sir John Spencer which if he had done £50,000 would not have redeemed him. He came over the Seas in a Shallop with twelve Musketeers and in the night went into Barking Creek and left the Shallop in the custody of six of his men and with the other six proceeded as far as Islington and there hid themselves in ditches near the path in which Sir John always went to his house but by the providence of God Sir John upon some extraordinary occasion was forced to stay in London that night, otherwise they had taken him away and they fearing they should be discovered returned to their Shallop and so proceeded safe to Dunkirk.' (*The Vanity of the Lives and the Passions of Men* by D. Papillion, Gent 1651, cited by Gregory.) His daughter eloped with William Lord Compton and the estranged father and daughter were only reunited (so it is told) by a strategem on the part of Queen Elizabeth who induced Spencer to adopt a baby which was in fact his own grandchild. Lord Compton was the heir to Compton Wynyates, the Marquess of Northampton's seat. He was driven out of his mind by his wife's wealth and by its responsibilities and at one time had to be kept bound.

RICHARD STAPER. Master 1590. Director of the East India Company. His monument tells that he 'was the greatest Merchant in his time, the chiefest actor in discovery of the Trades of Turkey and East India . . . '.

SIR WILLIAM STONE. Master 1607 when James I was entertained at the Hall. Mercer to the Queen, member of the Turkey Company.

THOMAS TUCKER. Clothworker scholar at St John's College, Oxford 'Prince or Lorde of the Revells in 1607' (Opie: Oxford Dictionary of Nursery Rhymes). It is suggested he may be the original 'Little Tommy Tucker'.

BARLOW TRECOTHICK. Fined for Master 1764, M.P. for London 1768, Lord Mayor on decease of William Beckford 1770. 'Mr. Alderman Trick-a-Trick,' as he is described in a lampoon inviting votes for him. 'He being a Gentleman zealously attached, both by Nature and Education to Boston Principles and Bostonian Maxim; a strenuous Promoter of Faction and Disobedience to the Mother Country; and upon all Occasions, a fast Friend to the Interests of America, as opposed to those of Old England.'

SIR JOSEPH WILLIAMSON. Master 1676–7. Keeper of H.M. Paper Office 1670, Clerk of H.M. Papers in Privy Council 1673. Succeeded Arlington as one of the Principal Secretaries of State. Committed to Tower by Commons for pro-popery, released by Charles II. Recorder of Thetford. M.P. for Thetford, also M.P. for Rochester at the same time. President of the Royal Society 1677.

JAMES WYLD, M.P. for Bodmin, 1851. Erected a Great Model Globe in Leicester Square. Geographer to the Queen.

(ii) CLOTHWORKER LORDS MAYOR

Sir William Hewet	1559
Sir Rowland Hayward	1570
Sir James Hawes	1574
Sir Edward Osborne	1583
Sir John Spencer	1594
Sir Thomas Skinner	1596
Sir Nicholas Moseley	1599
Sir John Watts	1606
The Rt Hon. Ralph Freeman	1633
Sir Robert Parkhurst	1634
Sir Richard Gurney, Bart	1642
Sir John Ireton	1658
Sir John Robinson, Bart	1662
Sir William Peake	1667
Sir Thomas Lane	1694
Sir Robert Beachcroft	1711
Thomas Winterbottom	1751
Sir Samuel Fludyer, Bart	1761
Samuel Turner	1768
Barlow Trecothick	1770
Sir John Perring, Bart	1803
Sir John Musgrove, Bart	1850
John Humphery (purchased into this Company the next year)	1842

(iii) MASTERS OF THE COMPANY FROM 1536 TO DATE*

The earlier Court Books were destroyed in the Great Fire (1666)

Andrew Fraunceys	1536
William Grenway	1537
John Tollous, Alderman	1538
Thomas Spencer	1539
Andrew Fraunces	1540
John Grymes	1541
John Davy	1542

*Square brackets indicate Masters formally elected but 'excused' service.

William Hewet, Alderman	1543
Rauffe Hamersley	1544
Augustine Hynde, Alderman	1545
John Halse, Sheriff	1546
John Machell	1547
John Petyngar	1548
John Watson	1549
Richard Folkes, Alderman	1550
Adam Wynthropp	1551
John Lute	1552
Nicholas Smalle	1553
Thomas Hunte	1554
Philipp Bolde	1555
Richard Maryatt	1556
Thomas Ormeston	1557
Richard Maryatt	1558
Sir Rowland Heywarde, Kt, Alderman	1559
William Armorer	1560
Sir James Hawes, Kt, Alderman	1561
Robert Christopher	1562
John Whitehorne	1563
William Ryxman	1564
Edward Bashe	1565
John Lacye	1566
Morris Longe	1567
William Wylson	1568
William Lambe	1569
Edward Dyeher	1570
William Petynger	1571
Edmonde Burton	1572
William Phillips	1573
John Clarke	1574
Richard Lyster	1575
Robert Howse, Alderman	1576
John Marwoode	1577
[Thomas Altham]	1578
Nicholas Parkynson	1578
Thomas Byarde	1579
[John Spencer]	1580

Thomas Gilbourne 1580
William Hardinge (*to September, decd*) 1581
John Kymber (*from October*) 1581
Richard Sleyforde 1582
John Lacye, Alderman 1583
Sir Thomas Skynner, Kt, Alderman 1584
John Sothall 1585
Thomas Willett 1586
Laurence Palmer 1587
Henry Tailforde 1588
William Heron 1589
Richard Staper, Alderman 1590
John Blounte 1591
Robert Coggan 1592
John Burnell 1593
[Henry Hewitt] 1594
Sir John Watts, Alderman 1594
[John Hawes] 1595
John Oldham 1595
[Launcelott Young] 1596
George Hanger 1596
John Robothom 1597
Cutbert Brande 1598
Abraham Campion 1599
Thomas Hussey 1600
Edward Pilsworth 1601
John Bayworth 1602
Richard Farrington, Alderman 1603
John Eldred 1604
Thomas Champney 1605
Sir William Stone, Kt 1606
Christopher Gaylor 1607
John Coleby 1608
Edward Coxe 1609
William Jennyns 1610
Hughe Morrall 1611
Richard Foxe 1612
Henry Walton 1613
Thomas Bastock 1614

Nicholas Salter	1615
[Richard Booth]	1616
William Kymber	1616
Thomas Hyde	1617
Thomas Amys	1618
Sir Thomas Hewett, Kt	1619
[Richard Beale]	1620
Rt Hon. Ralph Freeman, Alderman	1620
Richard Beale	1621
James Chapman	1622
Joseph Jackson	1623
Sir Robert Parkhurste, Kt, Alderman	1624
[Robert Reynolds]	1625
Thomas Normcott	1626
[Theophilus Brereton]	1626
Thomas Champney	1626
James Monger	1627
John Carpenter	1628
Thomas Wood	1629
Humfry Hawker	1630
William Walton	1631
Anthony Abdy, Alderman	1632
Sir Richard Guarnard *alias* Gurney, Kt, Bart, Alderman	1633
Edward Claxton	1634
Thomas Gipps	1635
William Hodges	1636
Francis Roberts	1637
Thomas Jennings	1638
[John Barcroft]	1638
Roger Drake	1639
Thomas Burnell	1640
Thomas Austin	1641
Marmaduke Rawden	1642
[Robert Austin]	1643
[John Beale]	1643
Ralph Hough	1643
[Roger Jones]	1644
[Mathew Alexandre]	1644

[Ralph Holmes]	1644
Robert Jackson	1644
[Thomas Boylston]	1645
Augustine Phillips	1645
Francis Thriscrosse	1646
Lawrence Holt (*decd August*)	1647
George Hanger (*remainder of year*)	1647
Thomas Wilson	1648
[William Webb]	1649
Robert Story	1649
[Edward Hudson]	1650
William Harris (*part of year*)	1650
Thomas Andrews (*remainder*)	1650
[Richard Brent]	1651
[Gregory Phillipott]	1651
William Caswell	1651
Sir John Ireton, Kt, Alderman	1652
Robert Rendor	1653
Edward Trussell	1654
Daniel Waldoe	1655
Sir John Robinson, Bart, Alderman	1656
[Thomas Sherston]	1657
William Penoyer, Alderman	1657
George Downes	1658
Valentine Pet	1659
Sir William Peake, Kt, Alderman	1660
Henry Bainbrigg, Alderman	1661
Arthur Hall	1662
William Ellwood	1663
[Richard Brown]	1664
[Thomas Browne]	1664
Nicholas Penning	1664
Nicholas Boufoy, Alderman	1665
Phillip Chetwind	1666
Sir Dennis Gawden, Kt, Alderman and Sheriff	1667
Sir Frauncis Chaplin, Kt, Alderman and Sheriff	1668
Michael Davison	1669

327

Richard Beckford	1670
John Lane	1671
Frauncis Dorrington	1672
James Burkin	1673
Edward Griffith	1674
William Edwards	1675
Sir Joseph Williamson, Kt	1676
Hon. Samuel Pepys	1677
Sir Robert Knightley, Kt	1678
Sir Thomas Beckford, Kt, Alderman and Sheriff	1679
John Harris	1680
Sir Benjamin Ayloffe, Bart	1681
Brian Boden	1682
Francis Burton	1683
Sir Edmund Wiseman, Kt	1684
Hon. William Bridgeman	1685
William Hewer	1686
Edward Gawdren (*to November*)	1687
William Gouge (*from November*)	1687
Thomas Strudwick	1688
Sir Thomas Lane, Kt, Alderman	1689
Samuel Lamott	1690
John Legg	1691
David King	1692
Bryan Bentham	1693
Thomas Mason	1694
Godfrey Webster	1695
Josias Dewey	1696
John Ward	1697
John Smith	1698
John Midgley	1699
[Sir Thomas May]	1700
Sir Robert Beachcroft, Kt, Alderman and Sheriff	1700
Augustine Dry	1701
[James Herriott]	1702
[John Harwood]	1702
Edward Milles	1702

[Robert Brough]	1703
Thomas Aspley	1703
Sir Thomas Webster, Bart.	1704
George Boddington	1705
[John Moore]	1706
[William Cockrum]	1706
[Humphry Willett]	1706
Francis Emerson	1706
John West	1707
John Crayle	1708
[John Mitford]	1709
Sir Randolph Knipe	1709
Samuel Cornock	1710
Stephen Mills	1711
Thomas Lediard	1712
Thomas Sherman	1713
Paul Sherman	1714
William Barnsley	1715
Richard Barnes (*part of year, decd*)	1716
William Andrews (*remainder of year*)	1716
Walter Ryan	1717
Sir John Bull, Kt	1718
Nicholas Hanbury	1719
John Blackall	1720
Launcelot Skynner	1721
Richard Savill	1722
John Hester	1723
Arundel Wastfield	1724
Thomas Harrington (*part of year*)	1725
Richard Hardwick (*remainder of year*)	1725
John Barwick	1726
Samuel Aaron	1727
Richard Chauncy	1728
Thomas Wilmer	1729
William Leach	1730
Richard Wilson	1731
John Nicholas	1732
William Jenkins	1733
Stephen Parry	1734

John Brittain	1735
William Langmore (*part of year*)	1736
Henry Clifton (*remainder of year*)	1736
John Whittle	1737
Stephen Roome	1738
Thomas Boddington	1739
John Welch	1740
George Smith (*part of year*)	1741
Henry Clifton (*remainder of year*)	1741
Walter Bernard, Alderman	1742
Benjamin Fleming	1743
John Wallis	1744
Thomas Winterbottom, Alderman	1745
George Davis	1746
Abraham Daking	1747
Thomas Sherlow	1748
William Whitaker, Alderman and Sheriff	1749
Mathew Newman	1750
Robert Lovick	1751
James Crawforth	1752
[Francis Gillow]	1753
John Skynner	1753
[Henry Stanton]	1754
Ambrose Asty	1754
[Henry Clifton]	1755
[George Taylor]	1755
Coles Fortrie	1755
Giles Vincent	1756
[George Boddington]	1757
Benjamin Boddington	1757
William Yerraway	1758
[William Farnworth]	1759
Joseph Taverner	1759
Jacob Shelton	1760
James Harding	1761
[John Lodge]	1762
[Thomas Hodges]	1762
[Robert Wastfield]	1762
Isaac Rawlins	1762

[Samuel Turner, Alderman]	1763
[Thomas Hurnal]	1763
Richard Peers, Alderman	1763
[William Boothby]	1764
[Barlow Trecothic]	1764
Phillip Griffin	1764
John Whalley	1765
John Ellicott	1766
[Reuben Foxwell]	1767
[Edmund Smith]	1767
Thomas Burfoot	1767
John Baptist Angell	1768
Richard Pepys	1769
John Hall	1770
[Charles Morris]	1771
Richard Locke	1771
[John Foxwell]	1772
Richard Griffiths	1772
Robert Overton	1773
John Favell	1774
[William Clarke]	1775
Philip Milloway	1775
William Stanton	1776
[John Spiller]	1777
[John Price]	1777
Francis Vincent	1777
Edward de Saute	1778
[Robert Frecland]	1779
Morphew Yerraway	1779
John Biggs	1780
[Nicholas Pearce]	1781
Robert Keene	1781
[Thomas Horne]	1782
Edward Ellicott	1782
Henry Rutt	1783
[John Tickner]	1784
[Edward Hill]	1784
Samuel Knight	1784
Richard Townsend	1785

331

Thomas Hunter	1786
[John Nash]	1787
[Stafford Briscoe]	1787
[John Taverner]	1787
Daniel Whalley	1787
[Samuel Marsh]	1788
Roger Mawdesley	1788
Thomas Cooper	1789
John Arnold	1790
Benjamin Wood	1791
[William Smith]	1792
[Gideon Herbert]	1792
Isaac Wiltshire	1792
[John Barnard]	1793
John Yarnton	1793
Francis Ruddle	1794
[John Clarke]	1795
[Edward Jeffries]	1795
John Everett	1795
William Knight	1796
Richard Hollier	1797
Anthony Wingfield	1798
[John Perring, Alderman]	1799
Richard Reeve	1799
[Thomas Newman]	1800
[Thomas Everett]	1800
William Chapman	1800
[John Worth]	1801
[John White]	1801
[George Archer]	1801
John White (*died before being sworn*)	1801
Willington Clarke	1801
Henry Cock	1802
[John Wansey]	1803
[Thomas Neatby]	1803
William Smiton	1803
William Alchorne	1804
John Rahn, M.D.	1805
[Thomas Rivers]	1806

James Renat Syms	1806
[John Cowley]	1807
[Charles Palmer]	1807
Charles Alsager	1807
Joseph Broster	1808
William Bloxham	1809
[John Rappenden]	1810
Thomas Latham	1810
Abraham Purshouse Driver	1811
Benjamin Fuller	1812
[John Calvert Clarke]	1813
Samuel Favell	1813
James Yerraway	1814
Robert Burchall	1815
John Towill Rutt	1816
[Joseph Partridge]	1817
[Henry Wilson Mills]	1817
Thomas Pearson	1817
Thomas Abbott Green	1818
Daniel Whalley	1819
George Hammond	1820
John Angell	1821
[Nathaniel Whalley]	1822
Thomas Husband Vincent	1822
Richard Turner	1823
John Ward	1824
[Thomas Haynes]	1825
[John Strange]	1825
[William Beach]	1825
[Abraham Evans]	1825
Joshia Kirby Trimmer	1825
George Rutt	1826
Thomas Hayter	1827
Ralph Clarke	1828
[Isaac Whiteing]	1829
John Wood	1829
Huntley Bacon	1830
[Daniel Mills]	1831
[Randle Jackson]	1831

David Griffin	1831
William Strange	1832
[William Thwaytes]	1833
Philip Perring	1833
Samuel Houston	1834
[Thomas Wiltshire]	1835
[John Herd]	1835
[William Bousfield]	1835
[Samuel Norman Cowley]	1835
[John Bott]	1835
Thomas Howard Randell	1835
[Robert Steers]	1836
[George Cowell]	1836
[John Henry Burchall]	1836
Thomas Massa Alsager	1836
Michael Thomas Atkins	1837
Matthew Percival	1838
[Edward Driver]	1839
[Robert Clarke]	1839
Thomas Horne	1839
William Horne	1840
Charles Francis	1841
[William Sandell Angell]	1842
John Richardby Bousfield	1842
[John Humphery, Alderman]	1843
Sir John Musgrove, Alderman	1843
Edward Gregory	1844
Samuel Blaxland	1845
James Horne	1846
George Cornell	1847
George Bousfield	1848
John Britten	1849
Samuel Preston Child	1850
[Robert Whalley]	1851
[Henry Robert Burfoot]	1851
Henry Alsager	1851
Lyon Falkener	1852
[William Kemp Evans]	1853
[Henry Rutt]	1853

John Scrafton Thompson	1853
James Edward Allen	1854
Thomas Leachman	1855
Arthur Wilcoxon	1856
Thomas Beachcroft	1857
Charles Frederick Angell	1858
Charles John Bloxam	1859
Charles Larkin Francis	1860
Josiah Wilson (*decd during Mastership*)	1861
Sir John Musgrove, Bart (*for remainder of year*)	1861
Samuel Wheeler	1862
Rev. Edward John Ward	1863
Robinson John Kitchener	1864
Edward Pritchard	1865
[Alfred Francis]	1866
John Dormay	1866
[Frank Farnan]	1867
Richard William Atkins	1867
John Gregory	1868
[George Burnell]	1869
[Thomas William Wing]	1869
[David Burwash]	1869
[James Evans]	1869
[Charles Warton]	1869
Thomas Bousfield	1869
Edmund Heysham Wood	1870
Samuel Strange	1871
[Samuel Bousfield]	1872
[Edward Falkener]	1872
[George Wood]	1872
John Bazeley White	1872
John Farnan	1873
Robert John Child	1874
[John Bousfield]	1875
James Wyld	1875
Francis Farnan	1876
Charles Reynolds	1877
[Robert Bousfield]	1878

[Thomas Christopher]	1878
Edgar Horne	1878
Lt-Col John Britten	1879
[John Brampton Perks]	1880
Robert Collier Driver	1880
Rev. Alfred Child	1881
[Walter Farnan]	1882
Edward Gregory	1882
Charles James Orton	1883
Richard Roberts	1884
John Neate	1885
John Mews	1886
[Edmund Collingwood Bousfield]	1887
James Self, M.D.	1887
Rev. Thomas Wiltshire	1888
[John Trinder Talmadge]	1889
Wyatt Papworth, A.V.S.	1889
[Arthur Farnan]	1890
Col John Charles Angell	1890
Gilbert William Child, M.D.	1891
William Hunter	1892
[Samuel Blaxland]	1893
[George Fisher]	1893
Nathaniel Wood Lavers	1893
Sidney Wilson	1894
Rt Hon. Viscount Cross	1895
John Walter Sugg	1896
William Latham, Q.C.	1897
GeorgeWyndham Hog Girtin	1898
Alfred Charles Cronin	1899
Rt Hon. Lord Kelvin	1900
Richard Francis Moore	1901
James Edward Horne	1902
Andrew Waugh Snow	1903
Sir William Bousfield	1904
Thomas Stanhope Kelley	1905
John Samuel Phene	1906
Francis Farnan	1907
Herbert Winstanley	1908

Sir Owen Roberts	1909
Rev. Joseph White Horne	1910
Frederick George Fitch	1911
Morton Latham	1912
[William Tucker Bloxam]	1913
[Col Edmund Garrett]	1913
[Henry Hamilton Howell]	1913
[John Farnan]	1913
[Robert Peel Humphery]	1913
Sir Richard Melvill Beachcroft	1913
John Mews	1914
John Astley Bloxam	1915
Sir William Edgar Horne, Bart	1916
Robert Manning Driver	1917
William Withers Moore	1918
Walter Mews	1919
[Frederick Herbert Davies]	1920
[George Sydney Waterlow]	1920
[Rev. Dr Charles Lett Feltoe]	1920
[William Perks]	1920
James Hutchinson Driver	1920
[Edward John Bowring]	1921
[Tyndale White]	1921
Herbert Mews	1921
Percy John Neate	1922
Col Owen Willmer White	1923
Herbert Mews	1923
Col Stephenson Robert Clarke	1924
Sydney Robert Maurice Townsend	1925
Col Frederick John Angell	1926
Alderson Burrell Horne	1927
[Frederick Pinckard Coles]	1928
Charles Bridger Orme Clarke	1928
Stephen Ambrose Child	1929
Arthur Bousfield, M.D.	1930
Nicholas Gilbert Louis Child	1931
[Lyon Falkener, M.D.]	1932
Rayner Maurice Neate	1932
Charles Herbert Hunter	1933

337

Beresford Rimington Heaton   1934
[Frederick Henry Whalley]   1935
Peter MacIntyre Evans, C.B.E.   1935
[George Norbury]   1936
[Richard Adam Ellis]   1936
[Frederick Stuart Morgan]   1936
Stanley Bousfield, M.D.   1936
John Edward Humphery   1937
Sidney Neale Horne   1938
[Cecil Bernard Morgan]   1939
Charles Ernest Wilson   1939
[Geoffrey Hope Pearson]   1940
[George Henry Pinckard]   1940
Thomas Girtin   1940
Sir William Henry Davison, K.B.E., M.P.
   (created Lord Broughshane 1945)   1941
Edmund Heisch (*decd March*)   1942
The Immediate Past Master (*remainder of
   year*)   1942
[Ernest Edgar Morgan]   1943
[Capt. Sir Beachcroft Towse, V.C.,
   K.C.V.O., C.B.E.]   1943
Geoffrey Courthope Bosanquet   1943
Sir Robert Waley Cohen, K.B.E.   1944
Major Philip Maurice Beachcroft, O.B.E.   1945
[John Wyatt Papworth]   1946
Henry Hawkins Turner   1946
William Foster Reeve   1947
Reginald Wellesley Britten, M.B.E.   1948
[Captain Guy Rixon]   1949
[Col Hugh Delabere Bousfield, C.M.G.]   1949
Harold Driver Jonas, O.B.E.   1949
Robert Bravery Attlee   1950
Robert Collier Jonas   1951
Major Walter Frank Pothecary, O.ST.J.,
   D.C.M., LL.D., J.P.   1952
[Henry Ward]   1953
Rt Hon. Viscount Hyndley, G.B.E.   1953
Major Henry Gibbon Moore, M.C.   1954

Owen Astley Bloxam   1955
Captain Frederick Arthur Lacey   1956
Major William Guy Horne   1957

(iv) TRUSTS AND GENERAL SUPERINTENDENCE COMMITTEE: LIST OF CHAIRMEN

Records and Trusts Committee (established 24 April 1837)

John Thomas Rutt	1837–41
William Horne	1841–8
George Bousfield (following the death of William Horne)	1848
George Neale Driver	1848

Superintendence Committee (established 3 February 1841)

Thomas Massa Alsager	1841–6
(Sir) John Musgrove	1846–8

These two Committees were amalgamated by the Court, 3 January 1849, as the General Superintendence Committee, and the title was changed to the present one of the Trusts and General Superintendence Committee in 1871

George Neale Driver	1849–52
Charles John Bloxam	1852–9
Charles Larkin Francis	1859–60
Charles John Bloxam	1860–2
Charles Larkin Francis	1862–5
Charles John Bloxam	1865–8
Charles Larkin Francis	1868–9
Charles John Bloxam	1869–70
Charles Larkin Francis	1870–1
Charles John Bloxam	1871–2
John Bazeley White	1872–91
Charles James Orton	1891–3
William Wiltshire	1893–1903
William Latham	1903–15
Morton Latham	1915–28
Herbert Mews	1928–9

Alderson Horne	1929–44
Arthur Bousfield	1944–56
Maurice Beachcroft	1956–

(v) ESTATE COMMITTEE: LIST OF CHAIRMEN

This Committee was established by the Court, 12 August 1829

The Master for the time being	1829–35
John Towill Rutt	1835–7
Thomas Massa Alsager	1837–46
(Sir) John Musgrove	1846–75
(Sir) Sydney Waterlow	1875–6
James Wyld	1876–87
Edgar Horne	1887–1905
James Edward Horne	1906–8
Herbert Winstanley	1909–12
(Sir) Owen Roberts	1913–14
John Mews	1915–23
(Sir) Edgar Horne	1924–6
Robert Manning Driver	1926–29
(Sir) Edgar Horne	1929–40
Sidney Neale Horne	1941–53
William Foster Reeve	1953–

(vi) FINANCE COMMITTEE: LIST OF CHAIRMEN

This Committee was established by the Court, 19 July 1871

The Master for the time being	1871–5
John Gregory	1875–7
Charles John Bloxam	1877–80
John Mews	1880–1
John Bousfield	1881–8
John Mews	1888–92
William Hunter	1892–1916
Francis Farnan	1917–32
John Edward Humphery	1933–46
Maurice Beachcroft	1947–56
Right Hon. Viscount Hyndley	1956–

(vii) CHAPLAINS TO THE COMPANY SINCE 1659

The Rev. George Gifford	1659–67
No details available	1667–86
The Rev. Wright Burditt	1686–94
The Rev. William Stringfellow	1694–1731
The Rev. John Branson	1731–50
The Rev. Richard King	1750–84
The Rev. John Whalley	1784–1827
The Rev. Charles Perring	1827–91
The Very Rev. R. W. Forrest	1891–1908
The Rev. A. B. Boyd Carpenter	1908–17
The Rev. C. L. Feltoe	1917–27
The Rev. Prebendary Tom Wellard	1927–43
The Rev. A. Powell Miller	1943–

(viii) CLERKS TO THE COMPANY SINCE 1541

John Brown	1541–70
John Humfrey	1570–1619
John Warren	1619–37
Thomas Rogers	1637–9
Maurice Blount	1639–64
Thomas Dutton	1664–75
Edward Gurney	1675–1703
John Chase	1703–14
Thomas Hennand	1714–34
Harry Pollard	1734–66
John Skinner	January to August 1766
Giles Crompe Snr	1766–1826
Giles Crompe Jnr	1826–37
Allen Pering	1837–45
Robert Beckwith Towse	1845–67
(Sir) Owen Roberts	1867–1907
Peter MacIntyre Evans	1907–33
Walter Frank Pothecary	1933–50
John Edward Coomber	1950–

(ix) BEADLES TO THE COMPANY SINCE 1523

George Coulman	1523–39
John Clerk	1539–63
Francis Kitchen	1563–6
Thomas Godfrey	1566–74
Peter Hayborne	1574–1610
Thomas Holte	1610–24
Rowland Ainsworth	1624–36
Thomas West	1636–40
Thomas Boulton	1640–53
Paul Isaack	1653–6
Edward Jones	1656–66
Arthur Hall	1666–9
Ambrose Frewin	1669–80
John Chase Jnr	1680–1704
Thomas Wade	1704–39
Ralph Toone	1739–42
Thomas Dikes	1742–5
Thomas How	1745–52
Thomas Grant	1752–66
Martin Capron	1766–7
Henry Hodges	1767–82
Christopher Havergill	1782–8
James Noon	1788–90
Thomas Hawkins	1790–1808
Thomas Wensley	1808–25
John Jasper Stone	1825–35
Joseph Hughesdon	1835–53
George Nicoll	1853–71
Benjamin Bates	1871–95
William Dyke	1895–1920
Percy Frederick Fenn	1920–37
Henry William Groves	1937–

APPENDIX G

SOURCE NOTES

* *
*

PROLOGUE

1. City Journal, 13, fol. 33.

INTRODUCTION

ORIGIN

1. *Reports of Municipal Enquiry Commissioners and Commissioners for Charities* (quoting Sir F. Palgrave).
2. P. M. Evans: *Brief Account of the Clothworkers' Company.*
3. Sir E. Pooley: *The Guilds of the City of London.*
4. D. M. Stenton: *English Society in the Early Middle Ages.*
5. G. Unwin: *The Guilds and Companies of London.*
6. A. H. Johnson: *History of the Drapers' Company of London.*
7. Thornley and Hastings: *The Guilds of the City of London and their Liverymen.*
8. City Repertories, 7 (1525–27), fol. 119b.

BACKGROUND

1. S. T. Bindoff: *Tudor England.*
2. W. Maitland: *History of England.*
3. S. T. Bindoff: *Op. cit.*
4. *Ibid.*
5. *Ibid.*

STRUCTURE

1. Anon.: *The Government of the Fullers, Shearmen and Clothworkers of London as Proved by their Charters.*
2. G. Unwin: *Industrial Organization in the Sixteenth and Seventeenth Centuries.*

343

3. Charter of the Clothworkers' Company, 19, H. VIII (1528).
4. G. Unwin: *Op. cit.*
5. A. H. Johnson: *Op. cit.*
6. *Ibid.*
7. Thornley and Hastings: *Op. cit.*

CHAPTER ONE

1. Clerk's Notes on Title on First Registration at H.M. Land Registry, 18 January 1943.
2. *State Papers Domestic*, 4 May 1528.
3. G. Unwin: *Op. cit.*
4. W. Herbert: *The History of the Twelve Great Livery Companies.*
5. J. R. Green: *A Short History of the English People.*
6. S. T. Bindoff: *Op. cit.*
7. *City Journal*, 15, fol. 414b and 415.
8. *City Repertories*, 11, fol. 330b.
9. *City Journal*, 16, fol. 116.

CHAPTER TWO

1. S. T. Bindoff: *Op. cit.*
2. *Ibid.*
3. *State Papers Domestic*, Eliz. XL, 15.

CHAPTER THREE

1. Henry Arth: *Provision for the Poor* quoted by R. H. Tawney and E. Power in *Tudor Economic Documents.*
2. S. T. Bindoff: *Op. cit.*
3. Letter from Hakluyt to Walsingham, 7 January 1585.
4. *State Papers Domestic*, Eliz. CVI.
5. J. Stow: *English Chronicles.*

CHAPTER FOUR

1. E. Lipson: *The Economic History of England.*
2. W. H. Price: *English Patents of Monopolies.*
3. E. Lipson: *Op. cit.*
4. *Petition of Fustian Makers*, Guildhall Broadside 24.32.
5. E. Lipson: *Op. cit.*
6. W. Maitland: *Op. cit.*

7. Sir E. Pooley: *Op. cit.*
8. G. M. Trevelyan: *English Social History.*
9. T. W. Moody: *The Irish Plantation.*

CHAPTER FIVE

1. G. Unwin: *Op. cit.*
2. T. Burton: *Diary.*
3. *State Papers Domestic,* March 1604.
4. Hakluyt to Morgan Hubblethorne, quoted by G. B. Parks in *Richard Hakluyt and the English Voyages* (American Geographical Society, special publication 10).
5. *State Papers Domestic,* April 1606.
6. *City Repertories,* 18 December 1613, 12 July 1614.
7. *State Papers Domestic,* 23 February 1615.
8. G. Unwin: *Op. cit.*
9. Bacon to James I, 12 August 1615, 23 February 1616.
10. *State Papers Domestic,* 7 February 1616.
11. *State Papers Domestic,* May 1616.
12. *Lansdowne Papers,* 152, fol. 271; State Papers Domestic, James I, lxxx; *Ibid.,* 29 November 1616; *City Repertories,* 2 June, 13 June, 4 September 1616.
13. *State Papers Domestic,* 12 August 1617.
14. G. Unwin: *Op. cit.*
15. *Privy Council Records,* 12 October 1617.

CHAPTER SIX

1. E. Lipson: *Op. cit.*
2. Vertue MSS, Index, Walpole Society, Vol. xxix.
3. W. Herbert: *Op. cit.*
4. Vertue MSS, Index, Walpole Society, Vol. xxix.

CHAPTER SEVEN

1. *State Papers Domestic,* Chas I, 1626, Vol. xli, 49.50.
2. *Ibid.,* Vol. ccccxcviii, 11.
3. T. Burton: *Diary.*

CHAPTER EIGHT

1. Guildhall Broadside, 19.11.
2. Prestwick: *Respublica.*

3. J. R. Green: *Op. cit.*
4. Thornley and Hastings: *Op. cit.*
5. G. M. Trevelyan: *Op. cit.*
6. J. R. Green: *Op. cit.*
7. G. M. Trevelyan: *Op. cit.*
8. E. Lipson: *Op. cit.*
9. *A New Discourse of Trade*, 1671.
10. E. Lipson: *A Planned Economy or Free Enterprise.*
11. E. Lipson: *The Economic History of England.*
12. W. Herbert: *Op. cit.*
13. *State Papers Domestic*, Chas II, 408.174.
14. W. Herbert: *Op. cit.*

CHAPTER NINE

1. W. Herbert: *Op. cit.*
2. E. Lipson: *Economic History of England.*

CHAPTER TEN

1. G. M. Trevelyan: *Op. cit.*
2. J. H. Plumb: *Op. cit.*
3. G. M. Trevelyan: *Op. cit.*
4. J. H. Plumb: *Op. cit.*

CHAPTER ELEVEN

1. G. M. Trevelyan: *Op. cit.*
2. J. H. Plumb: *Op. cit.*
3. *Ibid.*
4. *London Triumphs*, 1677.
5. R. and S. Redgrave: *A Century of Painters of the English School.*
6. Gregory Collection, III, p. 112.

CHAPTER TWELVE

1. Gregory Collection, I, p. 205–8.

CHAPTER THIRTEEN

1. D. Thompson: *England in the Nineteenth Century.*
2. 28 March 1860.

CHAPTER FOURTEEN

1. Thomas Nussey: *Report on Carded Wools at the Paris Exhibition of 1867.*
2. *Textile Manufacturer*, 15 June 1876.
3. Thomas Nussey: *Op. cit.*
4. ? *The Times* (the newspaper cutting is unheaded and undated).
5. E. J. Brown: *The Private Donor in the History of the University of Leeds.*
6. Thomas Nussey: *Op. cit.*
7. ? *The Times.*
8. Mr Watherston, a member of the Court of the Goldsmiths' Company.
9. *Ibid.*

CHAPTER FIFTEEN

1. *Leeds Mercury*, 10 July 1884.
2. Unheaded newspaper report (presumably Manx).
3. 26 September 1889.
4. 8 March 1893.

CHAPTER SIXTEEN

1. 19 September 1894.

BIBLIOGRAPHY

* *
*

IN addition to the original sources provided by the Minute Books and Account Books of the Clothworkers' Company, by the Gregory Collection in the Clothworkers' Library, the City Repertories, the City Journal, the Acts of the Privy Council, the State Papers Domestic, the Guildhall Broadsides, etc., the following works have been consulted:

T. M. Alsager: *Book of Irregularities. 1837.*

T. M. Alsager: *Register for the Year 1838.*

Anon: *The London City Livery Companies' Vindication. 1883.*

F. P. Barnard (ed): *Companion to English History (Middle Ages). 1902.*

S. T. Bindoff: *Tudor England. 1949.*

E. J. Brown: *The Private Donor in the History of the University of Leeds. 1953.*

C. M. Clode: *Early History of the Merchant Taylors' Company. 1888.*

F. H. Durham: *Relations of the Crown to Trade under James I.*

C. Golding: *London: The City. 1951.*

J. R. Green: *A Short History of the English People. 1908.*

R. Hakluyt: *The Principal Navigations. 1600.*

W. C. Haslitt: *The Livery Companies of the City of London. 1892.*

W. Herbert: *The History of the Twelve Great Livery Companies. 1836.*

Gordon Home: *Old London Bridge. 1931.*

A. H. Johnson: *History of the Drapers' Company of London. 1915.*

R. K. Kelsall: *Wage Regulation under the Statute of Artificers. 1938.*

E. Lipson: *The Economic History of England. 1947.*

E. Lipson: *A Planned Economy or Free Enterprise. 1944.*

T. W. Moody: *The Irish Plantation. 1839.*

G. B. Parks: *Richard Hakluyt and the English Voyages. 1928.*

J. H. Plumb: *England in the Eighteenth Century. 1950.*

B. Pontifex: *The City of London Livery Companies. 1939.*

Sir Ernest Pooley: *The Guilds of the City of London. 1945.*

BIBLIOGRAPHY

W. H. Price: *English Patents of Monopolies*. 1906.

L. F. Salzman: *English Trade in the Middle Ages*. 1931.

A. N. Shimmin: *Leeds University: The First Half-Century*. 1954.

D. M. Stenton: *English Society in the Early Middle Ages*. 1951.

R. H. Tawney: *Agrarian Problem in the Sixteenth Century*. 1912.

R. H. Tawney and E. Power: *Tudor Economic Documents*. 1924.

D. Thompson: *England in the Nineteenth Century*. 1950.

Thornley and Hastings: *The Guilds of the City of London and their Livery-men*. 1911.

G. M. Trevelyan: *English Social History*. 1946.

George Unwin: *Industrial Organization in the Sixteenth and Seventeenth Centuries*. 1904.

George Unwin: *The Guilds and Companies of London*. 1908.

G. Vertue: MSS. Index. Walpole Society Publication XXIX. 1947.

H. Ross Williamson: *The Gunpowder Plot*. 1951.

Dictionary of National Biography.

Extracts from *Reports of Municipal Enquiry Commissioners*.

Journal of Leeds Textile Association. 1951.

INDEX TO THE NARRATIVE

*　　*

*

This second edition of

THE GOLDEN RAM

was printed by Hunt, Barnard & Co Ltd, Aylesbury,

The plates were printed at the Chiswick Press,
London N 11.

The book was designed by
Hans Schmoller

* *
*